Stained Glass in Thirteenth-Century Burgundy

STAINED GLASS IN THIRTEENTH-CENTURY BURGUNDY

Virginia Chieffo Raguin

PRINCETON UNIVERSITY PRESS

Library of Congress Cataloging in Publication Data
Raguin, Virginia Chieffo, 1941-
Stained glass in thirteenth-century Burgundy.

Bibliography: p.
Includes index.
1. Glass painting and staining, Gothic—
France—Burgundy. 2. Glass painting and staining
—France—Burgundy. I. Title.
NK5349.A3B876   748.594'4   81-47946
ISBN 0-691-03987-9   AACR2

This book has been composed in Linotron Aldus
Designed by Barbara Werden

Clothbound editions of Princeton University Press books
are printed on acid-free paper, and binding materials are
chosen for strength and durability

Printed in the United States of America by
Princeton University Press, Princeton, New Jersey

Illustrations by Village Craftsmen, Inc.
Rosemont, New Jersey

To the Memory of My Mother
Margaret Kirby Chieffo

Contents

List of Illustrations

All photographs from *Archives photographiques* are copyrighted with Paris/ SPADEM/ VAGA, New York.

Acknowledgments

This book was written with the aid of the released time provided by a Faculty Fellowship awarded by the College of the Holy Cross. Grants from the College's Research and Publications Committee and the Committee on Professional Standards have supported additional research and the purchase of photographs. A grant from the National Endowment for the Humanities has enabled me to complete research on certain chapters, especially those concerning the glass of Saint-Germain-lès-Corbeil and the Sainte-Chapelle of Paris.

Although all the statements in this work are my own responsibility, I am grateful for the advice and assistance of many people. Acknowledgment of generous contributions of time and expertise is made to: Michael Archer of the Victoria and Albert Museum; Carl Barnes, Oakland University; Ellen Beer, Corpus Vitrearum Medii Aevi, Swiss Committee; Françoise Bercé, Archivist and Paleographer, Monuments Historiques Français, Paris; l'abbé Michel Boucher, curate of Saint-Pierre of Saint-Julien-du-Sault; Pamela Blum, Columbia University; the late Robert Branner, Columbia University, whose work in both architecture and manuscript studies has provided major assistance; Catherine Brisac, curator, Musée des Plans-Reliefs, Paris; Walter Cahn, Yale University; Madeline Caviness, Tufts University, whose contribution can be felt on every page of this work; Michael Cothren, Swarthmore College; Sumner McKnight Crosby, Professor Emeritus, Yale University, who supervised my dissertation; Alain Erlande-Brandenburg, Director, Cluny Museum; Gloria Gilmore-House, International Center of Medieval Art; Louis Grodecki of the Sorbonne, undisputedly the single greatest contributor in the field; Jane Hayward, Curator, the Cloisters, who has provided advice, encouragement and support from the very beginning of my studies in stained glass; the Reverend Robert Fisher Healey, S.J., College of the Holy Cross; C. Hohl, Director, Archives Départementales, Yonne; the late Jean Lafond, Corpus Vitrearum Medii Aevi, French Committee, whose perceptive insights and generous spirit have done so much to further investigation in this area; Meredith Lillich, Syracuse University; Jan van der Meulen, Cleveland State University; R. Moreau, glass painter of Auxerre, who shared much information with me about his and his predecessor's restorations of the glass of Auxerre Cathedral; the staff of the Musée d'Art et d'Histoire, Geneva, Claude Lapaire, Director, François Schweitzer and Françoise Hug of conservation and Jacqueline Dieboli, who provided me with much assistance in examining the glass of Saint-Fargeau in their collection; Linda Papanicolaou, whose work on the glass of Tours has provided important points of comparison; S. Pélissier; C. Penny, Verger, Church of Saint Mary and Saint Nicholas, Wilton, who enabled me to study the impressive collection of French glass reset in English windows; Françoise Perrot; persons attached to the Pitcairn collection, Bryn Athyn, especially Lachlan Pitcairn and the Reverend Martin Pryke; Harvey Stahl, University of California, Berkeley; Harry Titus; the late Raymond Vautrin, sacristan of Auxerre Cathedral, who provided me with ladders for access to walkways surrounding the cathedral ambulatory and even allowed me to study the exterior of the windows from vantage points in his garden; Philippe Verdier, University of Montreal; and Jeanne Vinsot, Honorary Head of Services, Archives photographiques, Paris, whose open-hearted assistance with photographs and advice made such an impression on a young scholar.

Of the many institutions that have provided documentation for this study, I would like to thank especially the libraries of Yale and Harvard Universities where the bulk of my research was carried out. I am also indebted to the New York Public Library, the Columbia University Library, the Cloisters, the Pierpont Morgan Library, the Bibliothèque Nationale,

Paris, the Bibliothèques Municipales of Auxerre and Dijon, the Archives of the Monuments Historiques, Paris, and the Département of the Yonne, Auxerre, the library of the College of the Holy Cross and Tufts University Library.

The following individuals and institutions have provided me with information or photographs or allowed me to examine works in their possession: the Bundesdenkmalamt, Vienna; the Cluny Museum, Paris; the Courtauld Institute of Art, London; the Dayton Art Institute, Dayton, Ohio; the Detroit Institute of Arts; Edouard Fièvet, Chartres; the John Woodward Higgins Armory Museum, Worcester, Mass.; the Krannert Art Museum, Champaign, Ill.; the Metropolitan Museum of Art, New York; the Musée Historique de l'Ancien Evêché, Lausanne; the Museum of Fine Arts, Montreal; the Österreichische Nationalbibliothek, Vienna; the Victoria and Albert Museum, London; the Wellesley College Art Museum, Wellesley, Mass.; the Worcester Art Museum, Worcester, Mass.

Pearl Jolicoeur's typing and editorial skills have been essential to the completion of this work. I am also indebted to Irene Cole's assistance in typing the appendices. I am particularly grateful for the support of relatives and friends both in Europe and in America. To my parents and brothers and sisters I owe the initial encouragement for beginning work in the field of art history. The late Raymond Macé and Jacqueline and Pierre Bricher provided assistance, hospitality and color photographs. My husband's parents, Monsieur and Madame Philippe Raguin, have given me much emotional and material support for the study of a culture that is so dear to them. To my two children, Daniel and John, I owe much. Their passionate attachment to the beauty of these monuments helped firm my purpose when obstacles seemed insurmountable. My husband, Michel, has provided not only support and encouragement but a much needed critical counterbalance for all of my work.

Stained Glass in Thirteenth-Century Burgundy

INTRODUCTION

A peine commençons-nous à entrevoir toute la diversité stylistique de ce domaine, plus vaste qu'aucun autre à la même époque. (Louis Grodecki)[1]

Grodecki's statement over twenty years ago that we had just begun to examine the stylistic diversity of stained glass in the first half of the thirteenth century is still true today. Despite significant contributions to our understanding of a number of monuments, vast areas of research remain virtually untouched. The cathedral of Auxerre, in particular, provides an unusual opportunity to study the development of the glazed window. Documentary sources, most importantly the *Gesta pontificum Autissiodorensium*, that since the ninth century recorded the biographies of Auxerre's bishops present references to the now lost windows of the successive buildings that preceded the construction of the Gothic cathedral.[2]

Burgundy also presents a rich collection of extant glass showing diverse glazing styles which demands scholarly attention. Even despite considerable loss over the centuries, stained glass still presents one of the most extensive collections of medieval painting of its period, a collection as rich for iconography as for style. It bears constant repetition that an understanding of any aspect of medieval life cannot be achieved by studying each element in isolation. The "mental habits," as Panofsky has termed them, that lie behind the production of a manuscript, sculptural program or theological treatise do not vary from subject to subject.[3] The import of a medieval religious edifice, the organization of the workshop, the development of styles in manuscript illumination, the innovation in iconographic motifs or the motivations for patronage cannot be understood in any general sense without the study of medieval glazing systems. Unfortunately glass has been one of the most neglected areas of medieval scholarship. Given the rapid deterioration of the windows caused by twentieth-century pollutants, it is all the more imperative that they be studied and made accessible to scholarly enterprise.[4]

---

[1] *Vitrail*, 115.

[2] See Bouchard (1979, 5-11) for discussion of *Gesta* authors. Under Bishop Wala (873-879) brief entries were also made for all of the bishops since the foundation of the see.

[3] Erwin Panofsky, *Gothic Architecture and Scholasticism*, New York (1957), 21.

[4] See Jean Taralon, "Problématique de la conservation et de la restauration des vitraux," *Les Monuments historiques de la France* (1977/1), 2-6, 97-100; Jean-Marie Bettembourg, "Problème de la conservation des vitraux de la façade occidentale de la cathédrale de Chartres," *ibid.*, 7-13, and other articles in this volume. These articles concerning the controversial restoration of the twelfth-century windows of Chartres are an indication of the pressing decisions faced by the guardians of all windows exposed to the elements. The international committee of the Corpus Vitrearum Medii Aevi, founded in 1952, has endeav-

Five Burgundian churches form the core of this study: the cathedral of Saint-Etienne of Auxerre, the collegiate church of Saint-Pierre of Saint-Julien-du-Sault, the church of Saint-Ferréol of Saint-Fargeau, all in the Yonne, and the churches of Notre-Dame of Dijon and Notre-Dame of Semur-en-Auxois in the Côte-d'Or. Attention is also directed toward many related monuments in the Ile-de-France, the Champagne, the Touraine and other areas.

The Burgundian style in architecture has been viewed as a corollary to the "para-Chartrain" development as defined by Bony.[5] Branner has focused attention on the impressive Burgundian systems of fluctuating space which flourished in the early part of the century before being engulfed by the influence of Rayonnant forms toward the middle of the century.[6] This evidence is summarized in a separate chapter. The evidence given by the glazing systems is at once less unified and more complex. There seems to be no one "Burgundian style" but a series of stylistic expressions under the direction of sometimes extraordinary and sometimes mediocre masters. The stylistic origins of these workshops are sometimes very clear, but each appears to have experienced a period of growth and development that significantly altered its approach to all aspects of painting while on Burgundian soil.

Perhaps the most significant characteristic of Burgundian glass painting is that it is almost totally dominated by Parisian styles. Although close to sixty churches, chapels and oratories were probably built and glazed in Paris between 1150 and 1250, Parisian examples of extant glass from this period are pitifully rare.[7] Only a handful of programs now remain, many dispersed in museums, of what must have been the dominant glazing center of its time.[8] The position of Burgundy assumes great importance when viewed as a documented repository of the style of glass painting developed in the capital. The dominant atelier of the cathedral of Auxerre, responsible for fifteen large windows, depended on the glass of the Saint Martin Master of Gercy (Seine-et-Oise), now in the Cluny Museum in Paris. Panels at Semur-en-Auxois, the cathedral of Troyes and in the cathedral of Auxerre give evidence that they were executed by the atelier of Saint-Germain-lès-Corbeil, slightly to the south of Paris. Another workshop, producing large quantities of glass at Saint-Julien-du-Sault and the cathedral of Auxerre, shows itself to be the work of the Isaiah Master who produced windows for the Sainte-Chapelle of Saint Louis. The Life of the Virgin workshop from Saint-Germain-des-Prés influenced two windows at Saint-Julien-du-Sault. Lastly, the Apocalypse Master, working at Auxerre, Saint-Julien and Saint-Fargeau, clearly depends on Parisian manuscript sources.

ored to focus attention on these problems, without reaching accord on how to halt the deterioration. At Chartres the windows were cleaned and a layer of plastic resin applied to the exterior. In the cathedral of Cologne, windows were placed between two additional layers of glass with a resin infill. There has been no long-term experiment determining the effects of such solutions. Some researchers are of the opinion that a simple second window placed on the outside of the medieval glass will halt much of the major deterioration until some of the more radical methods can be tested.

[5] 1957-1958.

[6] 1960.

[7] Jean Lafond, "The Stained Glass Decoration of Lincoln Cathedral in the Thirteenth Century," *Archaeological Journal* 103 (1946), 152-153.

[8] See especially *Corpus, France, Recensement* I, 15-16, and the references to particular sites in the catalogue.

This last workshop may also provide a much needed model demonstrating the relationship of small- and large-scale figure painting. In most of the great Gothic churches, Chartres serving as an example, the lower windows present extended narratives using many small figures in multiple-medallion formats. The upper windows (clerestory) display single standing figures of apostles, prophets, bishops, kings, etc., of colossal size. With rare exceptions, notably Caviness in 1977 and Grodecki in 1978, current scholarship has not demonstrated how a painting style employed for small narrative glass adapted to accommodate the massive proportions of the clerestory figures. At Auxerre, smaller figures such as personifications of the Sun and Moon, Virtues and Vices and the Liberal Arts appear in the clerestory windows and may be attributed to the workshop responsible for the Apocalypse window from the narrative style of the lower choir.

Monumental art has never appeared completely divorced from social and political motivation, and in thirteenth-century France the growing prestige of the monarchy bolstered the influence of Parisian styles. The patrons who followed the Parisian norms in architecture, manuscript illumination or stained glass were fully aware of their first manifestations in a royal context. In Burgundy, the archbishops of Sens and the bishops of Auxerre show a particularly close relationship to the royal house. Gauthier Cornut, archbishop of Sens, served as chaplain to Philip Augustus, Louis VIII and Louis IX. He performed the marriage uniting Saint Louis and Marguerite of Provence and supervised the reception of the relic of the Crown of Thorns, the immediate cause of the construction of the Sainte-Chapelle. The bishops of Auxerre, unusually generous patrons of their cathedral, were also staunch supporters of the monarchy. Guillaume de Seignelay eventually became bishop of Paris and Guy de Mello served as papal legate and counsellor to Charles of Anjou during the Sicilian crusade. Specific programs in stained glass reflect the relationship of churchman and monarch, especially at Saint-Julien-du-Sault and Auxerre.

Although by far the most important stylistic input, Parisian workshops were not the only ones working in the Burgundian area. The Good Samaritan workshop, active at Bourges and Poitiers from before 1205 to 1214, produced four windows at Semur-en-Auxois. A stylistic variant of the expression appears in the personality of the Saint Eustache Master working at Auxerre around 1233. This master brought to the cathedral stylistic concepts of vigor, movement and dramatic relationships clearly evident in five choir windows. Finally, a series of panels preserved in five lancets beneath the north rose of the church of Notre-Dame of Dijon show stylistic variants of the glazing patterns from the northeast, particularly around the Laonnais.

I have devoted the major portion of this study to an analysis of the stylistic identity of each workshop. This decision was dictated in large part by the need for work in this area. Earlier treatment of the glass has concentrated almost exclusively on the identification of iconographic themes. That has been useful for judging the accuracy of present programs and for assessing the extent of restoration in individual windows. To properly evaluate these research trends, it should be realized that only within the past three decades has serious work begun to be undertaken on the stylistic importance of glass. One of the great milestones in this respect is Grodecki's 1948 analysis of the glazing of Bourges by three distinct ateliers. This article set the tone for future research by establishing norms for the analysis of medallion schemas, decorative motifs, composition and painting styles. Lafond's work, notably his precocious perception of the importance of Paris as a dominant glazing center,[9] and his articles in the 1958 *Congrès archéologique* volume on Burgundy have also been major steps forward in the understanding of Burgundian glass. Adequate photographic resources are indispensable for a study of glass and the decision to photograph all the panels removed from buildings during the Second World War has changed radically the methodology of research in this area. The photographs of Auxerre (indicated by cliché number next to the diagrams in the Iconography Appendices) were made available to the photographic archives of the Commission des Monuments Historiques only in 1966.

Neither Grodecki's comments nor Lafond's article had access to this material.[10] Nonetheless both made important suggestions directing research toward comparisons with glass of the Parisian area, Chartres and Bourges. Lack of adequate photographic documentation has also limited the study of the glass of Semur-en-Auxois and Notre-Dame of Dijon. Only the windows of Saint-Julien-du-Sault, in addition to those of Auxerre, have been photographed adequately.

Descriptions of the iconography of almost all the Burgundian windows have appeared in various publications. Auxerre was treated by Guilhermy in manuscript notes during the mid-nineteenth century; by de Lasteyrie in 1841; by Bonneau in 1885, by Porée in 1926, and by Fourrey in 1929; Saint-Julien-du-Sault by Rheims in 1926; Notre-Dame of Dijon by Vallery-Radot in 1928 and Oursel in 1938; Saint-Fargeau's panels in the Musée d'Art et d'Histoire, Geneva, by Lafond in 1948; and Semur-en-Auxois by de Tervarent in 1938. In certain cases the descriptions have been inaccurate, and I have endeavored to present a comprehensive survey of these panels in an iconographical appendix indexed by saints' names. Saint-Julien-du-Sault's glass presents such extensive restoration that iconographic references would be too unreliable at the present, and so has been omitted from the catalogue. Even without this monument, the collection is vast. To simplify access to this material I have listed the references made to local hagiographic traditions, such as dedications of altars or churches, attention paid to feast days, relics, etc., under each window. I have also included a list of the same themes in twelfth- and thirteenth-century French glass. The chapter on iconography is therefore restrained, giving attention to general development of programs, unusual practices and specifically Burgundian themes. It is hoped that this publication will encourage scholars to develop many of these suggestions.

The determination of authenticity for glass remains one of the major issues of glass studies.[11] Despite long periods of neglect and even deliberate destruction, much

---

[9] See above n. 7. Lafond was at this time contradicting many statements about the importance of Chartres as the great center of its age.

[10] Grodecki, *Vitrail*, 139-140; Lafond, 1958a.

[11] For the most thorough treatment of this topic see Caviness, 1977, 13-22.

is visible in the Burgundian area. One of the chief indications of age in glass is the patina of the exterior surface, readily evident in the Auxerre window of Nicholas and Germain (fig. 63). This surface pitting produces a matt, whitish effect when seen in raking light. The darker areas, predominantly in the background, are strong indications of their relatively modern date. Unfortunately there is no precise pattern of aging for medieval glass. Windows will vary from one locality to the next, depending on the techniques of each workshop and on the raw materials available in each area. Even glass in the same window can exhibit differences since the method of manufacture produced relatively small amounts of glass from a single pot. Different colors also show various levels of resistance. At Auxerre, purples, commonly used for mantles, appear particularly impervious to pitting.

A visual examination of both the interior and exterior surfaces has been indispensable for a study of these windows. In most cases it has also been possible to gain a tactile understanding of the glass. The interior walkway around the ambulatory of Auxerre and the passage in front of the five lancets beneath the north rose of Notre-Dame of Dijon have allowed close examination of many panels, as well as the making of rubbings of lead patterns and tracings of painted surfaces. The Saint-Fargeau glass, in a museum context, has naturally been the most thoroughly studied. In the remaining churches ladders have sufficed to allow comparative study.

A study of the restoration campaigns has also been extremely important in assessing the extent of original glass. In addition, a survey of the destruction and attempts at restoration, sometimes resulting in the definitive loss of the original by the creation of a more legible modern substitute, reveals changing aesthetic attitudes as well. Information on the restoration campaigns at Auxerre, Saint-Julien-du-Sault and Notre-Dame of Dijon is contained in appendices as well as in references in the text.

It is hoped that this analysis of Burgundian developments will support recent inquiry concerning major questions of medieval artistic production. Perhaps most important is the definition of an "atelier" or workshop, its stylistic development and its methods of working. The Burgundian evidence also clarifies our understanding of the interaction between medieval manuscript painting and medieval glass painting as well as emphasizing the diversity of iconographic sources available to the workshop. Then, too, this rich collection alerts us to larger themes such as the relationship of the architectural framework to the glass and the influence of political motivation on patronage.

The growing tendency is to see glazing history as much more a part of a general Gothic development. Although dominated by Paris in every sense, social, economic, political and artistic, the Gothic world is essentially characterized by the disappearance of the regional styles that functioned so actively in the twelfth century.[12] Instead, glazing production became more and more the concern of itinerant work-

---

[12] See most recently Grodecki, 1977.

shops that moved to sites whenever and wherever they were needed. That Paris employed more artists and for longer periods is explained by the greater amount of work available, not its position as a new "regional" center. Although Burgundy can contribute to our analysis of these trends, a complete understanding of her position will not be achieved until the many adjacent sites are studied in greater detail.

I

THE ARCHITECTURAL FRAMEWORK

The Burgundian architect went a step further. He designed a support that appears to have normal parts, such as a capital, an impost, and the departure of the ribs directly above. But in reality the true function of the several stones often do not correspond at all with the apparent ones. Such concealment is the sign of the virtuoso designer and it marks the presence of a very complex and highly mannered point of view.

(Robert Branner)[1]

Burgundian Gothic architecture was a logical, if localized, outcome of a very general twelfth-century "renaissance."[2] The acquisition of wealth and new social institutions enjoyed by Western Europe throughout the twelfth century was the true foundation for the great "age of cathedrals" of the thirteenth. The development of commercial routes, urban centers and a vastly expanded agricultural system produced more goods and a means of distribution that wrought extensive changes in society. The rise of a new class, the bourgeoisie, with its attachment to the urban cathedral, deeply affected current medieval religious and artistic traditions. The great new buildings necessitated liturgical innovations, new iconographic programs, transformation of architectural practices, and in particular, the development of the stained glass window.

Burgundy in the twelfth and thirteenth centuries shared Europe's common prosperity. The burst of construction in large and small religious edifices around 1210, however, attests to an unusual degree of economic success. The wealth of the Burgundian region, and its subsequent population growth depended on an agricultural development largely independent of the monasteries that so dominated the Romanesque era.[3] The Cistercians had contributed to this development by their practice of settling in uninhabited regions and clearing the wilderness for new farmlands. The opening up of new regions for cultivation allowed Burgundy to exploit its particularly favorable climate and gently sloping hills for vineyards, a practice still very much in evidence today. The areas around Beaune and Auxerre were the two largest production centers of quality wine for export. Second to wines, but still notable, textiles were produced in a manufacturing and trading system that

---

[1] 1960, 7-8.

[2] Henri Pirenne, *A History of Europe* I, New York (1956), 183-272; Charles Homer Haskins, *The Renaissance of the Twelfth Century*, New York (1964).

[3] Branner, 1960, 1-5; E. Jarry, *La Formation territoriale de la Bourgogne. Essai de géographie historique (Provinces et pays de France, III: Monographies provinciales)*, Paris, 1948.

greatly favored the urban population. The rapid growth of towns and the acquisition of charters granting commune status to an increasingly vocal bourgoisie were natural results.[4] Population increased in both urban and rural areas, however, which accounts for the widespread pattern of church construction. Contemporaneous accounts recording the construction of the cathedral of Auxerre cited the population pressure as a motivation for the builders.[5] Guillaume de Seignelay, bishop of Auxerre, founded no less than three parish churches at La Charité-sur-Loire to accommodate the growing population in 1209.[6]

Concurrently with the economic progress of the thirteenth century, Gothic architecture in Burgundy in the first half of the century developed from the rich heritage of Romanesque innovation. Throughout the eleventh and twelfth centuries, two great monastic orders, the Cluniacs and the Cistercians, as well as secular patrons and ecclesiastics, contributed to the artistic and economic importance of the area with many buildings, some still extant.[7] The cathedral of Autun, the abbey of Sainte-Madeleine at Vézelay and the remnants of the abbey of Cluny and her dependencies all attest to the importance of the Burgundian region. One of the most notable buildings, the Romanesque cathedral of Auxerre, has been lost, but its crypt, preserved as the substructure of the Gothic cathedral, displays an impressive system of vaults and extensive murals.[8] The Gothic buildings reveal their connection to twelfth-century traditions in several ways. Some, like the cathedral of Auxerre, were constructed over twelfth-century foundations, whose disposition largely determined the limits of the Gothic plan. Others seemed to retain a Burgundian flavor, like the articulation of the wall surface so beautifully evident in the fluted pilasters and carved capitals of Autun.

During these years there was no clear stylistic frontier between Burgundy and Champagne, and trade routes linking Burgundian centers with the great fair towns of the Champagne, especially Troyes, emphasize the openness of this northern connection (text illus. 1). A trade route from the south of France followed the Rhone River, passed through Lyon and then Auxerre, before arriving at Troyes, site of one of the most prominent and well-documented regional fairs of the Middle Ages.[9] Burgundy was similarly linked with Paris through the Yonne River which emptied into the Seine at Montereau. The early development of the particular Burgundian Gothic style in architecture was largely a result of a series of borrowings from these northern areas, which resulted in a tapestry of richly varied responses in style.[10] The Burgundian system achieved coherence through its relationship to

[4] Dijon 1183 and 1187, Sens 1189, Auxerre 1194 (Branner, 1960, 3, n. 15).

[5] *Gesta*, LIX, 474-475; Vallery-Radot, 1958a, 45.

[6] *Gallia Christiana XII, Instrumenta*, col. 150.

[7] On Romanesque Burgundy, see Charles Oursel, *L'Art roman de Bourgogne*, Dijon (1928); Marcel Aubert, *L'Architecture cistercienne en France*, Paris (2nd ed., 1947); Kenneth J. Conant,

Cluny, les églises et la maison du chef de l'ordre, Macon (1968). Branner (1960, 10-37) discusses the twelfth century.

[8] Porée, 1926, 1-24; Branner, 1960, 106.

[9] Elizabeth Chapin, *Les Villes de Foires de Champagne des origines au début du XIVe siècle* (Bibliothèque de l'école des hautes études), Paris (1937).

[10] Hans Jantzen (''Burgundische Gotik,'' *Sitz-*

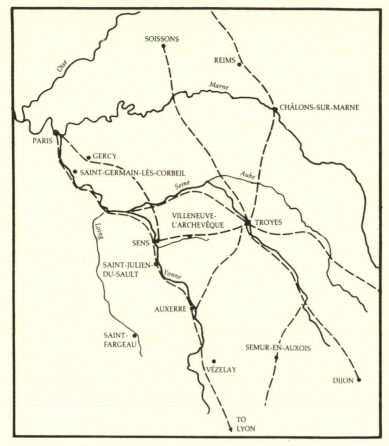

1. Map showing glazing sites and principal trade routes linking
Burgundy, Champagne and Paris.

large and varied group of Early Gothic monuments form part of this group stretching
across northern France and Belgium on an axis linking the cathedrals of Lausanne
and Canterbury. Bony was the first to single out this development of the Gothic
building, which presented many deviations in elevation, vaulting and facade from
the Chartrain solution of clarity in structure, equal balance of components and planar
articulation.[11]

The Burgundian buildings almost always gave equal height to the triforium
and the clerestory, which combined, almost equaled the height of the supporting
arcades. The Chartrain building, in contrast, favored a clerestory almost equal to
arcade elevation, with a short, dark triforium in between. In opposition to the clear
articulation of structure, as discussed by Panofsky in his analysis of the High Gothic
style,[12] Burgundian Gothic buildings consistently masked the actual function of the

*ungsberichte der Bayerische Akademie der Wis-
senschaften* [Phil.-hist. Klasse] 5 [1948], 1-38)
was one of the first art historians to recognize the
Burgundian development as a distinct stylistic
variant.

[11] Bony, 1957-1958, 35-52; Prache, 1978, 117-
120.

[12] Erwin Panofsky, *Gothic Architecture and
Scholasticism*, New York (1957).

supporting elements by the use of open passageways, arcaded screens and shifting surfaces. Most Burgundian buildings exhibit a lower height than their Chartrain counterparts. Especially evident in the long, low movement of the cathedral of Sens, the massive sobriety of the Cistercian tradition so firmly established at Fontenay and Pontigny may have contributed to the acceptance of measured, open spaces in the subsequent Gothic constructions.[13]

In the context of an analysis of Burgundian glazing ateliers, four major monuments correspond to the development of the style labeled Burgundian Gothic; Auxerre and Notre-Dame of Dijon where the style first appeared, Semur-en-Auxois, which witnessed an elaboration of the movement, and Saint-Julien-du-Sault where the Burgundian quality of the design gave way to the increasing influence of architectural forms of the Ile-de-France.

The complex fortification surrounding medieval Auxerre, ramparts, towers, moats and parapets, served as a massive frame for an unusual collection of religious edifices.[14] Auxerre was chiefly a city of clerics and administrators due to the energetic founding of monasteries by Auxerre's bishops of the fifth and sixth centuries. The churches of Saint-Amâtre, Saint-Julien, Saint-Marien, Saint-Gervais and Saint-Martin surrounded the city. Inside the walls the churches of Saint-Germain, Saint-Pèlerin, Saint-Eusèbe, Notre-Dame-de-la-Cité, Saint-Pierre-en-Vallé and Saint-Loup clustered around the cathedral, clearly the most notable architectural landmark. The beauty of Auxerre's cathedral owes much to its unusually striking site. The building rises up on the highest part of the city, overlooking a sharp embankment just above the Yonne River. From the curving bank of the Yonne the chevet of the cathedral presents a dazzling display of masonry substructure, glazed ambulatory and flying buttresses supporting the double lancets and roses of the upper choir. This great wall of glass and stone dominated the heavily traveled waterway and principal access to the rich Burgundian farmlands.

Guillaume de Seignelay, bishop of Auxerre from 1207 to 1220, appears to have taken strong measures to support the construction of the present Gothic building. He completely leveled the existing Romanesque building, except for the crypt and sacristy, due to the perceived "ancient style of its construction and small dimensions," as recorded in a contemporaneous account.[15] Guillaume accordingly assumed the major part of the expenses for the first years of the cathedral's construction, most probably underway by 1215.[16] The bishop's bold actions seem to have been

[13] Salet, 1955; Kenneth W. Severens, "The Continuous Plans of Sens Cathedral," *Journal of the Society of Architectural Historians* 24 (1975), 198-207. Henri Sanglier was probably influenced by Saint Bernard's conception of architectural norms for religious buildings.

[14] For medieval Auxerre, see Marguerite David-Roy, "Pierre de Courtenay, batisseur," *Archeologia* 30 (1969), 50-55; Odile Liebard, "Les maisons d'Auxerre au XVIe siècle," *Bulletin archéologique du Comité des travaux historiques*

et scientifiques n.s. 4 (1968), 155-159; Bouchard, 1979, 4-5, fig. 1.

[15] *Gesta*, LIX, I, 474-475; Mortet, 1911-1929, II, 202-209; Branner, 1960, 106; Porée, 1906, 239; Porée, 1926, 12; Vallery-Radot, 1958a, 45; Lebeuf, *Mémoires* I, 374.

[16] *Gesta*, LIX, 474-475; Lebeuf, *Mémoires* I, 392; Branner, 1960, 38; Vallery-Radot, 1958a, 45; also Guillaume's donation on his death in 1223, Molinier, 1919, III/3, 267.

matched by the character of the architect, whose eagerness resulted in the well-documented collapse of the Romanesque towers in 1217.[17] After Guillaume was named bishop of Paris in 1220, he continued to support the work, and to a lesser extent so did the new bishop, Henri de Villeneuve. Work on the chevet was probably completed before 1234 since Henri was buried in the choir in that year (fig. 1).[18]

The foundation of the Romanesque crypt determined the width of the Gothic choir, but the length of the choir appears to have been variable and was clearly altered even during the first construction campaign. The present choir comprises four oblong quadripartite vaults from the crossing to the beginning of the hemicycle, the hemicycle vaulted by means of eight ribs radiating from a single key. The original vaulting plan appears to have been sexpartite, and the elevation significantly lower than the present state, possibly similar to that of Notre-Dame of Dijon. The architect must have progressively enlarged and modified his plan as he progressed toward the crossing, a daring but dangerous course. The lighter, more harmonious vaulting system and the increased height, however, did much to produce the effect of great spaciousness and clarity.

Branner notes that the colonnette clusters in the ambulatory and triforium of the Auxerre choir appeared in much the same form in the triforium of Canterbury Cathedral some thirty years earlier.[19] However, the form had already appeared at Sens in the north tower dating from the final years of the twelfth century. At Sens, the earlier masonry piers were replaced by the same slender clusters of detached columns with open passageway behind that we find at Auxerre. At Auxerre, the cluster performs a very real function in carrying the weight of the ribs.

The axial chapel of the cathedral is at once a work of striking beauty and fascinating heritage (fig. 2). The concept of ambulatory with a single radiating chapel may have been inspired from the nearby cathedral of Sens, but was more likely based on the old Romanesque cathedral at Auxerre and the chapel in the crypt. Historians almost unanimously attribute the choice of two free-standing columns just before the chapel to the example of Saint-Remi of Reims of about 1170.[20] This plan of screening the ambulatory from the axial chapel gained popularity in the northeast of France with the south transept chapels of the cathedral of Soissons (1176) and Notre-Dame-en-Vaux of Châlons-sur-Marne (1185-1190). The general effect of such placement of detached columns rendered an interior space partitioned and yet unified, broken, but still harmonious.

Influenced by northern French architecture, Auxerre offers an example of wall space that becomes fluctuating in character (fig. 3). The wall is not a single but two thin layers, defined on the exterior by masonry pierced by windows, and on the interior by screens of columns and pierced passageways. On all levels the construc-

---

[17] *Gesta*, LIX, 475-476; Branner, 1960, 39-40; Robert of Saint Marien, 1882, 277, 283.

[18] Molinier, 1919, 248; *Gesta*, LX, 486.

[19] Branner (1960, 38-48) remains the most important statement on Auxerre's architecture. See,

however, Harry Titus, dissertation in progress, Princeton University.

[20] Branner, 1960, 52-53; Bony, 1957-1958, 43; Hautecoeur, 1927, pl. 11; Prache, 1978, 119-120, pl. 43.

tion of the wall space refuses to be confined by a single concept. The ambulatory wall, as well as restating the vaulting system by the continuation of the system of clustered columns, reflects the ambiguity of the over-all wall space through a blind arcade. At the window level, the wall fluctuates between the masonry and an open passageway completely surrounding the ambulatory. In the elevation of the choir, the arcades themselves define a space without really walling it in. Above, the ample triforium holds its own between arcade and generous clerestory by the clear and rhythmic progression of detached columns, three per side bay and two per bay of the hemicycle. The open passageway in front of the clerestory windows, like that surrounding the ambulatory, reflects the pervasive spatial tension characterizing Burgundian Gothic at its best.

Notre-Dame of Dijon (fig. 4), a parish church under the authority of the cathedral of Saint-Etienne, was begun some five years after Auxerre's cathedral.[21] Built on a much smaller scale, it nevertheless exhibits a superbly organized plan. The apse appears to derive from that of the church of Saint-Yved of Braine, one of the important buildings in the para-Chartrain axis.[22] Some attempt has been made to link patronage of the building campaign and the influence of Braine with the marriage of Hugues IV, Duke of Burgundy, with Yolande, daughter of Robert II, count of Braine and Dreux, but the lack of any specific documents makes the association highly conjectural.[23] Although the church was not dedicated until 1334, a document of 1251 mentions an altar in the church and indicates that the building must have been open for use, or that its use was envisioned in the near future.[24]

Robert Branner surmised that the building was the result of a unified campaign, working from east to west, and concluded about 1245.[25] Unlike Auxerre, whose choir is the only part of the church truly in the new style, the entire edifice in Dijon belongs to the Burgundian Gothic movement. The nave especially exhibits the openness and delicacy of the style, and has drawn praise from no less architectural authorities than Vauban, Soufflot and Viollet-le-Duc.[26] The lightness of the nave results from the distribution of the weight of the vaults through colonnette clusters. The double wall construction so successfully employed at Auxerre is recreated in Dijon through the continuous use of passageways.

In the choir, supported by the blind arcades of the dado, the elevation comprises a level of lower lancet windows, a triforium pierced by glazed oculi and a clerestory,

[21] Branner, 1960, 54-62; Oursel, 1938.

[22] Branner, 1960, 56-68.

[23] Charles Oursel, "Les origines monumentales de l'église Notre-Dame de Dijon," *Mémoires de la Commission des antiquités du département de la Côte-d'Or* 20 (1933-1935), 171-172, reprinted as "La question des origines architecturales de Notre-Dame de Dijon," *Annales de Bourgogne* 6 (1934), 299-300; Oursel, 1938, 18-22. Conditions were somewhat strained at this time. Courtepée (1847-1848, I, 137-141) and Petit (1884-1894, V, 40-46) show much contention between

Burgundy and Champagne, especially since the marriage of Hugues and Yolande defied dynastic accord between the Counts of Champagne and the Dukes of Burgundy.

[24] Oursel, 1938, 22; Branner, 1960, 132.

[25] Branner, 1960, 54.

[26] (Henri Baudot), "Rapport sur les travaux qui s'executent en ce moment à l'église Notre-Dame de Dijon," *Mémoires de la Commission des antiquités du département de la Côte d'Or* 7 (1865-1869), 31.

all provided with passageways like the nave. The transept, where the only extant glass of the church appears, exhibits a two-story elevation with two passageways. The two free-standing columns supporting the triple arcade of the inner wall connect with the columns of the dado. Just as the columns of the choir triforium act as a screen in front of the oculi, so the transept arcade screens the five lancets under the rose (fig. 5).

The columns cut across the lancets themselves instead of following the placement of the mullions. Branner pointed to the para-Chartrain origin of this screen in the Canterbury transepts where colonnettes cross the edges of the rose, an early design for the north transept at Lausanne, but most directly to the west facade of Saint-Remi at Reims where the architect has achieved a similar effect of fluctuating wall space somewhere between an inner screen of columns and an outer wall of glass.[27]

The picturesque setting of Semur-en-Auxois, a town still surrounded by its medieval fortifications, illustrates the elaboration of the Burgundian architecture in the priory of Notre-Dame (fig. 6). The restricted dimensions of the edifice notwithstanding, Notre-Dame approximates the proportions of a large cathedral.[28] Branner estimated that the building was begun about 1220-1225 under the direction of an innovative architect conversant with, but not limited to, established tradition. The building is essentially Burgundian in structure but with significant modifications, especially the extreme height of the clerestory which almost equals that of the triforium and arcades combined. None of the High Gothic monuments of the north have this feature and Branner suggested that the clerestory may have been conceived of independently as a way of giving distinction to a smaller-scale monument.

The architect certainly knew the cathedral at Auxerre, and his decision to raise the height of the clerestory may have been influenced by the Auxerre master's progressive elevation of the vaults of the cathedral's choir. Semur's architect retained, for the choir at least, the Burgundian three-part elevation with three passageways. The effect of the triforium screen and the double level of clerestory wall seems overshadowed by the dominance of the huge clerestory lancets that completely fill the width of the choir bays. The three radiating chapels that clearly disassociate themselves from the body of the choir are certainly not of Burgundian origin, but may have been influenced by the plan of the cathedral of Rouen. The remaining glass from the Gothic campaigns has now been grouped in four lancets of the axial chapel. The architect must have been concerned with the effect of the distortion of accustomed elevation proportions since the transept shows an increase in the height of the triforium at the expense of the clerestory, producing an elevation rather similar to the old Chartres style.

About 1235, however, with the construction of the nave, the architect delib-

[27] See also Prache, 1978, 53, 120, figs. 16, 19, 135.

[28] Branner, 1960, 66-68, 179-180. Little work has been done on the architecture of Semur.

erately moved away from the Burgundian style. He chose to completely eliminate the triforium, creating a two-story elevation, actually very close in feeling to the developing Rayonnant designs in the north. This style elevation in so small a church, however, creates a curious effect of compression quite distinct from the early Rayonnant striving for elegant ordering of continuous spaces. The application of columns to the nave piers and the use of three columns on the face of the wall effectively continues the weight descent from vault rib, to clerestory column, to arcade support. Such articulation of pier and rib may also be attributed to the influence of the newer styles being developed at Saint-Denis in the 1230s.

The collegiate church of Saint-Julien-du-Sault (fig. 7) marks the dissipation of the Burgundian style under the influence of the new Rayonnant style from the north of France.[29] The chapter at Saint-Julien was founded by Guy de Noyers, archbishop of Sens, shortly before his death in 1193.[30] Saint-Julien was the site of the archepiscopal château of Vauguilain, whose now ruined chapel also dates from the last years of Guy's tenure.[31] The château was one of the most popular of the archbishop's residences for its site commands an unforgettable view of Burgundian pastures and the sweep of the Yonne. Guy's foundation charter reveals that he chose the expediency of giving the newly founded chapter the already existing church in Domats, some twenty kilometers to the northwest, presumably in the expectation that a new collegiate church would be constructed in the near future. The actual building campaign, however, waited for the tenure of Gauthier Cornut (1222-1241). Although there are no documents relating to the construction of the present building, evidence from Saint-Julien's parish church would indicate that both buildings were supervised by canons from Sens.[32]

Saint-Julien's choir was probably begun about 1235, and exhibits many features common to Gothic construction in the Ile-de-France and Champagne. The choir contains three bays terminating in a hemicycle of five segments corresponding to the five chapels of the chevet. Although a much later building, Saint-Julien repeats the twelfth-century disposition of Suger's Saint-Denis in the progressive deepening of the chapels toward the east and the inclusion of the two western chapels into the vaulting of the ambulatory. The shallowness of the chapels reflects designs at Soissons and Chartres. The severity of the damages caused by the Hundred Years' War and the subsequent sixteenth-century restorations makes a reading of the elevation difficult.[33] Branner believed that the extant evidence indicates an original design of band triforium and tall clerestory without interior passageway, a clear abandonment of the traditional Burgundian elevation proportions as well as its fluctuating wall space.

Toward the middle of the century, paralleling developments across Europe, the

[29] Branner, 1960, 87-89, 171-172.

[30] Charters published by Quantin, 1854-1860, II, no. CDXLVI, and ibid., 1868-1873, II/G. G 1579.

[31] Quantin, 1868, 167; Tonnelier, 1842, 102.

[32] Branner, 1960, 4-5; Document published by Quantin, 1873, no. 620.

[33] Vallery-Radot, 1958b, 358-365; Tonnelier, 1842, 109.

Burgundian economic boom appears to have abated. The experience of Burgundy might serve as a microcosm for general tendencies affecting Europe as a whole.[34] The Burgundian towns ceased to expand in area or to increase in population. Pierre de Courtenay's late twelfth-century walls of Auxerre, which replaced the old Gallo-Roman wall that had formed such a tight circuit around the cathedral, remained the boundaries of the city throughout the Middle Ages. It was only in the late eighteenth century that the medieval walls were torn down and replaced with the wide boulevards that surround Auxerre's central city today.[35] The towns themselves hardened distinctions between a wealthier class of merchants and professionals and a poorer class of artisans and laborers. The trend toward emancipation of peasants abated and the overall economic situation of the peasant declined. With the disappearance of an agricultural frontier, there was no additional land for younger sons to cultivate, so that family plots became smaller and more intensely farmed. Thus a rotation of fallow and cultivated plots became more and more unlikely.

Political disunity, although perhaps not always violently evident, was clearly more a part of the general scene. In Burgundy, the disastrous quarrel between Vézelay and Provence over the identification of the relics of Mary Magdalene might be viewed as an indication of the divisive challenges to authority experienced during this time. Vézelay's relics were verified on 24 April 1267, and Erard de Lésignes, bishop of Auxerre 1270-1278, received a strand of the hair of the Magdalene, yet eventually the 1279 contention of Charles of Salerno that he had found the true resting place of the Magdalene eclipsed the Burgundian claim.[36] Vézelay had been Burgundy's most renowned pilgrimage site, located at the head of the Limoges-Perigueux road to Compostella and its discrediting in the late thirteenth century is an example of the general disruption of established traditions that had served so well during the past two centuries. Erard de Lésignes was also the last medieval bishop noted in the *Gesta pontificum Autissiodorensium*, in which the cathedral canons had recorded the actions of Auxerre's bishops for over four hundred years.[37]

Significantly, the spate of building in Burgundy and the development of a specifically Burgundian architectural style experienced simultaneous declines. Elsewhere, particularly in the north and the Ile-de-France, profound changes had already affected building styles. The derivative, but clearly independent style of the Rayonnant had already supplanted the High Gothic. Indeed the cathedral of Amiens, that "summa" of High Gothic expression, evolved a mid-century choir whose clerestory with glazed triforium and sweeping verticality convincingly articulated the new aesthetic.[38]

---

[34] Branner, 1960, 4, 83-101; Archibald R. Lewis, "The Closing of the Medieval Frontier, 1250-1350," *Speculum* 33 (1958), 475-483; see also Richard, 1954, 310-318 for indebtedness of nobility.

[35] Marguerite David-Roy, "Pierre de Courtenay, batisseur," *Archeologia* 30 (1969), 50-55.

[36] For verification see Lebeuf, *Mémoires*, I, 441-442 and Petit, 1891-1894, V, 95-97. The relic is recorded by Lebeuf (*Mémoires*, I, 454 and IV, 240). For the Provençal claim see especially *Acta sanctorum*, July vol. 6: July 22, pp. 207-216.

[37] Duru, 1850-1863, I, 511.

[38] Stoddard, 1972, 211-222; Branner, 1965, 138-140.

The vast and public cathedral, dependent on corporate action of canons and populace to insure its construction, no longer functioned as the dominant architectural model. The new exemplar was found in the small, private and royally funded Sainte-Chapelle of Louis IX, whose architectural style as well as glazing systems were to inspire so many imitators in Burgundy, other French sites and even abroad. The disappearance of Burgundian Gothic as an architectural style about 1250 must be seen as one element in a complex set of transformations affecting France socially and artistically at mid-century.

II

LES NEIGES D'ANTAN: THE LOST PRE-GOTHIC GLASS OF AUXERRE

> *Elegit etiam cum laude et cum gratiarum capituli sui actione, quosdam quos gratis canonicos ad prefinitam obedientiam constituit; presbyterum scilicet dignum et idoneum qui cotidie, pro defunctis canonicis nostris proprie offeret; aurifabrum mirabilem, pictorem doctum, vitrearium sagacem.* (*Gesta* account of the donation of Geoffroy de Champallement, bishop of Auxerre, 1052-1076)[1]

The art of stained glass windows has been linked to the development of the Gothic style. The gradual elimination of the wall as a weight-bearing member and the subsequent expansion of the window space allowed the art of the stained glass painter to reach its full potential. The art of glazing windows, however, developed gradually and by the Romanesque period had already become a major art form. The existence of the *Gesta* accounts of the bishops of Auxerre makes it possible to trace the history of glazed windows in the cathedral to Carolingian times. The information contained in the *Gesta* has been taken into account by historians and art historians alike. De Lasteyrie made a detailed inventory of *Gesta* references to the early glass at Auxerre but did not attempt to connect the references to windows to the particular building campaign or to incorporate these laconic descriptions into a discussion of the development of early glass in general.[2] His example was followed by Westlake, who listed the references to the Carolingian and Romanesque programs before describing Auxerre's Gothic program.[3] Lebeuf, Quantin, Louis, Vallery-Radot and Bouchard have all noted these passages when listing the accomplishments of individual bishops or describing lost buildings.[4] In order to provide a broadened understanding of the glazier's art in Burgundy, it seems important to see these textual references to now lost windows in the context of what we understand about window glazing of the period under review.

---

[1] *Gesta*, LI, 396, "He chose also with the praise and thanksgiving of his chapter, certain men whom he established without payment as canons within his prescribed jurisdiction; namely, a worthy and suitable priest who would daily offer Mass properly for our deceased canons, a clever goldsmith, a learned painter and an intelligent glazier." I am indebted to Rev. Robert Healey, S.J. for this translation.

[2] 1857, 184-185.

[3] N.H.J. Westlake, *A History of Design in Painted Glass*, London, I (1881), 86.

[4] Lebeuf, *Mémoires*, I; M. Quantin, "Restitution par les textes des cathédrales élevées successivement à Auxerre avant le XIIIe siècle," *Bulletin de la Société des sciences historiques et naturelles de l'Yonne* 4 (1850), 369-379; Louis, 1952; Vallery-Radot, 1958a, 40-50; Bouchard, 1979.

The Carolingian cathedral of Auxerre is the first to receive glazed windows. Bishop Héribalde, 824-857, restored the walls and ceiling of the building and decorated the church with murals and glass windows. The *Gesta* simply states that "vitreis quoque ac picturis" were added.[5] This concern for the embellishment of structures must be connected to the general revival of interest in liturgy and church-building that distinguished the Carolingian era. The abbey of Saint-Germain of Auxerre still retains a series of murals from this period and Auxerre's school of biblical studies was one of the most renowned of the ninth century.[6] The cathedral's windows may have been in the form of transennae: wooden, stone or stucco armatures that housed small pieces of glass. Carolingian artists seem to have favored this technique, which had the double advantage of strength and beauty without necessitating the use of large pieces of glass. Few extant examples of true transennae exist, but a window found in S. Apollinare in Classe has been dated to the eighth century.[7] A significant number of references by early medieval authors, Gregory of Tours, Venantius Fortunatus, Sidonius Apollinaris, bishop of Clermont-Ferrand, and others make it possible to conclude that glazed windows were commonly employed in France by the ninth century.[8] Since the *Gesta* omits references to figures, stories or pictures, Auxerre's windows might have resembled the stone lattice patterns from a window of a chapel built about 506 in Dijon by Gregory, bishop of Langres.[9] Extant Carolingian stucco and stone decorative work similar to early medieval transennae patterns further argue for an oriental source as the common inspiration for both art forms. Most authorities accept the importance of these early windows in establishing a tradition of decorative systems that continued throughout the course of the Middle Ages.[10]

[5] *Gesta*, XXVI, 354, "Ecclesiam Sancti Stephani et parietibus et laquearibus renovavit; vitreis quoque ac picturis optimis decoravit" (He renewed the walls and ceiling of the Church of Saint Stephen, decorating them with excellent windows and pictures); de Lasteyrie, 1857, 184; Lebeuf, *Mémoires*, I, 191; Vallery-Radot, 1958a, 41.

[6] Louis, 1952, 60-62; Henri Focillon, *Peintures romanes des églises de France*, Paris (1967), 13-16. For Auxerre's theological eminence see Beryl Smalley, *The Study of the Bible in the Middle Ages*, Notre Dame Press, Indiana (1978), 37-46; Henri Barré, *Les Homélies carolingiennes de l'école d'Auxerre*, The Vatican, 1962 (Studi e Testi 225).

[7] Descriptions of the technique of the transennae best handled by H. G. Franz ("Neue Funde zur Geschichte des Glasfensters," *Forschungen und Fortschritte*, 29 [1955], 306-312). The Museo Nazionale, Ravenna, preserves a portion of the window from S. Apollinare in Classe. Franz suggests that the grisaille patterns in later medieval windows hearken back to transennae patterns.

[8] For the most recent treatment of the subject of the development of early stained glass, including references to literary sources, see Grodecki

(1977, 37-49). See also Eva Frodl-Kraft, *Die Glasmalerei*, Munich (1970), 13-28. Discovery of a large quantity of window glass from the monastery of Jarrow (682-870), including a possible figural window, has been published by Rosemary Cramp ("Window Glass from the Monastic Site of Jarrow: Problems in Interpretation," *Journal of Glass Studies* 17 [1975], 88-96).

[9] Jean Hubert, *L'Art pré-roman*, Paris (Les éditions d'art et d'histoire) (1937), 139-142, pl. XXVII, fig. d. The object is now housed in the Musée d'Orléans.

[10] See Grodecki, 1977, 38-42, figs. 23-27. Robert de Lasteyrie (*L'Architecture religieuse à l'époque romane en France*, Paris [1926], 2nd ed., p. 86, fig. 67) connects the interlaced circles inscribing floral bosses at Germigny-des-Prés to patterns in grisaille glass of the twelfth century. See also Erika Doberer ("Die Ornamentale Steinskulptur an der Karolingischen Kirchenausstatung," *Karl der Grosse* III, ed. W. Braunfels, 1966, 3rd ed., 203-233) for discussion of decorative patterns, especially examples of tangent circles and interlace from Reichenau.

The Carolingian cathedral was added to through the episcopate of Guibaud (Wibaldus), 879-887, so that it stood complete in the 880s. The eastern end terminated in a vaulted hemicycle containing a mosaic with a gold background, very possibly like the mosaic of the Arc of the Covenant at Germigny-des-Prés.[11] A western apse had been added during the 850s, and Guibaud is recorded as having completed a two-storied westwork.[12] The architecture of the cathedral, therefore corresponds to the better documented, but also lost, example of Saint-Riquier, with elaborate westwork and chapels at both the eastern and western portions of the church.[13] The impressive crypt of the abbey of Saint-Germain had been completed by 859 and might have encouraged the bishops to press for improvements to their own seat.[14]

Unfortunately the Carolingian cathedral was ruined by a late ninth-century fire that also ravaged the three churches of the episcopal group as well as most of the town. Bishop Herfroi, 887-909, immediately began rebuilding, but again the church was destroyed by fire.[15] Gui the Venerable, 933-961, built a fourth cathedral and ornamented it with two lateral oratories with crypts and large glass windows, "vitreis magnis," again probably of the transennae type.[16] This building seemed no more privileged that its predecessors for in 1023 the church as well as a major part of the city went up in flames.

For the next thirty years, the bishops of Auxerre were temporarily without a church until the Romanesque cathedral was ready for service in 1057. Information about the glass for this building is fortunately more extensive than for the previous periods. Geoffroy de Champallement, 1052-1076, who consecrated the new building, employed an astute method to insure the proper embellishment of the edifice. He persuaded five officers of his household to give funds for five windows in the apse. Responsibility for the sixth and more considerable window in the chapel of Saint Alexander was suggested to Geoffroy's own chaplain. Geoffroy went beyond simply insuring the production of the windows; he set up prebends for canons who would insure permanent maintenance.

> He chose also with the praise and thanksgiving of his chapter certain men whom he established without payment as canons within his prescribed jurisdiction; namely, a worthy and suitable priest who would daily offer Mass properly for

[11] Louis, 1952, 18. For Germigny-des-Prés, see André Grabar and Carl Nordenfalk, *Early Medieval Painting*, New York (1957), 69-71, figs. on pp. 69 and 70. The mosaic is dated 799-818.

[12] Louis, 1952, 21. For Guibaud's contribution, see *Gesta*, XL, 359; Jean Hubert, " 'Cryptae inferiores' et 'cryptae superiores' dans l'architecture religieuse de l'époque carolingienne," *Mélanges d'histoire du moyen-âge dédiés à la mémoire de Louis Halphen*, Paris (1951), 352; Louis, 1952, 21.

[13] Kenneth J. Conant, *Carolingian and Romanesque Architecture*, New York (1978), 43-46.

[14] Ibid., 66-67, fig. 26c; Jean Hubert, *The Carolingian Renaissance*, New York (1970), 5-10, pls.

5-8, 48-50, 345.

[15] *Gesta*, XLI, 362-363; Louis, 1952, 22-23.

[16] *Gesta*, XLV, 381, "sicut enim predicta Sancti-Stephani aecclesia post incendium funditus est eruta, ita postmodum ad eo ab ipsis est elevata fundamentis et ampliori decore quam fuerat antea, vitreis magnis et camera exornata" (For just as the above mentioned Church of Saint Stephen was destroyed after a fire, so it was rebuilt from the very foundation. It was adorned with more ample decoration than before consisting of large windows and side rooms [oratories]); de Lasteyrie, 1857, 184; Lebeuf, *Mémoires*, I, 236; Vallery-Radot, 1958a, 42, nn. 4 and 5.

our deceased canons, a clever goldsmith, a learned painter, and an intelligent glazier.[17]

Geoffroy's donation is very similar to the action taken by Abbot Suger of Saint-Denis in the 1140s. Suger's donation is certainly more famous and deserves to be quoted in full:

> Now, because (these windows) are very valuable on account of their wonderful execution and the profuse expenditure of painted glass and sapphire glass, we appointed an official master craftsman (*ministerialem magistrum*), for their protection and repair and also for a skilled goldsmith for the gold and silver ornaments, who would receive their allowances and what was adjudged to them in addition, viz., coins from the altar and flour from the common storehouse of the brethren, and who would never neglect their duty to look after these (works of art).[18]

Both Geoffroy and Suger followed the same sequence; first the installation of the windows then the funding of resident experts to insure their proper care. In the many references to Suger's foundation, it should be more frequently stated that the abbot's actions were firmly grounded in tradition as well as setting an example for the future.[19]

Geoffroy's funding of three artisans provides additional insight into the division of crafts at a period when little is known about workshop practices. The *Gesta* text refers to three separate people: goldsmith (or metalworker), painter and glazier. The impression is that artisans were trained in a specific technique and that they did not easily move from one type of artistic production to another. This same division of labor appears some half-century later in the *De diversis artibus* of the monk Theophilus.[20] Through the careful descriptions of processes of all three crafts, Theophilus reveals that the early twelfth century possessed considerable technical expertise, which was essentially transferred through an apprentice system. Theophilus' description of the production of glass of various colors, the use of lead to hold sections of glass in place and the application of paint in three progressively darker washes "whether for the face, the robes, the hands, the feet, the border or any other place" indicates that the making of figural glass must have been commonplace.[21]

In discussing the glass of the late eleventh-century cathedral, despite the ref-

---

[17] *Gesta*, LI, 396, "quinque vero fenestras que sunt in supremi cancelli fornice, quinque de domo sua clientibus ut quisque suam vitrearet, distribuit: sextam quoque majorem, cunctarumque precipuam altare Sancti-Alexandri clarificantem, ut suus capellanus faceret, exoravit . . . elegit etiam cum laude et cum gratiarum capituli sui actione, quosdam quos gratis canonicos ad prefinitam obedientiam constituit; presbyterum scilicet dignum et idoneum qui cotidie, pro defunctis canonicis nostris proprie offerret; aurifabrum mirabilem, pictorem doctum, vitrearium sagacem.

. . ." See also de Lasteyrie, 1857, 184, and Lebeuf, *Mémoires*, I, 268.

[18] Panofsky, 1979, 76-77.

[19] Grodecki, *Vitrail*, 83; Louis IX also wished to guarantee the upkeep of the glass he had just had made for the Sainte-Chapelle and provided funding from the royal treasury (Dyer-Spencer, 1932, 337).

[20] Theophilus, *The Various Arts*, ed. C. R. Dodwell, London (1961), xxxiii-xliv; Theophilus, 1963, xv, xvi.

[21] Theophilus, 1963, 62.

erence simply to "fenestras . . . vitrearet," one might pose the question of the existence of true figural glass. Leaded glass of the figural type has been preserved in a few instances from the eleventh century. Fragments from a dramatic head found in the Ottonian abbey of Lorsch may even date from the ninth century.[22] A better preserved head from Wissembourg, now in the Musée de l'Oeuvre Notre-Dame at Strasbourg, has been dated by Grodecki to around 1060.[23] The three layers of paint mentioned by Theophilus are already apparent in the firm modeling of the planes of the face and the detailing of the hair and beard.

The text of the *Gesta* makes absolute statements difficult. The use of the term "vitrearius" is particularly frustrating. The medieval Latin makes no distinction between "glazier" and "glass painter," as we have been accustomed to doing in the English, and in the French terms "verrier" and "peintre-verrier." That "vitrearius" could mean a glass painter is demonstrated by the inscription at the bottom of the first Joseph window in the cathedral of Rouen, dated about 1235.[24] The artist identified himself as "Clemens vitrearius carnotensis" (Clement, glass painter of Chartres). Although Clement's "hand" has not been identified among the windows of Chartres, the complex medallion design, detailed iconography and meticulous working of paint in the Rouen window make it clear that Clement was a skilled glass painter during the very apogee of the practice of the art. Abbot Suger describes the windows of the ambulatory chapels of Saint-Denis as being painted "depingi." Later he refers to these same windows as containing "vitri vestiti," glass that has had a "covering," or "adornment."[25] Even for a single author, a consistently explicit vocabulary to describe true leaded and painted glass was not generally employed in the Romanesque period.

The *Gesta* text, however, uses a discreet list of adjectives to qualify each of the crafts that are mentioned in Geoffroy's donation. The goldsmith is qualified as "mirabilis," clever, wonderful, extraordinary. The words "mirabilis" or "mirabiliter" were very common terms to describe metalwork, especially during the Romanesque period.[26] The painter was to be "doctus," well-informed, learned, instructed. The glass painter should possess keen senses, be mentally acute, intelligent or shrewd, "sagax." One should also note that the three artisans were all to be ecclesiastics, canons, who must have been expected to have some understanding of church doctrines, religious themes and a familiarity with the liturgy. The combination of circumstances would argue that figural glass was quite possible, if by no means certain, at Auxerre and that the eleventh-century artist possessed a religious background as well as the requisite skills to enable him to participate in the elaboration of iconographic themes.

The Romanesque cathedral of Auxerre was a building of considerable size. The upper structure was completely torn down by Guillaume de Seignelay about 1214

[22] Grodecki, 1977, 45-48, figs. 30 and 31.
[23] Ibid., 49-50, fig. 35.
[24] Ritter, 1926, 43-45, pl. XIV; Grodecki, 1953, no. 22, idem., *Vitrail*, 143, fig. 108.

[25] Panofsky, 1979, 73-77.
[26] Edgar de Bruyne, *Etudes d'esthétique médiévale*, Bruges (1946), esp. II, 69-107, 406-420.

in order to construct the present Gothic building. The crypt, however, was untouched and preserved for the most part its eleventh-century disposition.[27] A wide nave of three bays, ambulatory, axial chapel and painted vaults distinguished Auxerre's construction as one of the most impressive of its period.[28] Similar to its crypt, the upper church had a nave, two side aisles and a single radiating chapel at the axis.[29] Throughout the late eleventh and twelfth centuries various bishops made improvements to the fabric, including the addition of several series of glass windows. Humbaud the Venerable, 1087-1114, donated a considerable number of windows:

> He further had made very beautiful glass for the four windows that illuminated the high altar, the two that opened onto the choir, and the twenty-three windows of the nave.[30]

Again, the *Gesta* makes no mention of figural glass, but the dates for Humbaud's donation make the glass contemporaneous with the first major series of windows still extant from medieval times. The four extant standing figures of prophets—Daniel, Osee, David and Jonas—and a sixteenth-century copy of Moses, once occupied the nave of the cathedral of Augsburg.[31] Dated around 1100, the figures are over two meters in height and remain in a relatively good state of conservation. Through a study of the inscriptions on the scrolls of the prophets, the placement of the figures in their architectural setting and the later programs such as the glass of Saint-Remi of Reims, the Augsburg series has been interpreted as a typological program relating the twelve apostles of the New Testament to twelve prophets of the Old Testament.

In the second half of the twelfth century two bishops added more windows to the cathedral. Guillaume de Toucy, 1167-1181,

> added an open balustrade to the exterior (of the cathedral) and rebuilt the front and rear gables as well as the windows that were a part of them.[32]

---

[27] Jean Hubert, *L'Architecture religieuse du haute moyen-âge en France*, Paris (1952), 56, pl. VII; Louis, 1952, 111-124. Hugues de Chalon was probably responsible for the plan of the crypt. Molinier, 1919, III/3, 239, 243.

[28] It is not possible to see the crypt frescoes as contemporaneous with the recorded donations of eleventh-century glass in the cathedral. Although the axial chapel was constructed about 1030, the extraordinary painting of Christ mounted as King and Emperor attended by four mounted angels disposed between the arms of a huge cross appears most probably to date from the mid-twelfth century. The very clear reference to Humbaud in the *Gesta*, "In crypta altare Trinitatis superius et inferius adornavit," 396, lead Paul Deschamps ("Peintures murales de la cathédrale d'Auxerre," *Congrès archéologique de France* 116 [1958], 56-59) to conclude that Humbaud was responsible for the vault fresco (superius) of Christ, and the wall fresco (inferius) of angels. Louis (1952, 111-124)

attributed the fresco either to Humbaud or to his predecessor Geoffroy de Champallement. However Otto Demus (*Romanische Wandmalerei*, Munich [1968], 71, 145-146, pls. 124-125) most convincingly points to the sensitive drapery rendering characterized by thin, elegant folds that indicates a date toward the mid-twelfth century.

[29] Branner, 1960, 106.

[30] *Gesta*, LII, 403, "Fenestras etiam quatuor seniori altari lumen prestantes mirabili opere vitreari fecit, atque in anteriori parte ecclesiae XXIII, juxta chorum quoque duas vitreavit"; de Lasteyrie, 1857, 184-185; Lebeuf, *Mémoires*, I, 281. Bouchard (1979, 17) gives Humbaud's dates as 1092-1114.

[31] Grodecki, 1977, 50-52, figs. 36-41; G. Frenzel, *Suevia Sacra, Frühe Kunst in Schwaben*, Exhibition Catalogue, Augsburg (1973), nos. 228-230, pls. I-IV.

[32] *Gesta*, LVII, 427, "anterius pignaculum et posterius cum vitreis ad ipsa pertinentibus fecit

Hugues de Noyers, 1183-1206, engaged in extensive renovations including a new, raised pavement, a new roof, and, as Branner suggested, possibly vaults over the side aisles.[33] He also completely reworked the west facade, enlarging the glass windows "in order to let in a brighter light."[34] These late twelfth-century renovations at Auxerre assume greater substance when taken in the context of the great wave of early Gothic construction and development of the stained glass window. The bishop of Auxerre was subordinate to the archbishop of Sens, whose cathedral had been completed by 1180.[35] Although the clerestory windows of Sens' choir date from a 1230 remodeling, and the nave windows date from a 1310 campaign, the Early Gothic of the archepiscopal seat must have presented a sharp contrast to the late eleventh-century Romanesque of Auxerre's cathedral. The choir of the abbey church of Vézelay was remodeled about 1185.[36] The clerestory windows at Vézelay have retained their original forms and provide an approximation of the twelfth-century disposition of Sens. The dark harmonies of Vézelay's Romanesque nave become even more apparent through their juxtaposition with the brilliant illumination of the Early Gothic choir. The Sens system spread north to the church of Saint-Quiriace at Provins, begun in all likelihood after the fire of 1188.[37] Auxerre's saturated market for church construction, with the exception of work on Saint-Eusèbe, seems to have limited the introduction of more progressive architecture.[38] The bishops of Auxerre appear to have contented themselves with remodeling the cathedral.

That Auxerre's late twelfth-century bishop would have been anxious to keep up with the tastes of the times in architecture and decoration is evident from the description of the life of Hugues, Count of Noyers. A nobleman of distinguished lineage, Hugues appears to have been paticularly zealous in maintaining the prestige of his office. He improved episcopal property through large purchases of land and building campaigns at the episcopal châteaux at Regnennes, Charbuy, Toucy, Cosne and Varzy, and the family château at Noyers. The author of *Gesta* biography, a canon named Eustache, and Robert of Saint Marien both describe the secular magnificence of his many journeys beyond his diocese, his large train of knights and ecclesiastics, numerous servants and his elaborate clothes and accouterments. Robert of Saint-Marien, a monk himself and a more critical observer than the cathedral's canons, even went so far as to accuse Hugues of luxurious living and a life style too profligate for a good bishop.[39] Despite his many expenses, however, Hugues must have been an able administrator for at his death he left only a small debt for the silver revetment of an old cross. Given the concern Hugues displayed for his status,

---

. . ."; de Lasteyrie, 1857, 184-185; Lebeuf, *Mémoires*, I, 335; Bouchard, 1979, 89.

[33] 1960, 160.

[34] *Gesta*, LVIII, 448. "Qualiter fenestras in fronte veteris operis ecclesie ac vitreas dilataverit, ut ecclesia . . . in lucem claresceret ampliorem."

[35] Salet, 1955; Stoddard, 1972, 113-119, figs. 139-142, 144, 146.

[36] Francis Salet, *La Madeleine de Vézelay*, Melun (1948); Stoddard, 1972, 116-119, figs. 148-153; Branner, 1960, 30-32, 192-194, pl. 9b.

[37] Stoddard, 1972, 150, fig. 197.

[38] Branner, 1960, 31, 108, pl. 9a.

[39] Bouchard, 1979, 99-119; *Gesta*, LVIII, 431-442; Robert of Saint-Marien, 1885, 270.

it seems very likely that the windows he placed in the cathedral would be leaded figural glass very like the examples still extant from twelfth-century campaigns in other churches.

The development of the art of painted windows in the Romanesque period has recently received a rich and scholarly treatment through Grodecki's *Le Vitrail roman*.[40] The glass of the cathedral of Le Mans, 1140-1145, and the abbey of Saint-Denis, 1145, figure as some of the earliest programs, but from 1150 through the end of the century examples of Romanesque glass survive in England, France, Germany, Switzerland, Austria and Italy. Vestiges of Romanesque glazing campaigns geographically closest to Auxerre, 1180 at Notre-Dame of Paris, 1160 at Bourges and 1170-1180 at Troyes, have been reinserted into later Gothic structures or dispersed in museums. Fragments recently discovered at the abbey of Vézelay have been associated with the Troyes series.[41] The Romanesque glass of Auxerre has never been mentioned in a description of the cathedral's present state. Two puzzling figures, however, appear in the westernmost choir bays. The standing female saints (figs. 82 and 84), one identified as Saint Camille, are clearly out of place amid the much larger and more dynamic figures of male prophets and apostles. Most of the prophets or apostles occupy four and sometimes even five panels in the clerestory window. The female saints extend over three panels only, the lower panels being filled by figures of kneeling bishops, both entirely of modern glass. The movements of the figures are restricted and their frontality is much more emphatic than that of their companions. Their robes fall in flatter and more vertical folds, and they present a more rectilinear format, keeping within the columns that surround the figures on either side. The closest comparison, despite stylistic differences, might be the arcaded figures of about 1190 from the cathedral of Strasbourg.[42]

The two subjects in the companion lancets of these bays had been destined for the two lancets of the axial bay of the choir. They must have been moved to the westernmost bays when the new hemicycle glass of the Crucifixion and Christ in Majesty was installed shortly after 1250. Thus these bays exhibit glass that has been reused. It is possible that when the Romanesque cathedral was torn down by Guillaume de Seignelay, the glass from Hugues de Noyers' donations, which could date as late as 1206, was taken out and preserved. Certainly it could have been considered as a valuable resource as a stop-gap measure during the construction of the cathedral, whose windows only date from the 1230s. The two female saints belong neither to the stylistic nor the iconographic programs of the Gothic building, and their inclusion "at the tail end" of the choir would not have seemed to disrupt seriously the effect of the Gothic ensemble.

The question of the reuse of "spolia" has recently been examined in architectural and sculptural programs.[43] Glass windows possibly provide one of the most common

---

[40] 1977.

[41] Charles Little, "*Membra Disjecta:* More Early Stained Glass from Troyes Cathedral," *Gesta* 20/1 (1981), 125-126, fig. 12.

[42] Grodecki, 1977, 168-180, figs. 144, 146, 153.

[43] Most especially, see Jan van der Meulen, "Sculpture and Its Architectural Context at Chartres around 1200," *Year 1200*, III, 509-560.

examples of this process as the fragments are both precious in nature and relatively easy to reinsert: they can be releaded, or reduced in size, or made larger by the addition of new borders. The late twelfth-century panels of the legend of Saint Matthew from the cathedral of Notre-Dame of Paris were reused in the mid-thirteenth century south rose.[44] In the cathedral of Rouen, a series of windows, probably made for the nave side-aisle windows, about 1210-1220, were recut and placed in the narrow lancets of the chapels built between the nave buttresses, about 1270. The expense of remaking windows after discarding such quantities of glass must have presented problems to church builders. The beauty of the early thirteenth-century work, despite its completely different aesthetic of fully colored medallion window design, also seems to have impressed the renovators. From the fourteenth century, these windows have been referred to as "les belles verrières."[45] Caviness reports that the same reuse of earlier glass of a radically different style appears in York Minster. When the nave was rebuilt in the fourteenth century, twelfth-century glass panels were provided with contemporary borders and set in the new windows.[46]

The well-known example of the large figure of the Virgin "Notre-Dame de la Belle Verrière" from the twelfth-century cathedral of Chartres shows a reuse of glass that is closer in time. The window must have been rescued after the fire of 1196 and retained in the glass painter's shop. About 1215-1220 it was given a border of censing angels, iconographically in accord with the themes of the seated Virgin and Christ Child, although in the style of the second decade of the thirteenth century.[47] Grodecki's recent work on the early Troyes glass affirmed the growing suspicion that the panels now dispersed in museums and private collections must have been made for a Romanesque building, but were rearranged, releaded and given borders sometime around 1260 and 1280.[48] Windows were made for the parish church of Gercy around 1220, following the established traditions of a series of medallions containing fully colored glass. Toward mid-century, probably at the time of the transformation of the parish church into an abbey, the windows were provided with grisaille borders that allowed the glazier to use the older glass in new window openings.[49] The reuse of old glass, obviously, was not uncommon and it is likely that this practice was far more widespread than has been supposed. Medieval builders, we may well assume, were as concerned with cost containment as their modern

[44] Lafond, *Corpus, France* I, 52-67, pls. 9-11.

[45] Ritter, 1926, 7, 8, 37-38, pls. I-VIII; see also glass in the Worcester Art Museum and the Pitcairn collection, *Year 1200,* I, no. 207, 202-204, and Jean Lafond, "La verrière des septs dormants d'Ephèse et ancienne vitrerie de la cathédrale de Rouen," *Year 1200,* III, 399-416.

[46] ("De convenientia et cohaerentia antiqui et novi operis: Medieval Conservation, Restoration, Pastiche and Forgery," *Intuition und Kunstwissenschaft: Festschrift für Hanns Swarzenski,* ed. Peter Block et al., Berlin [1973], 206) where Caviness has begun a very important reassessment of aesthetic attitudes in the Middle Ages. See also Caviness, 1977, 38.

[47] Delaporte and Houvet, 1926, 216-221, pls. XL-XLII, color pl. V; Chantal Bouchon, Catherine Brisac, Claudine Lautier and Yolanta Zaluska, "La 'Belle-Verrière' de Chartres," *Revue de l'art* 46 (1979), 16-24.

[48] Grodecki (1973, 200) dates the windows about 1180. See also ibid. (1977, 140, 147, pls. 118-125) where the date 1170-1180 is given. Caviness (1977, 154) concurs on the date of 1170-1180.

[49] Raguin, 1974, 38, n. 13, and below, Genesis Atelier.

counterparts. The medieval builder, in addition, was certainly not as oblivious to the beauty of monuments of preceding eras and in some cases even went beyond the reuse of ''spolia'' to the completion of fragmentary works in an archaizing style.[50]

[50] See above, n. 46.

III

MEDALLION COMPOSITION AND ORNAMENT: A BRIEF OVERVIEW OF THE BURGUNDIAN ATELIERS

In tracing atelier traditions, ornament is often more useful than figure compositions and style. Ornamental motifs tend to be very long-lived; their execution is less idiosyncratic than is that of the figures, but at the same time they are less responsive to a model. (Madeline Caviness)[1]

A study of the composition and ornament of the Burgundian windows and associated glass establishes a pattern of groupings by workshops, a pattern that accords in every case with workshop partition through an analysis of painting styles. In general, the Burgundian glass exhibits systems using straight armatures rather than curved irons. Such a predilection is typical of the movement away from more complex, and certainly more costly, armature patterns of the Early Gothic period. However, straight bars long had served to house complex medallion patterns constituting a parallel development to the curved armature system. Several windows at Chartres show how much the same groupings of circles and quatrefoils might be achieved through either method.[2] The Burgundian windows offer a variety of responses to design problems: simple horizontal systems of panels, medallion designs achieved within the straight armature format and true curved armature patterns.

Genesis Atelier

Auxerre's major atelier, responsible for fifteen of the cathedral's windows, uses only a horizontal system of successive panels in the narrative. Three of the windows in this group portray events from the Book of Genesis, an unusual concentration for a Gothic program. The workshop seems to have been under the influence of two distinct personalities. The Genesis Master set the early style of the atelier and was responsible for the story of Samson, that of Margaret and the legends of Mary of Egypt and Mary Magdalene, as well as two Genesis narratives. The second Master, called the Genesis Inheritor, seems to have controlled the later production of the workshop, producing nine windows (text illus. 2).

The first two Genesis windows, the Creation and Fall, and Noah, Abraham and Lot (figs. 8 and 12, pl. III) are identical in overall disposition. The narratives are

---

[1] 1977, 41.
[2] Ibid., 42-43, text fig. 3.

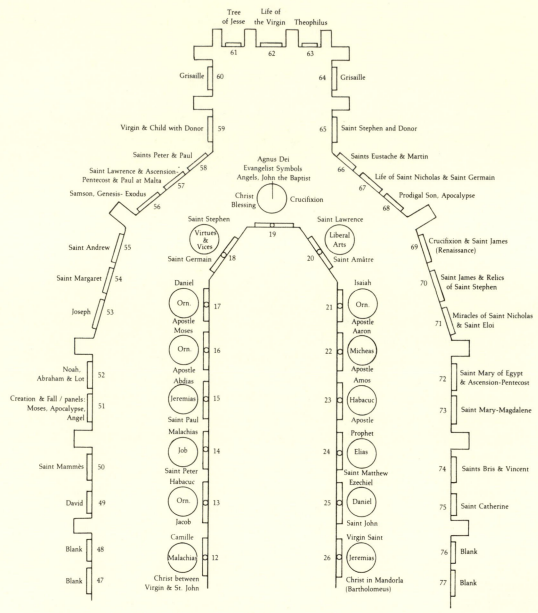

2. Position of windows in the cathedral of Auxerre after twentieth-century restorations.

framed in octagonal medallions whose interstices produce lozenge shapes filled with blue and yellow rinceaux patterns against a red ground, a decorative solution more typical of early thirteenth-century glass.[3] The vines curve in four circular patterns displaying leafy trefoil terminations and thick grape clusters near the borders of the medallions. The border motifs are much simpler. Against a red ground, blue and yellow fronds branch in oval shapes in regular intervals; grape clusters accent the upper interior of the oval. This disposition produces an unusual integration of

[3] Grodecki, 1948, 94-95.

medallion pattern and background. The overall effect is a series of interlocking successive polygons. Emphasis on surface patterning also extends to the treatment of foliage. The fronds are very thin, devoid of much grisaille modeling, and especially in the border, highly restricted in movement. Through the open decorative work and shifting polygons, these windows achieve a delicacy of overall treatment that distinguishes them from all other creations of the atelier.

The next four windows all show a progressive alteration of the systems employed by the Creation and Abraham windows. The Samson window (fig. 14) repeats exactly the same border design, but modifies the medallion format. The sharp angles of the octagons lose their precision, producing rounder, almost oval shapes, and the rinceaux between the medallions become somewhat heavier and radiate from a central focus. The Margaret window (fig. 15) uses circular medallions, shows a border of fronds in a zig-zag pattern, but retains the rinceaux systems between the medallions like the Samson window. The two windows of Mary of Egypt (fig. 35) and Mary Magdalene (fig. 34) are identical. Their medallion pattern follows the arrangement in the Samson window but the rinceaux between the medallions are replaced by quatrefoils around a square. The border is still narrow and extremely simple, but shows an alternation of a simple four-petaled flower and round boss very like the border of the Saint Stephen window of Chartres.[4] Despite the difference in motif, this system produces much the same effect as the geometrically ordered foliage of the Margaret window.

The windows of Saint Bris (fig. 27) and the Prodigal Son (fig. 25) appear to be transitional windows. Although its poor conservation makes an overall assessment rather difficult, the Bris window shows a rinceaux pattern between round medallions very similar to the Margaret window system. It introduces a new border pattern, however, consisting of fronds forming half-circular arcs. The Prodigal Son window also presents a new border pattern of successively curling fronds accented by grape clusters, a motif abstracted from the interior rinceaux of the Samson window. The Prodigal Son uses round medallions linked at the edges by the quatrefoils surrounding squares observed in the windows of Mary Magdalene and Mary of Egypt. In the spaces between the medallions, however, we find the foliate ornament of the Bris window, now inscribed by round bosses, a pattern similar to that at the Joseph window of Chartres.[5] Both the Bris and Prodigal Son windows achieve a much denser, more sporadic effect in their compositions. The medallions and decorative elements seem more relieved from their grounds and more insistent in their separate presentation.

This tendency toward greater contrast between medallion and ground is heightened in the remaining seven windows of the atelier, the work of the Genesis Inheritor. All of these compositions introduce a dense mosaic background between the medallions. The Joseph window (fig. 30) shows a red lattice system crossing blue circles painted with small grisaille fronds. An interlaced lattice with bosses at the inter-

---

[4] Delaporte and Houvet, 1926, pls. CXIX-CXXII.   Caviness, 1977, fig. 196.
[5] Ibid., pls. CLXII-CLXVI, color pls. XIV-XVI;

sections appears in the Andrew window (fig. 24). The window of Genesis and Exodus (fig. 29) shows a four-petaled flower lattice over a blue ground, and the Tree of Jesse window probably presented much the same pattern in the ground behind the half-circles of prophets. The window of James (fig. 32) shows a blue shell pattern with red borders and the David (fig. 36) and Mammès (fig. 37) windows complement each other with the same red vertical and horizontal lattice inscribing blue cinque-foils. The borders of these windows show the familiar thin, repetitious motifs of fronds in zig-zag, half-circles, ovals and curling patterns. Both the border and the mosaic background recall the design of the Peter and Paul window at Bourges.[6]

Eustache Atelier

The Eustache workshop uses very different formulas in medallion arrangement and decorative work. The border of the Eustache window (fig. 38) presents a system of triple leafy fronds accented by grape clusters, altogether a much fleshier design than the Genesis atelier's borders. An earlier variant of this motif is found in the Saint Stephen window of Bourges.[7] An overall medallion design is achieved within the straight armatures. On each level, the central rectangle is flanked by half circles connected by large bosses. The border of the central rectangle continues as an interlace surrounding the bosses so that the panels are linked in a continuous design. This treatment has been cited by Grodecki as a rare workshop expression that appears in the windows attributed to the Good Samaritan atelier at Bourges and at Poitiers.[8] The Passion and Saint Nicholas windows at Bourges and five windows at Poitiers (fig. 144) display such vertical bands connecting all of the medallions in a window.[9]

The medallion format of the Eustache window might be associated to the tradition established by its two immediate predecessors, the Eustache windows of Sens and Chartres. Chartres (fig. 39) alternates vertically ascending lozenges and paired circles.[10] The Sens plan uses medallions of four petals around a central lozenge inscribed in a circle.[11] Both windows are striking in effect. Auxerre's Eustache window, likewise, stands out among the ambulatory series. Both the unusual medallion pattern and color scheme command attention: clear sky-blue in the medallion backgrounds, dark blue and red floral mosaic surrounding the medallions, and bright pearl borders at the intersections. These contrasts achieve an exceptionally pleasing coloristic movement, one already noted by Guilhermy in the nineteenth century.[12] The Theophilus window (fig. 42) presents a medallion format similar to the Eustache window, but uses round bosses to weld the panels together, a pattern used in the Mary Magdalene window at Bourges (fig. 43), a product of the Good Samaritan atelier.[13] The mosaic background consists of tangent circles linked by smaller circles

[6] Cahier and Martin, 1841-1844, pl. XXIIA.

[7] Ibid., pl. XVIA.

[8] Grodecki, 1948, 94, 104, pl. 18.

[9] Papanicolaou (1977, 227) identifies continuous filleting in the Tours Infancy window. Jane Hayward (unpublished dissertation, "The Angevin Style of Glass Painting," Yale University, 1958,

237-250) sees the same technique in a Poitevin Master's work at Les Essards.

[10] Especially Grodecki, 1965; *Vitrail*, fig. 6; Delaporte and Houvet, 1926, pls. CLXVII-CLXXIV.

[11] Bégule, 1929, fig. 56, pl. XVI; *Vitrail*, fig. 9.

[12] Auxerre, fol. 693.

[13] Grodecki (1948, 93, fig. 18e) calls it an "un-

at the points of contact. The border presents successive ovals containing leafy fronds with grape cluster terminals.

The windows of Saint Lawrence (fig. 44, pl. IV) and the Miracles of Nicholas (fig. 47) do not present quite the same overall medallion formula, but still maintain a more unified system than the Genesis workshop's horizontal patterns. In the Saint Lawrence design, the central circles are flattened at the edges to blend with the flattened half-circles at the sides. The central medallions are further linked by a vertical connection that continues into the border of each medallion, a modified form of the continuous border design. The side border is unusually complicated with a zig-zag motif superimposed on a vertical progression of fronds and grape clusters, very like the Saint James window at Chartres.[14] The richness of the window is further enhanced by a mosaic background of a red lattice crossing blue circles decorated with small double fronds. The window of the Miracles of Nicholas shows much the same medallion organization, but uses quatrefoils. The decorative patterns, however, relate to the work of the Genesis atelier. The border shows a pattern of half-circles formed by arching fronds. The vegetative motifs are much thicker than those of the Genesis atelier and include a triple frond in the center of each arc. The interstices are filled not with a mosaic ground but with rinceaux stemming from a central focus, very like those of the Margaret window.

The remaining two windows of this workshop seem to derive as much from the Genesis Inheritor's designs as from those of the Eustache Master. Both show insistently horizontal successions of panels relieved against mosaic backgrounds. The Catherine window's mosaic (fig. 51) of four-petaled flowers against a blue background is common to the Eustache and Genesis ateliers. The Germain window's background (fig. 53) of vertical trellises whose intersections serve as foci for grisailled circles painted on blue glass is similar to the backgrounds in the Lawrence and Joseph windows. The Genesis atelier's Margaret window must have provided the pattern of fronds forming half-circular arcs found in the Germain window. The Catherine border, however, seems a conflation of the Theophilus and Lawrence designs presenting a succession of ovals superimposed on a central vertical motif of branching fronds. Almost the exact duplicate of this design appears in the Chartres window of Saint Nicholas (fig. 49) and a close variant in the Passion window of Bourges.[15] Although very similar to the Genesis Inheritor's designs, the quatrefoils in both the Germain and Catherine windows give the overall pattern a more undulating effect than the rhythmically insistent succession of circles.

Saint-Germain-lès-Corbeil Atelier

The workshop responsible for the Auxerre windows of the Life of Nicholas and the Relics of Stephen, the Troyes window of Andrew and the Peter window of Semur-

---

usual" composition and notes that it also appears in the Poitiers windows of the Childhood of Christ and the Passion. See also Cahier and Martin, 1841-1844, pl. XIA.

[14] Delaporte and Houvet, 1926, pls. CI-CIII.
[15] Ibid., pls. CLVII-CLXI, also window of Saints Theodore and Vincent (ibid., pls. CXI-CXIV). For Bourges see Grodecki, 1948, pl. 23b.

en-Auxois exhibits compositional and decorative characteristics that distinguish it from other Burgundian ateliers. Auxerre's Life of Nicholas window (fig. 62, pl. I) presents a medallion format with double pearled borders and complex bosses. Although straight armatures support the window, the overall design produced a medallion format that, if continued to the full extent of the original window, would produce a system of three large circles anchored at top by a half-circle. Despite its smaller scale, Troyes' Andrew window (fig. 60) exhibits the same system of vertically successive circles joined by large foliate bosses. The Peter window of Semur-en-Auxois (fig. 59) also presents a series of vertically organized medallions. At Semur, however, the medallions are quatrefoils and the armature actually follows that shape. The borders of the Auxerre Nicholas window and the Troyes window are identical.[16] It is an unusually rich design that integrates a succession of joined arches punctuated by foliate bosses and curling fronds. Although this same system has appeared in borders at Bourges, Chartres, and Canterbury,[17] the Troyes and Auxerre designs appear to be cut from exactly the same patterns. Typical of designs of the second quarter of the thirteenth century, the borders are more rigidly geometric and reduce the foliage to flatter, more abstract shapes.

A diaper mosaic of the background of the Semur-en-Auxois panels repeats the pattern found in the Nicholas window: a foliated quatrefoil inscribed in an alternating circle and diamond. The Troyes window and the Auxerre Relics window (fig. 66) also show dense mosaic backgrounds, at Troyes a four-petaled flower and in the Relics window an interwoven lattice inscribing four-petaled flowers. The Semur-en-Auxois borders are almost totally modern, but several extant portions show circular elements with leafy infill.

The Troyes and Auxerre borders and decorative bosses are unusual for their retention of thick, leafy forms. Indeed the closest comparison to the Relics border of continuous rinceaux whose rounded patterns encircle thick central clusters can be found in a group of monuments from a much earlier period: Châlons-sur-Marne, Canterbury and manuscript painting localized at Troyes and Cîteaux.[18] The Relics border shows much grisaille modeling, a technique singularly absent from the work of other ateliers discussed. Both the Relics and the Nicholas borders are by far the widest and most complex of any in the cathedral. The same lush foliage appeared in the bosses linking the Nicholas medallions at Auxerre and in their smaller counterparts in the Andrew window at Troyes. Such foliage treatment does appear in the Jesse Tree of Saint Germain-lès-Corbeil (fig. 54), which shows the same thick, sculpted leaves, gatherings of triple motifs and grape clusters.

Apocalypse Atelier

A study of the atelier responsible for the window of the Apocalypse at Auxerre is

[16] This group was cited by Lafond (1955, 31) and is most recently discussed by Caviness (1977, 43).

[17] Ibid., 1977, 84-95: discussed as part of a Sens-Canterbury development in border patterns, medallion formats and foliage delineation.

[18] Ibid., 1977, figs. 116, 121-124; *Year 1200*, I, no. 230. Illuminated initial, Bible, Paris, Bibl. nat. Ms. lat. 16743-6 (*Year 1200*, I, no. 247).

complicated by the radical rearrangement of the panels in all of the Auxerre windows associated with this group. The windows of the Apocalypse (fig. 67) and Eloi (fig. 73) now in portions of two south ambulatory windows were clearly not meant to present successive rows of three circular medallions. The extant ornament edging many of the panels indicates that the windows were once arranged in medallion formats, their joinings linked by large quadrilobed bosses inscribing a square. Between the medallions, space fillers of smaller quatrefoils appeared, very much like the quatrefoils between the medallions in the Prodigal Son, Mary of Egypt and Mary Magdalene windows. The original window design must have been almost identical to that found in the Simon and Jude window of Chartres (fig. 72) one of the works associated with the Saint Chéron Master.[19] Both the Chartres and Auxerre windows impose this quadrilobed design on a straight armature format. The windows of the Ascension-Pentecost (fig. 78) and Vincent (fig. 91) at Auxerre, and the windows of John the Evangelist (fig. 93) and Nicholas (fig. 92, text illus. 3) at Saint-Julien-du-Sault are also arranged without curving armatures. Despite the fragmentary conservations of these last two Auxerre windows, the half circles, quadrants,

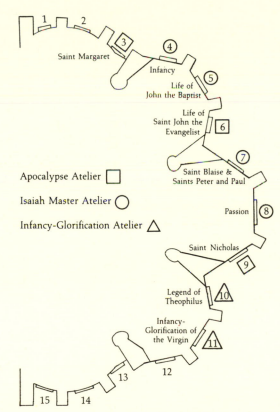

3. Disposition of windows at Saint-Pierre of Saint-Julien-du-Sault.

[19] Delaporte and Houvet, 1926, pls. XCVI-IC, color pl. X. This arrangement of two medallions per register is not uncommon. See the Theophilus and Typological Infancy windows in the apse of the cathedral of Laon, dated 1210-1215 (*Corpus, France, Recensement* I, 163, pl. 12). See below, Chapter IV, 6, n. 100, the Isaiah Master Atelier, for discussion of the Saint Chéron Master.

and pointed lobes of the extant panels indicate a medallion design involving central lobed medallions flanked by half circles.

The Saint-Julien-du-Sault Apocalypse atelier windows show simple horizontal dispositions of ovals and half circles. The one exception to this pattern is the Margaret window, whose medallion format is very similar to that of the Isaiah window of the Sainte-Chapelle (text illus. 4) discussed in the next section. Curved armatures support the central round medallions while the side trefoils are constructed with simple lead lines. The painting style shows more associations with the Apocalypse than the Isaiah Master atelier so that the window suggests a certain collaboration among ateliers. Perhaps the window was originally designed by the atelier of the Isaiah Master but executed by the Apocalypse atelier. The Saint-Fargeau panels are far too fragmentary to offer any hope of reconstructing medallion patterns. The variety of forms, however, suggests that systems using round, half-round and oval panels must have been used, all within a straight armature support.

Isaiah Master

The Isaiah Master's atelier responsible for four windows at Saint-Julien-du-Sault and two windows in the cathedral of Auxerre is immediately differentiated by its use of curved armatures, an unusual practice at mid-century. All of the Saint-Julien-du-Sault compositions mirror patterns already established by the glaziers of the Sainte-Chapelle (text illus. 4).[20] The Passion window is arranged in a simple vertical system of round medallions exactly like the framework of the Judith lancets in the Sainte-Chapelle. The Infancy window alternates central square panels with half

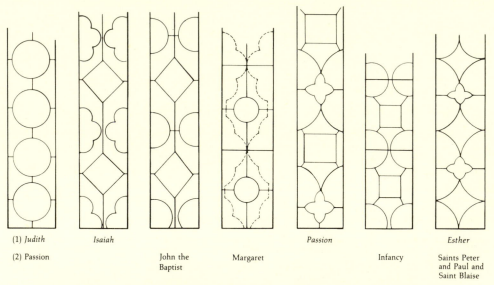

| (1) *Judith* | *Isaiah* | | | | *Passion* | | *Esther* |
| (2) Passion | | John the Baptist | Margaret | | | Infancy | Saints Peter and Paul and Saint Blaise |

4. Medallion patterns in the Sainte-Chapelle (1) and Saint-Julien-du-Sault (2).

[20] Grodecki, *Corpus*, France I, plan p. 75.

circles at the sides, a disposition similar to the succession of rounded and square panels in the Sainte-Chapelle's Passion window. The window of John the Baptist displays diamond shapes alternating with half-circles at the sides. The Sainte-Chapelle's Isaiah window differs only by substituting trilobed medallions for the half circles. The window of Blaise and Peter and Paul repeats the arrangement of quarter-circle medallions of the Sainte-Chapelle's Esther window. In both these windows a decorative central quadrilobe unites four central panels, giving the effect of a single medallion. Their borders show the same castles of Castille and fleur-de-lis found in the Parisian glass. The red and blue harmonies of the Sainte-Chapelle appear in all their intensity at Saint-Julien. Deep blues and, less frequently, reds fill the background of each medallion. At both sites red lattice patterns unifying a background of blue floral mosaic work complete the open spaces between the medallions. Even to the casual observer, the combination of medallion format and rich red-blue coloring immediately places the Saint-Julien-du-Sault glass within the Sainte-Chapelle's orbit.

Windows in the cathedral of Auxerre are products of this atelier. Both the windows of Martin and of Peter and Paul show variations on a quadrilobed medallion format, but accomplish this in the straight armature system. Although the Martin window (fig. 125) suffered the loss of many panels, those remaining have been grouped in a very plausible system of four vertically oriented petals around a central round medallion. At the sides quadrant medallions produce a half-circular effect, a system used in the Chartres windows of the Prodigal Son and the Life of the Virgin (fig. 126) and at other locations.[21] The Peter and Paul window (fig. 129) organizes the four lobes in an "X" shape around a central quatrefoil filled with fronds radiating from a square trellis. This disposition can be found in much earlier windows such as the John the Baptist window in the cathedral of Bourges and the Saint-Eustache window of Sens.[22] Saint-Julien's Blaise and Peter and Paul window (fig. 120) provides the canted square with blue and gold fronds against a red ground that appears again, with only the slightest of variations, in the Auxerre Peter and Paul quatrefoil. Both the Saint-Julien and Auxerre windows present precisely the same color schemes of balancing blues against reds and scattering touches of yellows throughout the backgrounds, borders, and mosaic infill. The use of these large motifs to connect angled figural medallions produces a visual impact that links these windows to a common artistic concept.

Infancy of Christ—Glorification of the Virgin Atelier

The atelier responsible for the Infancy of Christ—Glorification of the Virgin (fig. 103) and the legend of Theophilus (fig. 102) at Saint-Julien-du-Sault does not seem

[21] Delaporte and Houvet, 1926, pls. CL-CLIII and XXII-XXV. The use of almost exactly the same system for the Last Judgement window in the choir of Soissons, dated about 1220 (*Corpus, France, Recensement* I, 171, pl. 13), testifies to the widespread popularity of the arrangement.

[22] Cahier and Martin, 1841-1844, pl. XVIc and above, n. 11.

to have produced other glass in Burgundy. Arranged in insistently vertical patterns of small independent panels, the two windows show the same artistic thinking and workshop habits. The Infancy—Glorification panels are characterized by quatrefoil medallions. The Theophilus window shows another variation on the quatrefoil by surrounding it with four trilobed accompaniments and flanking them by segments of circles. Both windows, however, use straight armatures. The great deal of space between the small medallions is filled with diaper mosaic and small bosses, giving both windows a very dense, but essential superficial, spread of ornament. The border in the Theophilus window is a very restricted zig-zag pattern while the Infancy—Glorification window show a repetitious pattern of vertically successive fronds. Both windows reveal a workshop interested in repetitive symmetry that conceived of a window as a series of small isolated medallions held together by a decorative web.

Magdalene Master

The three windows in the axial chapel of Notre-Dame of Semur-en-Auxois relating the story of Mary and Martha may be assigned to a single workshop. All three windows (figs. 136-140) use an armature that conforms to the shape of the panels: a succession of circles, lozenges, or tangent half quatrefoils. Between the medallions, mosaic backgrounds of red and blue produce the dark coloration that dominates the windows. The borders are narrow and show geometric designs or stylized fronds.

Since the windows are much narrower than most of the windows under discussion, their formats show little direct correspondence. Our understanding of Semur is further restricted by the effects of various restoration campaigns and the resultant loss and rearrangement of the panels.

Notre-Dame of Dijon

The windows of Notre-Dame of Dijon (figs. 5, 146 and 148) do not exhibit any strong links with the extant glass in the rest of Burgundy. The five lancets underneath the north rose are the only surviving examples of Dijon's program. The narrow lancets present a series of vertically arranged medallions: the first a quatrefoil with points, the second and third, octagons, the fourth an alternation of circles and canted squares and the fifth simple quatrefoils. A vertical armature, however, cuts the panels in half, providing as well horizontal divisions above and below. The medallions are full, taking up most of the space allotted between the iron work and the side borders, although the fifth lancet's plan seems to allow somewhat greater background space. The sprouting fronds or circular rinceaux between the medallions are particularly lush and verdant. The borders of the lancets are similarly provided with unusually detailed foliage, bending toward the outer border, sprouting on a vertical axis, arched, or contained in wishbone or lyre shapes.[23] All of the medallions use blue for medallion backgrounds and red for the grounds of the ornament. The

[23] Suggestions concerning the provenance of such ornament are found under the discussion of Notre-Dame's style.

fifth medallion presents some variation (fig. 160). It uses a blue, not red, ground for its border, and shows a predominance of green and yellows in the foliage and the bosses linking the quatrefoils both vertically and to the side borders. This produces a distinctly warmer tonality than in the first four lancets, where a fine balance among yellow, white, green and blue foliage, red and blue grounds, and purple, gold and green tints for the figures creates a more variegated harmony.

IV

THE ATELIERS

*In the Middle Ages, artists very generally did more than they
had to. They indulged the impulse to embellish . . . and built
up a tremendous range of technical powers for executing their
embellishments.* (Daniel V. Thompson)[1]

1. The Genesis Atelier (Auxerre)

The production of the major portion of ambulatory glass in the cathedral of Auxerre
may be ascribed to a single atelier working under the direction of two distinct
personalities.[2] As discussed in the section on style and ornament, the Genesis Master
probably began with the windows of the Creation (51) and Noah, Abraham and Lot
(52) in the north ambulatory, after which the windows of Samson (56), Margaret
(54), Mary of Egypt (72) and Mary Magdalene (73) followed. The influence of the
Genesis Inheritor, whose style links him to later trends, appears first in the windows
of Saint Bris (74) and the Prodigal Son (68). His contribution becomes even more
pronounced in the windows of the Tree of Jesse (61), Joseph (53), Andrew (55),
James (70), Genesis and Exodus (56), David (49) and Mammès (50).

The Genesis Master is distinguished by highly individualistic drapery techniques. Most noticeable is an oval pattern, or "plantain-leaf" fold, most commonly
found in the lower portions of the mantles as they are pulled from the back of the
legs upward toward the waist (figs. 8 and 13, pl. III). The Genesis Master also uses
horizontal folds at the waist area that are immediately counterbalanced by long
vertical loops of drapery on the cuffs of the sleeves and the portions of the mantle
falling across the chest, as displayed in the porters in the Samson window (fig. 20).
He favored elongated facial types, elegant gestures and open, spatially ambiguous
compositions. The earliest productions of the atelier show the most individualization
in character portrayal and sense of actuality in the narrative. In the panel showing
Abraham confronting the angels (fig. 13) the figures appear engrossed in realistic
dialogue. Abraham thrusts out his hands in a heartfelt gesture of supplication as
he begs the angels to spare the people of Sodom. The gently articulated porters
carrying Samson's bier (fig. 20) actually seem to be moving forward at a mournful
pace. Drapery by the Genesis Master shows shading and an indication of depth.

[1] *The Materials and Techniques of Medieval
Painting*, New York (1956), 20-21.
[2] A major portion of the following chapter has
been published by Raguin (1974). Some of the
material was presented at the session sponsored
by the International Center of Medieval Art at the
Eighth Conference on Medieval Studies at Western Michigan University, Kalamazoo, Michigan,
1973.

Bold strokes of the brush in the garments of Abraham and the angels are softened by additional lighter accents, creating a spatial fluctuation. Figures relate to each other in three-dimensional space, frequently pushing beyond the medallion borders as if reluctant to be hemmed in on a single plane, evident in both these Samson and Creation details.

The style of the Genesis Master is intimately related to that of four well-preserved panels showing the life of Saint Martin made for the parish church of Gercy now in the Cluny Museum in Paris.[3] At present, three round panels showing Christ in Glory flanked by angels, the Death of Saint Martin (falsely restored as Saint Martin's dream),[4] and the Miracle of the Tree (fig. 17) have been united in a single lancet. The final panel, showing Martin dividing his cloak, although rectangular in format, belongs to the cycle both for iconographic as well as stylistic reasons.[5] All of these panels are flanked laterally by a handsome grisaille border which was probably added to the figural glass at the time of the transformation of the parish church into an abbey in 1269.[6] The narrow panels must then have been adapted to fit into contemporary wider openings. The original windows surely contained a far more complete account of the life of the saint that now remains at Cluny. In this case the mixture of round and rectangular panels would not seem unlikely.

The styles of Gercy's Martin Master and of Auxerre's Genesis Master show many similarities: clear open compositions, oval folds and fishhook indentations in the drapery patterns and long, narrow faces marked by wide staring eyes. The

[3] Gercy is located near the city of Brie-Comte-Robert, old Seine-et-Oise now Seine-et-Marne. The panels are catalogued 59 A, B, and C. Besides the Life of Saint Martin, the narrative windows at Gercy included a Tree of Jesse, Miracle of Theophilus and a Typological cycle. The panels were transferred to three windows of the sanctuary of the church of Varennes at least before 1758: Lucien Magne, "Les vitraux de l'ancienne abbaye de Garcy, Département de' Seine-et-Oise," *Commision des antiquités et des arts* 7 (1887), 75-98, and Olivier Merson, *Les Vitraux*, Paris (1895), 39-40, fig. 10. The glass was in the Palais du Trocadero: Magne, *Palais du Trocadero, Musée de la sculpture comparée, Galerie des vitraux*, Paris (1912), nos. 47-52. For complete illustrations, see Jules Roussel, *Les Vitraux du XIIe au XVIe siècle d'après les clichés des archives de la Commission des monuments historiques*, I, Paris, n.d. (1910), pls. 6-9. Recently the glass has been a part of several exhibitions (Grodecki, 1953, nos. 12 and 13, Tree of Jesse and Legend of Theophilus; idem, 1962, nos. 149-154; *Year 1200*, I, no. 210 and ibid., III, 417-425, Tree of Jesse).

[4] Martin lies on a well-draped bed, his head, restored, resting on his hand. An angel stands at the head of the bed gesturing with one hand and reaching toward Martin's head with another. The

cloak hanging over a crossbar to the right is a modern interpolation. Most probably the demon, commonly depicted waiting at the foot of the bed, has been replaced with a modern reconstruction of the vision of Saint Martin's mantle. Martin's death at Auxerre (fig. 125) and at Chartres (Delaporte and Houvet, 1926, pl. LX) show opposing angel and demon.

[5] Cluny Museum no. 49.

[6] Jeanne de Toulouse, sister-in-law of Saint Louis, made this possible through an endowment and transferred the parish seat to a newly built church in Varennes. For foundation charter, see *Gallia Christiana* VII, *Instrumenta*, CLII, cols. 113-114. See also Alain Erlande-Brandenburg, *Revue du Louvre* 21 (1971), 246, n. 51. The grisaille border should be compared with two grisaille windows from the abbey of Gercy now also in the Cluny collection, illustrated by Grodecki (1962, nos. 153 and 154). Compare also the grisaille patterns in Chartres window 48, dated 1260-1270 (Meredith Lillich, "A Redating of the Thirteenth-Century Grisaille Windows of Chartres Cathedral," *Gesta* 11/1 [1972], 13-14, fig. 6). I am indebted to Professor Lillich for calling to my attention the disparity between the figural and grisaille work at Gercy.

painting at Auxerre, however, has clearly transformed the Parisian style through a flattening, elongating and codifying of the figures. A comparison between the seated Christ of the Gercy window (fig. 10) and the seated Creator of the Creation window of Auxerre (fig. 9) summarizes some of the similarities and differences between the two masters. The origin of Auxerre's "plantain-leaf" fold visible in the knee of the seated Creator is found in the drapery patterns across the Gercy's Christ's lap. The fishhook folds so prevalent in the Auxerre figure have developed from the looped terminations best evident in the Gercy figure's lap to the left and in the edge of the mantle falling over the left arm. The facial type of Auxerre's Creator is more closely related to the elongated three-quarter view found in the angel from the same Gercy panel (fig. 21). The same long, narrow proportions, thin nose, open, staring eyes and strong line of the neck characterize both works. Differences are evident, however. At Gercy the drapery retains a feeling of fullness and depth, while at Auxerre the fold patterns have become more dominant. The thick lines of grisaille actually flatten the figure to create a strong linear pattern. Auxerre has transformed the lingering "muldenfaltenstil" loops found at Gercy into a surface design favoring calligraphic pattern over sculptural effect.

A reference to the figure of Humility from the sketchbook of Villard de Honnecourt (fig. 11) confirms the strong dependence of the Gercy artist on other thirteenth-century Parisian styles.[7] The numerous small scoop folds at the waist extending upward to articulate the torso, the semicircular loop across the upper lap and the fall of the mantle across the left shoulder all spring from a common artistic mold, repeated in both the Villard and Gercy figures. However, even at Gercy, the glass painting is more evolved, more delicate and linear, the face far less sculptural and the sleeve drapery of the right arm already marked by a concern for surface patterning.

Invariably, figures protrude over the borders of the panels in work attributed to both the Genesis and Gercy masters. The funeral of Samson (fig. 20) shows the hands, feet and heads of the two porters as well as the ends of the bier overlapping the simple red border. The head and hands of the angels confronting Abraham (fig. 13) and the soldier's feet and sword from the Saint Margaret massacre panel (fig. 16) also display these characteristics.[8] One might compare such compositional workshop habits with the position of Saint Martin in the Miracle of the Tree at Gercy (fig. 17); the saint's head, crozier and feet protrude over the round border.

This insistence on breaking through the frame imposed by a panel's border helps to create a highly distinctive concept of space in both masters' work. In general, the figures stand apart from each other, with a clear display of background glass to

[7] Paris, Bibl. nat. Ms. fr. 19093, fol. 3v., about 1235; Hans Hahnloser, *Villard de Honnecourt, Kritische Gesamtsausgabe des Bauhüttenbuches*, Vienna (1935), 19-21, 225-237, pl. 6. See comparison with sculpture from Reims, Ingeborg Psalter, Missal from Noyon, Missal from St. Corneille in Compiègne.

[8] A drawing of this window published by Cahier (1875, 67-73, pl. IV) shows only one reclining martyr in the foreground. The figure to the left may be attributed to the restorations of the glass painter David between 1925 and 1927.

emphasize the clarity of the compositions. In the funeral of Samson, the figures are set apart from one another save for the billowing scarf of the central mourner which brushes the porter's sleeve. The great expanse of sparkling blue background isolates the figures while their protrusion over the panel's border further develops this feeling of spatial ambiguity. Here the artist has not attempted to define the locale through groundlines or elements of foliage or architecture. The relationship of the central mourner to the two porters is aesthetically sound but realistically imprecise.

The harmoniously designed panel of Abraham's confrontation with the angels (fig. 13) repeats this fluctuation of space resolving the composition solely through the dynamic relationship of Abraham and the densely grouped angels. The Gercy Miracle of the Tree demonstrates the origin of such a composition through the relationship of Martin to the fallen pagans and the astonished onlookers (figs. 17-19). As at Auxerre, clear expanses of blue background separate the figures and the form of the tree. When several persons appear in a group, they huddle together, forming a dense mass with one unified outline. Such compositional devices occur again in the Saint Margaret massacre panel from Auxerre (fig. 16). Both soldiers are briskly silhouetted against the blue ground, thus isolating the tightly knit group of martyrs in the center.

Specific drapery techniques were also inspired by the Gercy Master's style, perhaps best evident in the figure of Martin redirecting the tree (fig. 18). The fall of the mantle over his left arm shows the characteristic terminal cuff with upper indentation and deep curves along the lower part of the sleeve. At Auxerre the central female martyr in the Saint Margaret panel displays the same wide cuff accented by boldly curved lines as well as the broad surface folds of the mantle across the shoulders and arms (fig. 16). The porters in Samson's funeral procession show many of the same characteristics in their rolled cuffs and sleeve loops (fig. 20). Yet here it is even more evident that the natural depiction of fold patterns by the Gercy artist have become abstractions functioning primarily as rhythmic designs.

Facial types perhaps best illustrate the unity of the Genesis atelier and its dependence on the Gercy Saint Martin panels. As in the Auxerre Creator, a long placid oval characterizes the faces both of Samson's mourners and the attending angel of the Gercy Christ in Glory panel (figs. 9, 20 and 21). All figures show a continuous line for the nose and eyebrow which serves as a counterweight for the great sweep of the jaw. A fully modeled brushstroke articulates the upper lip while the lower achieves definition through a small curve perched on the lower half circle of the chin. The hair flows back from a central part in parallel waves, curling in several loops as it reaches the ears. The eyes, the most dominant feature of the face, are large, oval shaped and bordered by a strongly outlined upper and lower lid. Emphatic brows repeat the curve of the lid.

The rather delicate treatment of Martin's features (fig. 18) introduces a slight variant of this type. Here one finds more subtlety in the sensitive delineation of the nose and the slightly askew eyes. As in the face of Christ in Glory (fig. 10) the Gercy Master demonstrates a clear preference for the asymmetrical. He seems to hesitate between depicting Martin's mouth from a front or a three-quarter view. The mouth slants downward and the eye line slants upward. The face of the worried female martyr in Auxerre's Saint Margaret window shows the same delicate off-center balance, especially in the wide, concerned eyes. Again, the eyes appear to be the most expressive part of the face. The angels clearly engage Abraham with a look that complements the gestures of their hands. The first angel appears to instruct, while the outstretched palm of the angel to the left may refer to the futility of Abraham's compassion.

The later work of this atelier, attributed to the Genesis Inheritor, reveals the direction in which this Parisian-inspired style developed. Despite obvious similarities to the style of the Genesis Master, such as the same long oval faces, plantain-leaf and fishhook folds and treatment of gesticulating hands, a distinct personality change seems indicated. Certainly, chronological changes may affect an artistic style, but the transformation of Auxerre's glass seems to be due to more than the passage of time. The compositions now appear more crowded and on one plane. Dramatic action, despite much the same hagiographic subject matter of miracles and heroism, is largely submerged in the static arrangement of the characters. Even when the Genesis Inheritor appears to borrow dynamic drapery patterns from another atelier, the compositions are not noticeably more dramatic. No movement or sense of confrontation occurs. The figures appear to be carrying out a well-rehearsed and completely predictable dialogue. Whereas in the previously discussed panels events were presented as happening, here symbols of these events are presented.

The drapery patterns, typically, reveal the major tendencies of this new direction. Long tunics show a swifter and more simplified fall of pleats, ultimately deriving from the Genesis Master's designs as in the female figures serving the angels (fig. 12) from the Noah, Abraham and Lot window. The father from the Prodigal Son window (fig. 26), Pharaoh gesturing to Joseph (fig. 31) or David with his harp setting out to welcome the Quadriga of Amminadab (fig. 36) show the types favored by the Genesis Inheritor. In these figures, the folds are much broader and their vertical fall is almost devoid of any counterbalancing horizontal accents. Even when the Genesis Master's patterns are more carefully preserved, the effect is still subtly different. The plantain-leaf folds of the robe of the servant bringing Joseph to Pharaoh (fig. 31) or of the mantles of Saint Andrew and his follower in the panel of the exorcism of the demons of Nicea (fig. 22) are very similar to those employed in the Creation, Samson or Margaret windows, but the patterns are simplified and flatter.

A comparison between the funeral of Samson and Saint Andrew's exorcism should clarify the atelier's development. The oval folds of material accompanied by small fishhook accents are the same for both Andrew and Samson's two porters. The robes in front of the figures fall in the same weighty folds. The long placid faces and the well-regulated undulations in the hair also point to a common workshop tradition. Yet, whatever the superficial similarities may be, the underlying organization and the psychological import of the scenes differ radically. The Samson panel conveys the feeling of an actual funeral procession, the hero's bier raised aloft by tall stately porters while an additional figure strikes a pose of subdued mourning at the side of the procession. Significantly the action of the scene extends beyond the borders of the panel as the head and feet of both porters overlap the oval frame. In the window of Saint Andrew, the artist is much more prone to limit the narrative to the confines of the medallion. The figures are conceived as flat shapes that interrelate as abstract forms, not as bodies in space. To this later artist, figural alignment, flatness of picture plane and the resulting symbolic nature of the action have become dominant artistic concerns.

With the later development of the Genesis workshop, we are certain to be dealing with a style very close to the artistic matrix of the mid-thirteenth century. A comparison with the window of Saint Vincent from Saint-Germain-des-Prés about 1245 brings into focus this tendency toward stiffness and linear stylization.[9] In the panel showing Dacien ordering two servants (fig. 23), now in the Metropolitan Museum in New York, the figures all stand on the same plane. There is almost no indication of depth, either through drapery rendering or position of the figures in space. Indeed, a swift, cursory brushstroke equalizes rather than differentiates among facial features, hair drapery and architecture. Borders are thinner and foliage attenuated. Mosaic backgrounds are reduced to surface patterns organized on predominantly vertical and horizontal trellises.

Transformations in the atelier are due to more than the march of time, however, for the Genesis Inheritor was influenced by another Auxerre atelier. The Eustache atelier, as discussed later, must have been active in the cathedral at about the same time as the Genesis workshop and its use of dynamic drapery forms and linear compositions must have had great appeal. Many panels of the Genesis Inheritor show clear borrowings of workshop habits of the Eustache atelier repertoire, particularly in the energetic handling of drapery with loop, swirls and windblown material. The guards forcing Saint Mammès into the blazing furnace (fig. 37) show exaggerated loops of drapery over the belt and a strong movement in the tunic skirt. In the David window the figure of Saul falling on his sword (fig. 36) wears a long flowing mantle. The agitated drapery of Moses descending from Mount Sinai (fig. 29) or the exaggeration of almost all of the drapery over the torsos of the male figures in the Prodigal Son window (fig. 25) would indicate that another stylistic influence was at work.

The baptism panel from the Saint James window (fig. 32) presents some of the best evidence for such interaction between ateliers.[10] The faces, especially that of Saint James, still retain their indebtedness to the Genesis atelier's forms. Yet the exaggerated size of the heads and their heightened expressiveness link them to the faces of the two robbers replacing stolen gold before the statue of Saint Nicholas (fig. 48). This panel from the Eustache atelier shows the particularly energetic sweep

[9] Grodecki, 1957; Verdier, 1962-1963.
[10] The lower triangle in Saint James' tunic and the lower part of the tunic of the acolyte are modern.

of drapery across the chest noted in many of the Genesis Inheritor's productions. All of the garments in the Saint James panel seem to have been influenced by these new forms: the fall of the mantle of the first kneeling man, the loop of fabric around the chest of the acolyte with the holy water bucket and the billowing drapery falling from the saint's upraised arm.

These observations coincide with recent scholarly opinion concerning the organization of artistic workshops. Ateliers appear capable of borrowing designs, sharing workmen and even experiencing a mutual growth that sometimes may have lead to the creation of a common style. For the atelier engaged in the immense task of producing the illuminations for the Parisian Moralized Bibles of the early thirteenth century, Branner noted that painters frequently copied one another's styles of drawing.[11] He observed that painters could step up, or down, to a more or less complicated manner probably depending on the pressures of time or finances. Caviness has noted that in the genealogical series of large clerestory figures at Canterbury a figure designed by the Methuselah Master was actually executed by another artist.[12] Oakeshott had earlier presented evidence that certain drawings in the Winchester Bible were made by the Master of the Leaping Figures but painted by the artist called the Morgan Master.[13] Caviness further observes that there must have been a "productive interaction" between the large number of artists working on the Chartres windows, a process that led inevitably to the formation of a new stylistic amalgam.[14] The acceptance of such processes in Gothic artistic production would explain the difficulty so far in tracing the Chartrain style to any one local school.

I think it acceptable to suppose that such an interaction between ateliers took place at Auxerre. These artists responded to external influences, and also experienced internal evolutions of personal artistic development, subtly shaped by the general stylistic transformation of painting toward a mid-century emphasis on linearity and abstraction.

2. The Eustache Master (Auxerre)

The atelier of Auxerre's Saint Eustache Master executed the ambulatory windows of Saint Eustache (66), Saint Lawrence (57), Legend of Theophilus (63), Miracles of Nicholas (71), Saint Catherine (75) and Saint Germain (67). Named after his most distinguished production, the Eustache Master shows the same elegant elongation of the figure, the linearity of the drapery folds and the emphasis on calligraphy at the expense of modeling that characterized the later work of the Genesis group. The glass of the Eustache atelier (pl. IV) concentrates on surface detail and abstract relationships between figure and ground, almost totally negating any realistic sense of space. Quite clearly the long ovals of the faces and the slender limbs of the Eustache figures might stem from a close association with the style of the Genesis

---

[11] 1977, 47.
[12] 1977, 52, figs. 8, 9, 12, 13 and 66.
[13] Walter Oakeshott, *The Artists of the Win-* *chester Bible*, London (1945), 7-8, 13-15, pls. XXIX, XL.
[14] 1977, 96.

Master, as do many of the modes of indicating specific position of drapery and expression. However, it is immediately evident that a new concept and personality is present, one far more dynamic and extreme.

The Saint Eustache window itself presents quite clearly the dramatic power of this Master. Although a traditional part of the Saint Eustache legend, the Auxerre representation of the saint witnessing the lion and wolf carry off his sons (fig. 38) becomes a vividly animated scene. Eustache raises both arms in despair while his cloak billows out around his shoulders. The water flows violently down from Eustache's knees, while the two animals bound upward. Even the relatively simple schema shown in the side panels of horrified peasants is enlivened by the Eustache Master's ability to arrange figures gracefully in space and to utilize gesture and drapery artistically. This dramatic effect is achieved through an unusual ability to suit composition to medallion frame.[15] In the story of Eustache losing his sons, the saint's pivotal figure anchors the central medallion, as trees bend in from the left and right and the animals carrying off the boys leap outward. This action is brought to a halt through the side medallions: the shepherds' bodies curve along the borders of the frame as their faces turn inward. Similar compositional sophistication appears in the confrontational arrangements of the Saint Lawrence window (pl. IV). The central medallions present compositions that are resolved along reciprocal curves (figs. 44 and 46). The body of the prone saint curves upward and the executioners' forms become complementary arcs that follow the shape of the medallion. In the side medallions the compositions employ strong verticals at the outer edges, but direct attention inward with gesture and look. The panel showing Theophilus distributing money to the poor (fig. 41) shows the same stabilized composition formed by the convex curves of Theophilus and the demon and the group of suppliants. The suppliant to the extreme right presents the characteristic movement of the body away from the center but with head turned back, as in the two Eustache shepherds.

Drapery assumes a new expressive role in this atelier even while the concept of the body beneath the clothing becomes better defined. A comparison of drapery treatment in each of the windows associated with the Eustache atelier reveals similar workshop methods. In the detail of the two robbers from the Miracles of Saint Nicholas window (fig. 48) fabric sweeps across the chest to fall in deep loops over the front of the waist bands. Swift, decisive brushstrokes delineate the pull of material over the shoulder and down to the bend of the elbow. In the window of Saint Germain (fig. 53) the man beseeching the mounted saint displays the same energetic pattern over his torso. The two guards flagellating Catherine (fig. 50) closely resemble the two robbers of the Miracles of Nicholas window. Enormous deep folds cascade over the belt while strong indentations mold the torso. The figure of Saint Eustache expelled from the boat (fig. 38) presents this characteristic drapery

---

[15] Such compositional skill recalls a great personality of the twelfth century, the Methuselah Master of Canterbury. His balanced interplay of medallion format and figural composition dramatically itensifies the depth of some of the cathedral's most iconographically complex programs. (Caviness, 1977, 49-58, figs. 12-63.)

pattern, as do the men wielding clubs from the Saint Lawrence window (fig. 46). In the panel showing the building of Theophilus' church (fig. 42), the first laborer carrying the stretcher and the man mounting the ramp with a load on his back show the forceful brushwork and vivid curves of the Eustache Master's style. Indeed, the position of the man mounting the ramp recalls the stance of the robber from the Nicholas window who stoops over and thrusts his head forward, letting the heavy drapery fall to the front and also surge over his legs.

The origin of the Eustache Master poses intriguing problems. Primarily, he exhibits strong links to the window of the Good Samaritan at Chartres (fig. 45).[16] In the compositional organization of the Samaritan's rescue of the wayfarer, the Chartres Master shows much the same concern for dynamic balance as the Eustache Master. The central circle and the two side medallions produce an effect similar to Auxerre's horizontal systems. The movement of the horse and the Samaritan to the right is anchored by the curving tree and flowing draperies on the left. The side medallions display identical concepts: standing figures pushed to the outer edges with the languishing wayfarer and the stable filling the remaining space. Both the Samaritan and the innkeeper face inward and direct attention to the central image, as in many of the Auxerre compositions. Facial types, figural proportions and drapery patterns also seem similar. The long narrow face of the Samaritan leading his horse seems to be repeated in the figures of Saint Eustache in the stream and the second shepherd to his right (fig. 40). The elongated proportions of the priest and Levite ignoring the beaten traveler from Chartres appear again in the figure of Theobista accompanying Eustache's two children and the figures of Lawrence being lead to and from prison (fig. 44). The sophisticated drapery pattern of many thin pleats fluidly draping the figure evident in the Chartres innkeeper are seen in Lawrence's garments and the drapery of the Eustache shepherds. One might also compare the scene of the robbers setting upon the wayfarer with the scene of torture from the Lawrence window. The sweeping drapery over the torso terminating in a long loop over the belt, so characteristic of the Eustache Master, is present in the figures of the robbers. Both the Chartres and Auxerre scenes exhibit highly active compositions; three figures, their arms stretched upward grasping clubs forming a moving "ballet" around their victims. The attenuated proportions of the figures and the interplay of the slender legs and arms emphasized by their silhouettes against the blue backgrounds give a similar flavor to both windows.

The Good Samaritan window itself may be the product of a complicated evolution. Grodecki supports much of Quiévreux's thesis linking the Good Samaritan window to an early group produced by the Master of Saint Lubin.[17] The Saint Lubin

---

[16] Delaporte and Houvet, 1926, 168-170, pls. XVIII-XXI, color pl. III.

[17] François Quiévreux, "Les vitraux du XIIIe siècle de l'apside de la cathédrale de Bourges," *Bulletin monumental* 102 (1942), 254-275. Because of the author's confusion of the windows of the Relics and the Good Samaritan Masters, it

is difficult to be precise about which traits he saw in the Saint Lubin glass. Quiévreux's insistence, however, on the Chartrain Master's love of figures in action, boldness, and energy in individual characterization, and fondness for thick application of grisaille indicates that he possessed a good awareness of the Good Samaritan Master's style.

group includes the Chartres windows of Saint Lubin, Noah and Saint Nicholas.[18] Grodecki dates the group about 1210 and admits to the possibility of a "rapprochement" between the Saint Lubin Master and the Bourges Good Samaritan atelier, since both display late Romanesque tendencies of the art of western France.[19] The dramatic energy of the Auxerre windows has much in common with the great tension and bold exaggeration of the Bourges windows (figs. 101 and 141). Compared to the fluid elegance of the Auxerre style, the broken lines and bunched drapery of the earlier painter achieve much the same effect of theatrical impact. In the context of the massive campaign to fill the Chartres openings, the Saint Lubin Master probably assimilated influences from more progressive ateliers. It is possible that he might have produced the Good Samaritan and Saint John the Evangelist windows during a later phase of his career.

This linking of the Saint Eustache Master's style to both Chartres and Bourges supports the assessment already presented in the discussion of composition and ornament, where common border motifs, medallion patterns, mosaic backgrounds and the unusual technique of joining medallions through a continuous border were seen at all three sites. It is evident that the Eustache atelier developed out of a web of interlocking influences, most probably from a style ultimately traceable to western France but transformed by the experiences of Bourges and Chartres. At Auxerre, the Eustache Master's style was further modified through contact with the major atelier of the cathedral, that of the Genesis Master. The influences were reciprocal, however, as we have seen, and much of the verve and flourish of the Eustache Master surfaced in the later windows of the Genesis workshop.

Despite the broad similarities linking these six Auxerre windows as the products of a single atelier, we may be able to distinguish specific hands responsible for individual windows. In this case, the comparison of composition and general figural proportions may be of greater use than the isolation of facial types. Any one of the panels of the Saint Lawrence window immediately impresses the eye with a sense of great space and clarity. The medallions are no larger than the size commonly used for Auxerre windows, but the elegant proportions of the figures and the superbly balanced compositions give the impression of great space. The backgrounds of the panels are singularly uncluttered by localizing details, even Lawrence's rack being considered superfluous. Likewise, the Theophilus legend presents figures of tall graceful proportions. The seated Theophilus distributing the ill-gotten wealth (fig. 41) shows the same dramatic flow of drapery, long limbs and noble heads. Leprévost did not ignore the specific quality of the figural style of this window during his restoration. Significantly, the modern panels at the beginning of the legend show the same general proportions and composition as the original glass.[20]

---

[18] Delaporte only recognized the hand of the Saint Lubin Master in the window of Saint Nicholas (Delaporte and Houvet, 1926, 394, 408).

[19] Grodecki, *Vitrail*, 129, fig. 96; idem, *Year 1200*, III, 343; idem, 1978, 50.

[20] Leprévost appears to have traced the original figure of the Jew who brings Theophilus his money (63:7) to create the nineteenth-century figure of the Jew receiving Theophilus at his door (63:5).

The compositional and figural aspects of the three windows of the Miracles of Saint Nicholas, Saint Catherine and Saint Germain present a wavering indecision between the more powerful expression of the Saint Eustache Master and the more reticent orderly arrangements of the Genesis atelier. The windows display a common shortening and broadening of the figures, an exaggeration of the features and a different concept of spatial composition. The two faces of the guards flagellating Catherine (fig. 50) possess extremely large eyes, huge jaws and generally caricatured features. These same traits immediately catch the eye in the panel of the two robbers returning the gold to the Jew's storeroom (fig. 48). Moreover, the patterning on the tunic skirts of all four figures displays a broad insistence on verticality, with wide columns of fabric articulated by deep, well-painted folds. A small flip at the bottom to the left and concave and convex undulations at the hem articulate the tunics' edges. The violent pull of the drapery across the robbers' chests is perhaps less exaggerated than the movement in Catherine's guards, but the energetic impression remains the same.

The compositions are far more crowded and confused than those of the Lawrence, Theophilus or Eustache windows. The three robbers listening to Saint Nicholas (fig. 47) seem jammed into an inadequate area. In the panels of the Lawrence window, there are exceptionally clear distinctions between one body and the next, even when three or four figures are grouped in a medallion. In the Saint Catherine window (fig. 51), the malleable contours of the medallion seem to compel the figures into an inadequate space, resulting in stiffer, more awkward compositions. Clearly these two windows, Catherine and the Miracles of Nicholas, derive from a personality quite distinct from the Saint Eustache Master himself. This Master, who may be named the Saint Catherine Assistant, used much of the Eustache Master's facial types and drapery patterns, but implanted them in a narrower format with murkier compositions and imprecise relationships.

Many of these same characteristics appear in the six panels of Saint Germain, which have unfortunately suffered the greatest damage of all the windows connected with this atelier.[21] The central panel of the lowest register (fig. 53) appears to retain some feeling for the original composition. The figures are bold and dynamic and engage each other in meaningful debate. However, as commonly found in the Catherine Assistant's work, the two figures to the right are conflated, the two torsos apparently sharing one pair of legs. The cleric behind Saint Germain stands flattened against the saint's back, a harsh vertical line dividing the two figures. The drawing of the cleric's figure, as well as that of Saint Germain in this as well as the four additional panels show an increased stiffness and a very definite retreat from the elegant proportions that so characterized the Saint Eustache Master. The saint's cloak appears to constitute an independent element, giving no indication of a believable body concealed beneath. Germain's face particularly seems quite lifeless and devoid of expression.

[21] One might wonder if this extensive destruction was motivated by the Huguenots' recognition that Saint Germain was the political and spiritual model for the power of Auxerre's bishops.

The panel showing God admonishing Adam and Eve from the Genesis-Exodus window (fig. 28) may explain some of the puzzling aspects of the Saint Germain legend. The stiff and independent cloak wrapped around the figure of the Creator must surely have inspired the cloak worn by Germain as he prays for the resurrection of the son of Volusian. Similarly, the placid, expressionless face and long, narrow nose so much a part of Saint Germain must have derived from the Genesis facial type here visible in the calm features of the Creator.

In assigning a date to the Eustache atelier, the glass at Bourges, before 1214, and at Chartres, at the latest in the early 1220s, offers little assistance. The differences separating the Eustache Master from the Genesis atelier do not necessarily reflect a distance in time. Perhaps the Genesis and Eustache Masters were called to work on the cathedral at the same time, about 1233. Their contemporaneity as well as proximity might explain some similarities in drapery patterns and facial types. The high quality of both the Creation and Saint Eustache windows would designate them as "prime objects" as well as name pieces from which the ateliers drew their inspiration. The inspiration for each workshop, however, was frequently qualified by the other's influence, extending perhaps even to an exchange of painters. The three windows of the Miracles of Saint Nicholas, Catherine and Germain exhibit the influence of the Genesis workshop. The later work of the Genesis Inheritor was seen to have incorporated many of the Saint Eustache Master's drapery techniques and heightened expression. Although the power of the Master's compositions remained inimitable, his reliance on linearity and surface values profoundly affected the Genesis Inheritor's style. Thus the Eustache atelier served as both recipient and inspiration for much of the glass created for the Auxerre Cathedral ambulatory.

3. The Atelier of Saint-Germain-lès-Corbeil and Burgundian Windows (Troyes, Semur-en-Auxois, Auxerre)

The windows associated with the atelier responsible for the glass at Saint-Germain-lès-Corbeil, several kilometers northeast of Corbeil in the Seine-et-Oise, illustrate a more direct link between glazing workshops of the Parisian area and Burgundian productions.[22] Over a period of a little more than a decade, the atelier furnished windows for the church of Notre-Dame at Semur-en-Auxois and the cathedrals of Troyes and Auxerre. The strikingly high quality of the glass at Saint-Germain presents a surprising contrast to the modest scale of the architecture of the church.[23] An unassuming flat chevet contains three lancets and a central oculus of narrative cycles. In the oculus single medallions contain "identifying scenes" for Saints Lawrence, Gilles, Agatha, Martin, Margaret and John the Baptist.[24] The central window

---

[22] Much of the material in this study was presented by Raguin (1976).

[23] The church dates from the late twelfth and early thirteenth centuries. *Corpus, France, Recensement* I, 83; L. Vollant, *L'Eglise de Saint-Germain-lès-Corbeil*, Paris (1897).

[24] Saint Lawrence is on the grill; Saint Gilles says mass while Charlemagne kneels to the left. The banderole held by the angel presumably represents the unutterable sin of the emperor, a representation remarkably like the last roundel of the Charlemagne window of Chartres (Delaporte and

recounts the Passion of Christ, and the right has been identified as the story of Saint Germain of Paris.[25] The Jesse Tree on the left is the best-known example of the glass since it appeared in major exhibitions in Paris and New York (fig. 54).[26]

Framed by the vine, the Virgin sits in the traditional frontal pose associated with the Jesse Tree from its inception in the mid-twelfth century. The striding, gesticulating poses of the flanking prophets also adhere to the expected format. This established iconography, characterized by Caviness as the "symbolic" mode,[27] must have influenced the style of the painter, for despite the artist's exceptional skill, the figures remain stiff, hieratic and restricted to two distinct facial types. Mary and the other seated personages have round faces with delicately drawn features, whereas the standing prophets exhibit much larger and more elongated heads with highly exaggerated facial traits.

In the Passion window the narrative treatment breaks away from the hieratic formula of the Jesse Tree.[28] Heightened activity and more varied compositions distinguish the scenes of the Passion depicted in three quatrefoil medallions supplemented by half-roundels at the sides of the window. The lowest medallion in the window pictures the events leading up to the mocking of Christ. Half-roundels to the left and right show Christ arrested and Christ carrying His cross.[29] The well-preserved central medallion (fig. 56) presents the scourging of Christ in the bottom lobe, Ecclesia and Synagoga in the lobes to the left and right and the Crucifixion in the center. The upper lobe depicts two angels crowned with the sun and the moon, variants on the personification of Sol and Luna, as witnesses to Christ's redemptive sacrifice. The half-roundels and the quatrefoil in the summit of the window follow logically with scenes from the Resurrection and Ascension.[30]

The Passion panels at Saint-Germain attain an intensity of style through whorls of drapery undulating in self-contained patterns and by swaths of drapery seemingly

---

Houvet, 1926, 313-314, pls. CVI-CX). The third medallion shows Saint Agatha in a long gown, her hands affixed to a crossbar while men tear at her breasts with pincers (cf. medallion N2 of the Sainte-Chapelle: Robert Branner, "The Painted Medallions of the Sainte-Chapelle in Paris," *Transactions of the American Philosophical Society*, n.s. 59/2 (1968), 25, figs. 22 and 23). To the left Martin divides his cloak with a beggar, then Saint Margaret is beheaded, and finally John the Baptist suffers martyrdom, while Salome, holding the platter, watches the scene. In the center of the window the Agnus Dei supports a red banner. See photograph, *Corpus, France, Recensement* I, pl. XIV.

[25] Neither Perrot (1975, 418) or *Corpus, France, Recensement* I, 84, explain the identification, although it seems a logical assertion because of the church's dedication. The upper and lower medallions are modern.

[26] Catalogue, *L'Europe gothique*, Paris, Musée du Louvre (1968), no. 195; *Year 1200*, I, no. 219.

[27] Caviness' analysis (1977, 53ff.) of symbolic and narrative subject types and their effect on a painter's style has coincided with my initial discussion of the Saint-Germain-lès-Corbeil windows and differences between the Martin and Jesse Tree windows at Gercy, now in the Cluny Museum (Raguin, 1974, 35).

[28] *Corpus, France, Recensement* I, 69, 83, color pl. 6; *L'Europe gothique*, Paris, Musée du Louvre (1968), no. 194.

[29] The panel of Christ Mocked is quite well preserved while the two side medallions show a good amount of restoration. The panels of the Entry into Jerusalem, Washing Feet, Last Supper and Agony in the Garden are modern.

[30] The half roundel to the left probably refers to Christ meeting Mary Magdalene, which would then form a complement to the roundel on the right, Christ appearing to Saint Thomas. The central medallions show the Holy Women at the Tomb and the Ascension.

swept by gusts of wind. The mantle of the Virgin in the Jesse Tree, the tunics of the men flagellating Christ, and the drapery of the Crucified Christ exemplify these traits. The Saint-Germain Master frequently depicted striding figures with their robes stretched taut by the pressure of the knee. Like that of the Virgin of the Crucifixion, mantles billow behind them as if reflecting their own action or that of the wind. The female and the youthful faces, often quite full with sloping chins, seem melancholy; see, for example, Saint John or the pensive Ecclesia (fig. 56). Older bearded faces appear almost anxious. Elongated, concave facial silhouettes, characteristic of the prophets of the Jesse Tree, also recur in the face of the Crucified Christ. The hair consistently resolves into a thick mass of soft curls that exposes the ears and often extends over the forehead. Shading that articulates the drapery and faces creates the illusion of volumes and round forms associated with painting of the early thirteenth century in the Parisian tradition.

A comparison with a large and highly productive manuscript workshop of Paris confirms the stylistic matrix within which the production of the Saint-Germain-lès-Corbeil glass took place. Branner has named this shop the atelier of the Vienna Moralized Bibles, after the two impressive manuscripts now conserved in Vienna.[31] The atelier probably began shortly after 1210 and continued working to around 1245, producing not only four Moralized Bibles, but missals, prayer books, psalters and works of literature.[32] The scope of the Moralized Bibles, which were made for the king and for members of his court, called for over 13,000 images in the four manuscripts, and must have necessitated a highly organized method of production.

I do not think that the same artists or even the same ateliers were involved in both manuscript and glass productions, yet the Vienna Bibles offer numerous analogies with the dynamic forms of the windows. Like the glass, the manuscripts show a predilection for dramatic tension among the formal as well as the psychological elements of the composition. In both, heightened color contrasts, formal balance and active surface patterns are set against uniform backgrounds. The atelier uses actively opposed diagonals in its compositions. In the manuscript illustration of the First Days of Creation and the Establishment of the Church (fig. 57), the striding

---

[31] Vienna, Österreichische Nationalbibliothek, 1179 and 2554. ÖNB 2554 is reproduced in a facsimile edition with commentary (Reiner Haussherr, *Bible moralisée*, Graz, 1973). Branner suggests that the ÖNB 1179 was commissioned by Philip Augustus about 1212/1215 and ÖNB 2554 for a member of the royal family about 1225. The location of the atelier might well have been the monastery of Saint-Victor or that of Saint-Germain-des-Prés. The atelier was also responsible for a Moralized Bible in the cathedral of Toledo (with several folios in the Morgan Library, New York) and another divided among the Bodleian Library in Oxford, the British Museum in London and the Bibliothèque nationale in Paris. (Branner, 1977, 32-57, figs. 26a-64.)

[32] I have earlier linked the Saint-Germain-lès-

Corbeil glass to a Parisian psalter, Paris, Bibl. nat. Ms. nouv. acq. lat. 1392 (Raguin, 1976, 267). Branner (1977, 45-46, fig. 64) believed that the psalter was painted by the chief illuminator of ÖNB 2554, or an artist very closely related to him. It is a manuscript of exceptional quality; "an individual, highly personal work of art that stands out from the routine of the atelier" (ibid., 46). Indeed the quality of the Saint-Germain-lès-Corbeil panels may associate them more closely to the Parisian psalter than to the many less well planned or executed illustrations in the Moralized Bibles. It seems important, however, to establish that the Saint-Germain glazing style is linked to an extremely well-known and productive atelier, clearly the most influential Parisian expression of its period.

figure of God separating light from darkness, a parallel to Mary of the Crucifixion window, resolves into a balanced system. Flying drapery, arms and inclined head are all stabilized by the powerful diagonal from shoulder to outstretched foot. The lavish technique for delineating drapery shows particularly strong analogies to the glass painter's style. Both glass and manuscript painters have articulated the deeply recessed folds through strong contrasts between light and shadow. The heavy fall of drapery over arms and shoulders in the seated figure of the Church assailed by a "sea" of worldly concerns (lower right, fig. 57) is similar to the mantle of the Virgin of the Jesse Tree window (fig. 54). The Virgin's legs, however, set at different heights, create a drapery movement like that cloaking Daniel in the Story of Susanna from the second Vienna Bible (fig. 55). Drapery loops easily over the lower leg before sweeping upward in eloquent curves. In the richly patterned folds of the seated Jews or of Susanna, the manuscript painter shows the same concern for lush painterly effects observable in the swirling drapery of the men flagellating Christ, of the Crucified Savior or of the mourning Virgin of the Crucifixion window. The long narrow faces of the Jesse Tree prophets appear again in the images of the Jews in both Susanna medallions. The rounded youthful types of Mary, John and Ecclesia from the Crucifixion window (fig. 56) are similar to the fully modeled faces of Daniel and Susanna.

Characteristics of the style common to the Saint-Germain atelier appear again in the Burgundian site of the church of Notre-Dame of Semur-en-Auxois.[33] Today the axial chapel contains only pitiful remnants of an extensive program of glazing. Whether through active destruction, fire or simple neglect, the windows at Semur appeared in a very poor state of conservation even in the sixteenth century. In one of the rare publications concerning the glass, Maillard de Chambure reported that in 1729 windows of white glass had been substituted for the Gothic glazing, except for several chapels, where even there complete subjects were rare.[34] The Revolution apparently damaged the church even more extensively; much sculpture, glass and other furnishings were either removed or destroyed in 1794 by the architect Clénet who had been charged with transforming the church into a Temple of Reason.[35] In 1833 the panels were dispersed in several windows in the two ambulatory chapels to the north, and de Chambure described certain scenes without identifying any connecting themes.[36] In 1847 Viollet-le-Duc directed the regrouping of panels in the axial chapel following a strong stylistic division among the windows.[37] He later published in his *Dictionnaire* a drawing of Saint Peter holding the keys.[38]

The window connected to the Saint-Germain-lès-Corbeil atelier relates the story of Saint Peter in six quatrefoil medallions (see Iconography Appendix: Peter).

[33] See above, Chap. I.

[34] "Histoire et description de l'église de Notre-Dame de Semur-en-Auxois," *Mémoires de la Commission des antiquités du département de la Côte d'Or* s.1/1 (1832-1833), 65.

[35] Pierre de Truchis, "Semur-en-Auxois," *Congrès archéologique de France* 74 (1907), 67.

[36] *Mémoires Commission des antiquités Côte d'Or* (1832-1833), 72. I believe the references are to panels I:2, 3, 5, 7, II:5, V:2, 5.

[37] Commission of the Monuments Historiques, Archives: Dossier 375, sec. 1.

[38] 1875, 429, fig. 28.

Two figures showing the same style of painting have been inserted into lancets I and IV.[39] The lowest panel (V:1), shows Saint Peter instructing Mary the Mother of John Mark, who listens attentively, her hands placed palms outward over her breast (fig. 58). A comparison of the heads immediately reveals similarities between Mary listening to Saint Peter, the mourning Virgin and the Ecclesia from Saint-Germain (figs. 58 and 56). Exceptionally large and rounded eyes offset a strong jaw and large head. The figures all wear similar headcoverings that curve softly over the forehead into gatherings at the temple. It is, however, the striding figure of Saint Peter that fully incorporates the Saint-Germain hallmarks. The strong diagonals of the drapery pulled across the knee, the generous allowance of sleeve and the drapery billowing behind, all have appeared in the figure of God separating the light from the darkness from the Vienna Bible, and in the Virgin of Saint-Germain's Crucifixion (figs. 57 and 56). The same vigor and sense of purpose animates the movements of the figures at Semur and Saint-Germain. In the following panel at Semur (fig. 59), an angel guides and instructs the liberated Saint with explicit gestures and a movement toward the right. At Saint-Germain, the swaying figures, whether in action (the Flagellation) or at rest (the Virgin at the foot of the Cross) evoke a similar feeling of animation.

A window dedicated to Saint Andrew in the fourth bay of the ambulatory chapel of Saint Nicholas in the cathedral of Saint-Pierre at Troyes belongs to this group. Several windows at Troyes show glass of about 1225-1235 regrouped after the nineteenth-century restorations. Grodecki earlier pointed out that the fragments of the life of Saint Andrew show a style indebted to Parisian currents.[40] Six of the eight medallions are old and show few restorations (see Iconography Appendix: Andrew). The figures in the panel that shows Andrew entering the city display all the essential characteristics of the glass at Semur and Saint-Germain (fig. 60). Andrew strides forward with drapery pulled taut across the knee. The sharply defined folds across the chest and over the legs of the man with flowers compare with the drapery of Mary at Semur (fig. 58) and Synagoga at Saint-Germain (fig. 56). One might easily substitute the reversed figure of the striding Saint Peter at Semur for the Saint Andrew at Troyes. The same sweep of drapery over the leg, deeply looping tunic and gesticulating arm characterize both representations. One might also compare the figure of Saint Andrew from the panel showing the exorcism of a child (fig. 61) with the prophet to the left in the Saint-Germain Jesse Tree (fig. 54). In both figures, drapery of the sleeve and mantle show strong similarities. The dramatic stance and elegantly flowing garments of the man witnessing the exorcism brings one back to the dynamic drapery patterns and active stances of the figures in the Vienna manuscript medallion of the Church surrounded by the sea of worldly concerns.[41]

---

[39] Both figures show a characteristic light purple glass in the mantle precisely the same shade used for the standing Saint Peter (fig. 58). All of the remaining glass in the chapel can be attributed to the Magdalene Master (see below).

[40] *Vitrail*, 140, "un art plus raffiné, plus 'parisien'; figures allongées, silhouettes flexibles, visages un peu déformés." See also Lafond, 1955, 30-31.

[41] An even closer comparison is found in the

The rounded eyes, thick caps of hair, wide noses and arched eyebrows of the Troyes figures all strike a familiar note. Equally remarkable are the similarly fixed stare and the arrangement of the head covering on the woman in front of the city gate, when compared with Mary from Semur (fig. 58). However, one also notices at Troyes a slightly more rigid stance to the figures and a less dramatic presentation on the narrative. A more cluttered composition resulted from the addition of architectural details such as the city gate and the masonry ground line.

Similar figural and compositional characteristics appear in the glass of the cathedral of Auxerre in two narrative cycles attributable to the same workshop. The first (70) contains nine panels recounting the story of the Relics of Saint Stephen (see Iconography Appendix: Stephen) (fig. 66).[42] The other window (67) presents the Life of Saint Nicholas in large quartered medallions (see Iconography Appendix: Nicholas) (fig. 62, pl. I).[43] The essential characteristics of the Saint-Germain style appear at Auxerre in the careful articulation of deep folds and the sense of volume the figures evoke. The detail of Saint Nicholas (fig. 64) shows the same energetic drapery treatment as that of the Jesse Tree Virgin (fig. 54). As if blown by violent gusts of wind Nicholas' mantle whips around his body just as the Virgin's garments surge across her legs and billow out to the side. In the head of Nicholas in this scene and the tracing of the angel's head from the Relics cycle (fig. 65) we see the same youthful face with full cheeks, broad jaw and heavy modeling. Both the head of the angel leading Saint Peter at Semur-en-Auxois (fig. 59) and the face of Saint John at Saint-Germain-lès-Corbeil (fig. 56) display similar generous proportions and rounded features.

Features of the Auxerre windows also recall the atelier of the Vienna Moralized Bibles. The taut pull of the mantle across the full extent of the back visible in the bishop praying over his deceased colleague (lower left, fig. 62) or in three figures in the Relics window (to the left and bottom center, fig. 66) appears again in the light colored mantle of the Jew immediately to the right of Susanna (fig. 55). One example of the older bearded figures, the bishop who seizes the hand of the overly modest Nicholas (upper right, fig. 62), shows an astonishing similarity to the man greeting Saint Andrew at Troyes (fig. 60) ultimately going back to the manuscript image of the bishop who assails the church (fig. 57). The anxious expression, the somewhat concave face and the extremely sharp pleats of the mantle and tunic all indicate a common workshop tradition. Like the Troyes panels, the Auxerre glass displays a more complex composition involving larger numbers of figures in each panel and more extensive architectural settings. The figures are less agitated and

---

figure of Cain, from the first Vienna Bible (ÖNB 1179, fol. 5C; illustrated in Branner, 1977, fig. 26a).

[42] The severe truncation of the Relics window is a result of the Huguenot destruction of 1567. The panels were only reunited in their present position during the 1926 restoration. See Restoration Appendix: Auxerre.

[43] Because of the striking medallion format of the Nicholas window, it has attracted some scholarly attention, although all of the discussion has concentrated on the iconography. Cahier, 1875, 42-54, pl. 1; Fourrey, 1929, illustration on p. 48; idem, "Auxerre et ses richesses artistiques," *L'Illustration*, 3 October 1941.

place a greater emphasis on verticality. Probably this modification arose from the atelier's association with another stylistic tradition. The Saint-Germain atelier undoubtedly arrived at Auxerre after the Genesis atelier had already established a stylistic vocabulary favoring restrained drama and a more linear conception.

The windows are further linked by an identity of border motifs and mosaic backgrounds at all four sites, as discussed in the section on composition and ornament. A chronological assessment of the atelier, however, depends on information about architectural development, and especially development of composition and figural style. The Saint-Germain medallions frequently present highly simplified compositions using but one or two figures per panel. Only minimal references to backgrounds occur, and those are of a decorative nature such as the little trees filling the panels beside Ecclesia and Synagoga. The date of about 1225 traditionally associated with the glass seems reasonable since Branner assigned a date of 1212-1215 and about 1225 for the flowering of the Vienna Moralized Bible atelier.[44] Due to the fragmentary conservation of the glass at Semur, dating is difficult, but one does sense an economy of figures per panel, a laconic narrative and a strong emphasis on diagonal composition.[45] The composition of the Troyes panels appear close to the Saint-Germain format, although architectural details are more common. The figural style, however, approaches that of the Auxerre panels, with more vertical emphasis and less dynamic relationship among the figures. I am inclined to date the Semur glass at about 1228, shortly after the Saint-Germain-lès-Corbeil windows. Troyes must have closely followed, and Auxerre should be placed at about 1237, perhaps four years after the establishment of the dominant atelier of the cathedral.

4. THE APOCALYPSE ATELIER
(Auxerre, Saint-Julien-du-Sault, Saint-Fargeau)

The Apocalypse atelier is possibly the most interesting of all the Burgundian glazing workshops.[46] Its evolution can be traced from narrative windows in the ambulatory of the cathedral of Auxerre to large-scale standing figures in the axial chapel, to the clerestory saints apostles, and prophets, to, finally, work at two nearby sites, Saint-Julien-du-Sault and Saint-Fargeau. The work of the Apocalypse atelier is particularly noteworthy because it provides a much needed model for the understanding of the transition from small- to large-scale figure painting. In monuments of this period, the lower windows comprise multiple small-figure medallions designed to present the life of a saint or biblical personage in great detail. The clerestories usually display

[44] 1977, 48.

[45] Branner (1960, 66) estimates that Semur's chevet was begun about 1220-1225, and the glass of Semur's Magdalene Master should be dated about the same time (see below, Magdalene Master).

[46] Portions of this study were presented at the Eleventh Conference on Medieval Studies, at Western Michigan University, Kalamazoo, Michigan, 1976, and "A Symposium: Problems in Stained Glass," in conjunction with the exhibition, *Medieval and Renaissance Stained Glass from New England Collections*, April 1978, The Busch-Reisinger Museum, Harvard University and the Department of Fine Arts, Tufts University.

single figures of apostles, prophets or saints of colossal size. To date only Caviness and Grodecki have explained convincingly how a painting style employed for one scale of work could have been adapted to fit another.[47] The Apocalypse atelier not only demonstrates that a single atelier could respond to the demands of different size windows in different areas of a building, but through its use of grisaille and colored glass heralds the beginning of the next phase of Gothic glazing.

The first windows of the Apocalypse workshop are the Saint Eloi window (71) and the Apocalypse window (68).[48] As discussed in the section on composition and ornament, the windows seemed so similar that restorers actually intermingled them at one time.[49] The painting styles of both windows are absolutely identical. Short, solid figures with rather large round heads are the rule. Gestures are restricted, as witnessed by the laconic movements of the Apocalyptic Christ (fig. 67) and the mechanical positions of the kneeling Saint Eloi and Saint Ouen (fig. 74). Drapery patterns display deep scoop folds with heavy grisaille modeling. The folds over the laps of seated figures such as the Apocalyptic Christ fall in heavy sculptural masses, smoothly draping the knees and creating deep indentations across the laps. Standing figures (figs. 70 and 73) continue the same generous massing of folds especially when material caught at the waist falls in deep recesses. The garments give the impression of being made of heavy woolen material, which in the standing figures achieves a sense of columnar rigidity, evident in the figures of John and Aristodemus (fig. 70) and the two clerics from the Saint Eloi window (fig. 74).

Tracings made of the angel adoring the Son of Man and the head of Saint Eloi (fig. 76) display identical formulas for every feature. The heads turn at exactly the same angle showing a full, almost square cut of cheek and jaw. The nose is extremely broad, emphasizing the rounded tip of the nostril. Paralleled by the fold of the upper lid and brow, the eyes follow the same simple curves.

Both windows show identical color schemes, deep blue silhouetting the figures and solid red between the medallions (pl. II). Although gold is frequently used, purple and green find unusual favor in the figures. The Apocalyptic Christ wears a deep green tunic and purple mantle in all the panels. Saint Eloi, likewise, except in the consecration panel, consistently appears in a green tunic under a purple mantle. Green is also used to highlight many decorative motifs, a color unusual for Auxerre.

The style of the Apocalypse Master can be loosely associated with a Parisian manuscript group of around 1230.[50] Of this group, the Evangeliary of the Sainte-Chapelle emerges the most extensive and impressive example.[51] In the illustrations

---

[47] At Canterbury (Caviness, 1977, 52ff., the Methuselah Master, c. 1178-1180; 71ff., the Jesse Tree Master, c. 1180-1198) and at Chartres (Grodecki, 1978, the Saint Chéron Master, c. 1220-1230).

[48] A unique representation. See iconographic discussion in text and Appendix.

[49] In Auxerre windows 70 and 71. Guilhermy, Auxerre, fols. 694-695; Bonneau, 1885, 338-339.

The present panels 68:8 and 9 were recorded by Bonneau as forming a single panel before the twentieth-century restorations.

[50] Branner (1977, 61-65, figs. 105-111, color pl. IX) refers to the manuscripts as the Leber group, after the earliest work of the group, Ms. 3016 (Leber 6) of the Bibliothèque municipale of Rouen; idem, "Manuscript Painting in Paris around 1200," *Year 1200* III, 175, fig. 7.

of the Three Kings before Herod and the Circumcision (fig. 75), the manuscript figures show facial types and drapery influenced by "muldenfaltenstil" patterns. Despite the difference in media and atelier, Herod (fig. 75) and the Apocalyptic Christ (fig. 77) show the same heavy, substantial drapery. Material is pulled across one knee and massed over the other, producing vertical folds on the right and deep indentations across the lap. Restrained gesture, particularly exemplified by the mechanical movement of the three kings again corresponds to elements observed at Auxerre. Arms are bent at the elbow and kept close to the body, emphasizing the solidity of the isolated figures. Saint Eloi's short curly bangs and wavy masses of hair (fig. 74) find their counterpart in the hair style of Herod. The eloquent folds of the long garment in the scene of the Circumcision appear again in the drapery undulating over the torso of the Son of Man seated on the Apocalyptic lamb (fig. 67). Both figures display extremely rich shading of the deep pleats, and animated pattern that heightens the interest of the scene. The standing figures of the Three Kings wear traveling cloaks characterized by deep vertical folds, similar to the modeling observed for the kneeling saints and the first acolyte (the second is restored) of the Saint Eloi panel (fig. 74) and Saint John and Aristodemus from the Apocalypse series (fig. 70).

It is possible that the Apocalypse atelier arrived in Auxerre a few years after inception of the glazing by the Genesis and Eustache ateliers. The Apocalypse atelier's closeness to a Parisian painting style of the 1230s would argue for the same pattern of artistic dissemination as that demonstrated by the Genesis atelier, but slightly later in time.

I suggest that the Apocalypse atelier experienced a progressive maturation of style first evident in the window of the Ascension and Pentecost followed shortly by the clerestory figures. Restorers had used the figures of seated apostles, angels and the Ascending Christ as stop-gaps to complete the narratives truncated by the Huguenot destruction.[52] David regrouped the panels into the lower portions of two separate windows producing one window containing six seated apostles (57), and another with two apostles, three panels with angels and one panel showing Christ surrounded by clouds (72).[53] The seated apostles (fig. 78) are very close to the figure of Christ enthroned from the Apocalypse window (fig. 77). Drapery in these figures shows the same sculptural massing, smooth over knees and deeply indented across laps. At the same time, these seated figures may be compared with the images of prophets placed in the central medallions of many of the clerestory roses (fig. 79). The figure of Jeremias (15) repeats the apostles' frontal position on a low bench complete with architectural frame of columns with foliate capitals supporting a simple arch. This small clerestory figure exhibits the same flow of mantle across the

---

[51] Paris, Bibl. nat. Ms. lat. 8892. See esp. Branner, 1969.

[52] The panels had been distributed among windows 51, 66, 68, 72, 73 and 74 (Guilhermy, Au-

xerre, fols. 693, 694, 695v., 689; Bonneau, 1885, 322, 335, 337, 340, 341, 346-347).

[53] See iconographic discussion in text and Appendices.

knees from left to right commencing with taut folds and terminating in a heavy cap of material over the right knee.

The angels in the Apocalypse window may be compared to the angels surrounding the Lamb of God in the rose of the axial bay (19) (fig. 80). The same prominent noses and broad mouths characterize the impassive faces. The treatment of the hair in both windows favors the same thick waving masses that flow close to the rounded forms of the head. Both clerestory and ambulatory figures show the same heavy drapery forms and scoop folds of the mantle.

Small-scale figures in the clerestory lancet of the triumphant Christ (12a) belong to this group. The personifications of Sol and Luna (fig. 81), each holding a celestial orb in their arms present the same facial types and drapery forms as the angel of the axial rose. Even these two images of Christ, despite the vast differences of scale between ambulatory narrative and clerestory icon, have the same dignified frontality and impassive stares. Both figures have almond-shaped eyes accented by strong brows and thick waves of hair framing the face. The lower portions of the face, with deeply shadowed beard and downward sloping mouth, display common workshop habits. The underlips are defined by a sharp curve from which the schematicized lines of the beard echo the form of the chin. The extant portions of the clerestory Christ surrounded by the tetramorph (26b) (fig. 82, Saint Matthew and the torso and arms of Christ) show the same stylistic approach. Both these lancets were originally designed to fill the axial bay of the cathedral, immediately under the rose of the Lamb of God.[54]

The patron saints of the cathedral are still in their original places to the left and right of the axial bay. Stephen and Germain (18) (fig. 89) as befits their preeminent position are to Christ's right, under the rose depicting the Virtues and the Vices. Lawrence and Amâtre (20) (fig. 86), their complements, fill the bay to the south, under the rose of the Liberal Arts. As befits a less symbolically impressive representation, these faces are more natural than the images of Christ. The comparatively narrow brushstrokes delineating Lawrence's features reproduce the same long curve of the nose, graceful almond eyes, firm mouth with narrow lower lip and rounded chin observed in the heads of Saint Eloi and the angel from the Apocalypse window in the ambulatory.

In the axial chapel of the cathedral two large-scale figures framed by grisaille panels appear in the side windows. On the north, the Virgin and Child face an image of Saint Stephen, patron saint of the cathedral on the south. The window of the Virgin and Child has been heavily damaged and restored, but that of Stephen (65) is in a good state of conservation. Stephen (fig. 87) is almost as large as a clerestory figure and is accompanied by a donor presenting a model of the window accompanied by an inscription. The vigorous face of Saint Stephen, impassively confronting the worshiper, attests to the further evolution of the Apocalypse atelier's style toward

[54] Lafond (1958a, 65) came to the same conclusion. See iconography chapter and Appendices.

the abstract effects of mid-century France. The mouth is a straight line articulated by three curves at the upper lip. The short lower lip leads one's attention to the firm half-circle indicating the chin. A predictable uniformity of features and a canon of proportion emphasizing broad curves and structured immobility become more evident in the workshop's later production.

The attribution of these large-scale figures to the same workshop that produced the Apocalypse and Eloi panels in the ambulatory is corroborated by the prevalance of the same color schemes. Christ surrounded by the tetramorph is clothed in a deep purple mantle over a green tunic. Saint Stephen in the axial chapel wears a dalmatic of deep green and the donor is given the purple complement. Both lancets then produce the same rich harmonies of green and purple against blue backgrounds that so characterized the smaller narrative panels.

Before continuing with a discussion of the narrative glass of the Apocalypse atelier, some remarks on the expansion of the atelier's work into the remaining clerestory windows and the innovative use of grisaille borders is in order.[55] The prophets and apostles in the remaining ten bays of the clerestory are in poor states of conservation. It appears that much of the darkened thirteenth-century glass was considered too illegible by subsequent restorers, and modern copies were used as replacements.[56] This appears to have been the case of much of the figural work in the three complex roses of the hemicycle. Such practices might conserve something of the original iconographic program, but are devastating for style.[57] The head of Ezekiel (25) (fig. 88), however, appears to be original and shows the typical exaggerated features of most of the figures outside of the hemicycle bays. Most noticeable is the dramatic enlargement of the eyes. One might compare the head to that of the clerestory Saint Stephen, where, despite the different use of the lead outlines, the same huge eyes, long nose and tapering chin are evident. Such manipulation of the normal proportions of the face seems typical of many artists working in the clerestory. Evidently, a common desire to make the figures readable from the ground, and to imbue these images with stark iconic power, led one of the Reims Masters to exaggerate the features of the apostle Philip (fig. 90), dated about 1240 by Grodecki, a date very close to the execution of Auxerre's clerestory figures.[58] One sees the same immense eyes framed by successive strokes of grisaille. The hair of both

---

[55] Bonneau (1885, 306) and Lafond (1958a, 62) noticed the difference in execution in the clerestory figures. For Lafond the hemicycle glass was "raffiné" while that of the remaining choir "assez rude."

[56] Bonneau (1885, 306) and Fourrey (1929, 7) speak of Vessière's reglazing of the lower parts of the choir glass after Steinheil's designs. This was the part of the glass that had presumably been destroyed when the Huguenots mounted ladders and broke what glass they could reach. This glass is easily recognizable for its clear and frequently garish colors. Many of the heads were also restored, however.

[57] Since only modern cleaning techniques allow darkened pieces of glass to be restored to acceptable transluscence, much of the nineteenth-century campaigns engaged in repairing windows by discarding old glass for new. See especially Caviness (1977, 17-19) for George Austin Jr.'s restorations at Canterbury.

[58] *Vitrail*, 143, fig. 107; See also Hanns Reinhardt, *La Cathédrale de Reims*, Paris (1963), 183-184.

figures is arranged in coherent clumps and the beard terminates in a rounded area below the chin.

The innovative use of grisaille panels surrounding the central figures in the clerestory and in the axial chapel figures has great significance in the development of a late thirteenth-century aesthetic concerning the intermingling of colored and grisaille glass. On the basis of the relative proportion of grisaille to colored panels, and the use of colored borders in the windows, Lillich has dated the clerestory figures to 1240-1245, a date that corresponds precisely with a dating based on stylistic evolution.[59] Significantly the only clerestory lancets, aside from the later Crucifixion and Majesty panels presently in the axial bay, that contain only fully colored glass are the original axial pair showing Christ surrounded by the tetramorph and the triumphant Christ flanked by Sol and Luna. In the mid-century experimentations of grisaille and colored arrangements, the axial bays were invariably glazed with fully saturated panels, as evidenced in the Virgin Chapel of Saint-Germain-des-Prés, and at Saint-Père of Chartres.[60] Auxerre, then, must be considered one of the pioneers of the formula that was to dominate the later development of the Gothic window.[61]

The ambulatory window of Saint Vincent (74) marks the last stage of the Apocalypse atelier's narrative productions in the cathedral. Nine panels in extremely fragmentary condition survive. However, the panel representing the torture of Saint Vincent with metal rakes (fig. 91) shows excellent examples of this later style. The head of the tortured saint shows an increase in breadth, very similar to the broad regularity of the face of Saint Stephen from the axial chapel. The guard to the right turns his face at the same angle as the donor below Stephen. The nose line, almond-shaped eyes, mouth and beards are almost identical and both heads show the same sweep of hair away from the forehead to form thick clusters at the ears. The scoop folds noticeable in the Eloi and Apocalypse panels still linger in the drapery of Vincent's guards.

The style of the Saint Vincent panels appears at another Burgundian site, Saint-Julien-du-Sault, where the atelier produced three of the extant ambulatory windows: the legends of St. Nicholas (9), Saint Margaret (3) and Saint John the Evangelist (6) (text. illus. 3).[62] In the Nicholas window panel showing the Jew striking a statue of the saint (fig. 92) we see the same facial type as the image of Dacien observing Saint Vincent's torture. The head is turned at precisely the same angle, and the similarity of features, hair and beard would argue that not only the same workshop model was employed, but that the Auxerre and Saint-Julien-du-Sault windows were painted very close in time. The Jew's garments, with lingering scoop folds in the

---

[59] 1970, 28. See also Cahier and Martin, 1841-1844, Grisailles pl. G.

[60] Grodecki, 1957, 34, and Lillich, 1978.

[61] Lafond (1958a, 63) whose knowledge of later Gothic glass was unparalleled, stated succinctly "on conviendra que la formule du XIVe siècle annonce ici avec un précocité remarquable." See also Viollet-le-Duc, 1875, 435-436, fig. 33.

[62] Rheims, 1926; Lafond, 1958b.

torso and cloak and swift fall of pleats in the skirt, are similar to the clothing of the guard on the left and Dacien.[63] The panel of John blessing the poisoned cup that had been handed to him by Aristodemus (fig. 93) shows two standing figures. The stiff gestures and the columnar verticality of the long figures recall the techniques used in the Saint Eloi window of Auxerre. Above all, this image should be compared with the panel of John drinking poison from the Auxerre Apocalypse window (fig. 70) which shows not only much the same iconography but similar drapery patterns and facial types. The face of Aristodemus is also a repetition of the type used in the Nicholas and Vincent panels. The face of Saint John, with its great jaw, full mouth and impassive features, recalls the head of the tortured Saint Vincent. The third window, that of Saint Margaret, appears the more evolved of the group. It is also the only one of the three using a curved armature system and a more varied medallion format. I would suggest that the more open, fluid painting style as well as the medallion schema are results of the influence of the atelier of the Isaiah Master working at Saint-Julien at the same time (see discussion following).[64] The medallion of Saint Margaret led from prison (fig. 94), like all of the compositions in this window, shows a more monumental concept of space. The draperies continue the lingering scoop folds evident in the Nicholas or Saint John windows, but they move with the actions of the figures, adding to the sense of Margaret and her guard walking forward. Even a more vigorous stride in the guard, and Margaret's more reticent, decorous pace are suggested. The identity of the two heads, as products of the Apocalypse Master's atelier, however, is undeniable. The characteristic round heads, broad features and unusually unvarying facial types of the Apocalypse atelier are very much in evidence.

The Apocalypse atelier worked on another Burgundian site, Saint-Fargeau, a small town on the Loing forty-five kilometers southwest of Auxerre. The parish church dedicated to Saint Férreol retains only the nave and side aisles from the thirteenth-century building. The choir was torn down and rebuilt in the fifteenth century. It was during this reworking that the glass must have been recut and set in the central and left lancets of the axial chapel where it was observed by Quantin in 1868.[65] Removed from the windows to accommodate new panels signed and dated, E. Didron, 1877, the glass must have been sold to a Parisian dealer sometime after 1881.[66] In 1885 twenty panels were acquired by Gustave Revilliod for the Musée

[63] The upper right half of the Jew's skirt is restored.

[64] See also discussion of the interaction between the Eustache and Genesis ateliers at Auxerre.

[65] 1868, 164.

[66] The story of the Saint-Fargeau panels points out the worst of abuses involving the fate of small parish churches in many areas of France. Due to the patient researches of Madame S. Pélissier, it is now evident that the decision to modernize the church in the 1870s necessitated its declassification as a historical monument which allowed local intervention to destroy the fifteenth-century wooden roof and substitute vaults of brick and stucco and to remove the thirteenth-century glass and install new windows. Although legally the local authorities had no power to effect the removal of the windows before the official declassification of 1877 (in fact the declassification permission specifically retained historical monument status for the windows), the windows had been taken down and Didron's installed by this date. The old glass remained for some time in Saint-Fargeau since in a letter dated October 20, 1881, now in the Town Hall of Saint-Fargeau, the sub-prefect of Joigny asks that the glass not be transferred to the ju-

Ariana of Geneva. These were transferred in 1960 to the Musée d'Art et d'Histoire.[67] Other panels have surfaced in the Pitcairn collection and the Wellesley College museum.[68] Identification of the iconographic themes in the Saint-Fargeau glass remains difficult, but one of the windows must have represented the story of the Passion, since there remain panels of the Flagellation, Kiss of Judas and a panel that fuses portions of a Crucifixion and a Descent from the Cross. I am inclined to accept Lafond's identification of a Last Judgment window in the various panels of bust-length apostles.[69]

In assessing the relationship of the early Auxerre glass to the Saint-Julien and Saint-Fargeau production, Lafond's precocious observations must be mentioned. Lafond stated in 1948 that he had drawn capitals from the stained glass at Auxerre that were similar to the capital in the Saint-Fargeau Flagellation.[70] Lafond could have meant the capitals in the Saint Eloi weighing panel (fig. 73) or those in the Ascension-Pentecost panels (fig. 78), since these scenes are in the lowest register and were therefore accessible before the present Monuments Historiques photographs were available. The prophet panels in the clerestory show capitals of the same form. Similar capitals can be found in the window of Saint Nicholas at Saint-

risdiction of the "Président de la Fabrique." Given the illegal nature of the removal of the windows, it is no wonder that to date records of their sale and departure from Saint-Fargeau have not been discovered. The glass must have been transferred to Paris, however, because of the presence of a well-known twelfth-century head from the collection of the Parisian glass painter Alfred Gérente reset into fragments of Saint-Fargeau's borders, figures, and backgrounds. Viollet-le-Duc has illustrated the head in his *Dictionnaire* (1875, 414-416, fig. 19 bis) enabling Lafond (1948, 120) to rediscover the "tête Gérente" in the Musée Ariana medallion. Research on the head and the problems of nineteenth-century restorers have been continued by Grodecki (1977, 282-283) and Catherine Brisac ("La 'tête Gérente,'" *Revue de l'art* 47 [1980], 72-75). See most recently, S. Pélissier, "L'ancienne vitrerie du XIIIe siècle de l'église de Saint-Fargeau," *Bulletin de la Société des sciences historiques et naturelles de l'Yonne* 112 (1980), 71-84.

[67] Claude Lapaire has discovered a document in the files of the Musée d'Art et d'Histoire speaking of the 1885 purchase of eight windows by Gustave Revilliod from Charles Töpffer, a painter of Geneva origin then living at 3 Cour de Rohan, Paris. The description of the windows corresponds to the eight more or less "full panels" numbered 71 to 78 in the Musée Ariana catalogue. The panels numbered 79-90 are preserved in a far more fragmentary condition, often distorted by the inclusion of fifteenth-century additions stemming from the reworking of the glass into the rebuilt choir of the church, conflated compositions and

recreation of false episodes by the juxtaposition of sections from disparate panels. That all twenty panels come from Saint-Fargeau, however, is attested to by the identical patination, color harmonies and draftsmanship. (W. Deonna, *Catalogue du Musée Ariana*, Geneva, [1938], 173-175). Lafond (1948, 115) erroneously believed that the glass was purchased at the 1891 Vincent sale in Constance. He included in his study two medallions of angels, nos. 91 and 92, to which he assigned a slightly later date, pointing out affinities with the glass of Notre-Dame of Paris (ibid., 127). Lafond later modified this opinion (*Corpus, France* I, 38), demonstrating that the angels come from the same atelier that painted the north rose of Notre-Dame. Since Alfred Gérente died in 1868, the identity of the glass painter responsible for releading the Saint-Fargeau panels and for the inclusion of the "tête Gérente" and a head of about 1200 called "Abraham" (Lafond, 1948, 130-131) remains unknown.

[68] The identity of the panel in the Pitcairn collection, Bryn Athyn, Pennsylvania, was recognized by Jane Hayward. Wellesley, Mass., Wellesley College Museum, 1949-19c; *New England Collections*, No. 10.

[69] Lafond (1948) identified sufficient iconography to allow him to suggest that Saint-Fargeau must have had windows representing the Passion, Childhood of Christ, Life of the Virgin, Apocalypse or Last Judgment, Saints Peter and Paul, Saint Vincent and Saint Blaise. The glass deserves a far more thorough study, for authenticity, iconography and style than can be presented here.

[70] Lafond, 1948, 127-128.

Julien-du-Sault, in the panels of the death and resurrection of the three clerics. We owe then to Lafond, so frequently a pioneer in unchartered territory, the first indication of a connection between these three Burgundian sites.

The Flagellation panel in Geneva (fig. 95) contains a figure with immediate associations to both Auxerre and Saint-Julien. The guard to the left displays the same stance as the Jew striking the statue of Saint Nicholas. Both figures show the same forward loop of material over the belt as the torturer in the Saint Vincent panel. The guard's face repeats the pattern found in the Jew and Auxerre's Dacien. The energetic profile with parted lips and jutting nose of the guard on the right appears in the torturer at Auxerre. Precisely the same systems of drapery and facial delineation appear in the unusually well-preserved Kiss of Judas panel in Geneva (fig. 96). Here it seems appropriate to look back to the manuscript associations discussed for the early work at Auxerre. The close arrangement of figures, the grouping of heads in a dense mass and the proportions of the figures link the Kiss of Judas panel to a representation of Christ exorcising a demon from the Evangeliary of the Sainte-Chapelle (fig. 97). Even the facial types are similar; the profile of Judas and the possessed man show the same curve of eyebrow, prominent nose, wide mouth and protruding lips. The faces of Christ and the apostles show similar squarish heads, broadly curving noses and hair flowing away from the face in thick waves. The Saint-Fargeau panel obviously has transformed much of the volumetric treatment of the drapery into a more linear expression, as well as simplifying the facial delineation, an expected development after more than fifteen year difference.

Three panels of half-length figures, in Geneva (fig. 98), Wellesley College (fig. 99) and the Pitcairn collection (fig. 100) may relate to a Last Judgment window at Saint-Fargeau. In the Geneva and Wellesley panels Saint Peter is recognizable by his short curly hair and beard, very much the duplicate of Saint Peter stooping to pick up the ear of Caiphas' servant in the Flagellation panel. Saint Paul's bald pate stands out in the center of the Geneva medallion. The Pitcairn panel also shows Peter to the right. The lower portions of this medallion consist of reused background mosaic, and the material below Christ's waist shows another reuse of drapery fragments. There is nothing in the iconography to insist on a Last Supper identification. A comparison with the Apocalypse window from Bourges, although it was produced before 1214, reveals striking similarities with compositional techniques used by the Saint-Fargeau painter.[71] Especially in the four lobes surrounding the Son of Man (fig. 101) the artist has packed groups of seated apostles, prophets and elders, even using the unusual device of overlapping profiles to give a greater sense of density. The several representations of the apostles in the same grouped poses, all somehow truncated, and the presence of Saint Paul would lead one to accept that these panels must have belonged to a window of a Last Judgment or Apocalypse, the only themes that would allow for so many groups of figures.[72]

[71] Dating by Grodecki, *Year 1200* III, 339, and ibid., 1948. These articles do not carry illustrations pertinent to this discussion.

[72] It is possible that the recutting in the sixteenth century was responsible for the loss of the lower portions of the figures. I believe that the

The relationship of the Apocalypse window, a product of the Good Samaritan Master's atelier, to the Saint-Fargeau glass raises some important questions. Are the similarities in composition merely coincidental, or did the Apocalypse atelier possess copybooks reproducing models that furnished inspiration for both the Bourges and the Saint-Fargeau work? Possibly because of our own period's dependence on written material, we tend to overemphasize the importance of the "portable" book. Were not windows that were so large, colorful and prominently displayed much more available as sources to the medieval artist? Perhaps, like mosaics, stained glass was visited, and lessons drawn from its composition, iconography or style.[73] A Burgundian atelier would not be too far away from the Berry for a border to be crossed, at some time during its twenty-year activity in the region, and monuments of the great masters studied and admired.

5. The Infancy of Christ-Glorification of the Virgin Atelier (Saint-Julien-du-Sault)

Although all of the windows at Saint-Julien-du-Sault have suffered from extensive restoration campaigns, the two windows of the Infancy of Christ-Glorification of the Virgin (11) and the Legend of Theophilus (10) have lost the most of their original glass.[74] This is apparently due as much to theft as it is to the effect of the Hundred Years' War and subsequent neglect (see Restoration Appendix: Saint-Julien-du-Sault). These two windows were the last of the series restored by Leprévost and Steinheil. A bill from Steinheil of 1901 ascertains that he replaced with new glass one-quarter of the Theophilus windows and one-third of the Infancy-Glorification panels. In reality, the replacements must have been much greater, for close study reveals that most of the panels at Saint-Julien are modern. Very probably many thirteenth-century panels were duplicated in modern glass and substituted for the originals.[75] Original panels, or more frequently a combination of old glass mingled

---

figures were seated, and a comparison with the size of the figures in other panels would argue that these showed full figures.

[73] See especially Ernst Kitzinger (*The Art of Byzantium and the Medieval West, Selected Studies*, Indiana University Press [1976], 365ff.) who suggests that the migration of artists might have far more importance than the arrival of a portable object (reliquary, manuscript or model book) for the dissemination of artistic ideas.

[74] Ideas basic to this study were presented at the 1975 Meeting of the College Art Association: Medieval Art, Session II. For iconography, see Rheims, 1926.

[75] The Saint-Julien-du-Sault windows are not isolated examples of such practices. In the decade after 1925 the Redemption window from Montreuil-sur-Loir was replaced by a copy, the original passing into commerce and eventually being pur-

chased by the City Art Museum of St. Louis, Mo. (Jane Hayward, "The Choir Windows of Saint-Serge and their Glazing Atelier," *Gesta* 15 (1976), 261-262, figs. 8 and 10). Léon Pressouyre has reported the substitutions of copies for Romanesque and Gothic sculpture in numerous French churches. Capitals from La Charité-sur-Loire appear in the collections of the Museum of Fine Arts, Boston, and the City Art Museum, Saint Louis, while copies remain in the church. A false capital is similarly in place in Saint-Martin of Candes, and the original on exhibit in the Memorial Art Gallery, Rochester. However, the process sometimes involved the making of duplicates that were then placed in commerce, leaving the originals in their places of origin (review, "La Renaissance du XIIe siècle," *La Revue de l'art* 7 [1970], 98-100).

[76] For Detroit panels see note following. The panels in the Higgins Armory Museum, Worces-

with copied portions have appeared in commerce, some panels rearranged to appear as entire windows in the Detroit Institute of Arts and the John Woodman Higgins Armory Museum.[76]

Although few of the panels date from the original glazing, the restorers appear to have copied faithfully the original format of the window. Arranged in insistently vertical patterns of small independent panels, the two windows display the same workshop solutions discussed in the section on composition and ornament (figs. 102 and 103). Simplicity dominates the compositional schemas of both windows. In the Theophilus window there are never more than two figures in a scene, a pattern that emphasizes the episodic and symbolic sequence of the narrative. Even in the Infancy-Glorification window the interaction of the figures is reduced to a minimum. Where tradition necessitates the grouping of several figures, such as the Adoration of the Magi, the episode is spread out over two panels.

The proportions of the figures are highly distinctive, as for example in the panel of the Magi before Herod (fig. 104). Unusually large heads dominate bodies characterized by stiff, formalized gestures. Symmetrically arched brows draw attention to exceptionally wide foreheads. Widely opened eyes accented by grisaille shading produce a worried, almost sleepless look. Tight curls at the end of the jaw-length coiffures draw attention to the short chins accented by scrubby beards. The marionette quality of the faces is also characteristic of the poses of the figures. Atrophied arms and legs assume prearranged positions, such as the crossed legs of Herod. The heavy bunched drapery contributes to the sense of the incorporeality of the bodies. The cloaks fall in massive insistency from shoulder to calf, their heavily shadowed folds repeating the impression of solidity of the tunics underneath. The haphazardly bunched folds over the first king's arms and to the right of the seated Herod emphasize the bulk of the material and totally subjugate the delineation of the body underneath. Such an unrealistic pictorial expression seems well adapted to the highly stylized medallion format. Harmonizing with the energetic outlines of the quatrefoil, the gesturing arms, Herod's legs and the architectural canopy create a sprightly pattern.

Original glass and modern copies from the Theophilus window were reworked into a four-medallion window incorrectly labeled "Scenes from the Life of John Chrysostom" in the Detroit Institute of Arts.[77] The lowest panel shows Theophilus

---

ter, Mass., contain very little original glass. Unfortunately, the panels at Saint-Julien-du-Sault are also mostly modern copies. The Higgins Massacre of the Innocents window was created by placing duplicate panels of Saint-Julien's panels 15, 16 and 14 in a vertical alignment, culminating in a rose of modern invention. A small figure from the Theophilus window was added to fill out one of the quatrefoils. Museum records list the window as from the collection of Daguerre of Paris, who sold it to Arnold Seligman, Rey and Company, New York, where it was expertised by Paul M. Byk, who sold it to International Studios on

7 February 1934. It then became no. 1102-8 of the William Randolph Hearst collection. Gimbel Brothers bought the window in 1941 and sold it to the Higgins Museum in 1943.

[77] Acquisition no. 44.82. The window was no. 106-52 of the William Randolph Hearst collection, bought by Gimbel Brothers, New York, 1941. The Detroit border uses the pattern of successive fronds shown in the Infancy-Glorification window. The first medallion is a duplicate of Theophilus' panel 17. The second duplicates panel 5, showing Theophilus speaking with the demon, but it eliminates the pointed quatrefoil medallion sur-

kneeling before his bishop to confess his contract with Satan (fig. 105). A totally modern copy of this episode is now located near the center of the window in Saint-Julien-du-Sault. The restorer, as seems to be the custom, has used old and new glass in the Detroit panels and also must have repainted much of the effaced detail, probably in the belief that the worn condition of panels like that of the Magi before Herod would have less market value. The Theophilus panel shows the same atelier solutions, particularly the broad foreheads, symmetrically arched brows and sloping chins. The seated bishop displays the same parallel waves in the hair, simple beard and tilt of head as in the figure of Herod. The bunched drapery with its deeply shadowed and awkward folds over the bishop's arm repeats the forms of those in the mantle of the first Magus.

The scarcity of authentic panels from the Theophilus and Infancy-Glorification windows makes necessary an unusual approach to the localization of the style. I am willing to accept the nineteenth- and twentieth-century restorations as based on tracings of the original glass. Such a practice has been well documented by Caviness.[78] Certainly, the modern panels are far removed stylistically from the originals, yet they give an indication of the proportions, cut lines and painting methods used by the Gothic atelier. This Burgundian atelier appears to have derived its inspiration from the Master of the Life of Saint Anne and the Virgin from Saint-Germain-des-Prés. On the basis of current research, it seems unlikely that Leprévost or Steinheil were involved in producing copies of Saint-Germain-des-Prés glass. The similarities, therefore, between the copies from Saint-Julien and Saint-Germain-des-Prés panels can be seen as corroborative evidence for a stylistic interpretation first suggested by the original panels.

Saint-Germain-des-Prés was one of the most important institutions of mid-century Paris. The glass from the great abbey has not withstood the clerical neglect or the revolutionary animosity culminating in the demolition of the Refectory and the Chapel of the Virgin in 1794 and 1805.[79] The Refectory was glazed entirely in grisaille glass but the Chapel of the Virgin presumably contained four-lancet side windows of grisaille dominated by a hemicycle of seven double-lancet windows of traditional fully saturated medallions against a rich mosaic background.[80] Both buildings were begun about 1245 under the direction of Pierre de Montreuil, an architect of unusual refinement.[81] The combination of colored glass in the apse and grisaille glass in the side windows allowed the inclusion of a narrative program as well as increased illumination that relieved the finely detailed interior surface of the building, clear evidence of the increasingly effective combination of glazing innovations

rounding the scene. The third medallion combines the sower from the Miracle of the Wheatfield, panel 17 from the Infancy-Glorification window, with a demon from panel 1 from the Theophilus window. The panel in the summit combines the seated figure of Theophilus from panel 6 with the little figure of a cleric emerging from a building from panel 15.

[78] 1977, 17-19.

[79] Grodecki, 1957; idem, *Vitrail*, 144, 149; *Corpus, France, Recensement* I, 46-47, for most complete bibliography.

[80] Branner (1965, 68-69) follows Verdier (1962-1963, xxv-xxvi) by ascribing the extant panels to the refectory. Grodecki (1957, 34) argues more convincingly that the glass came from the Chapel of the Virgin.

[81] Branner, 1965, 143-146, figs. 54, 73, 82.

and architecture that marked the later thirteenth century. The same disposition was used at Auxerre in the cathedral's axial chapel a few years earlier.

Grodecki has estimated that the Virgin Chapel originally contained a program of more than four hundred panels, grouped into two hundred scenes of which only thirty-four panels remain, dispersed among American, Canadian, English and French collections.[82] The atelier of the life of Saint Anne and the Virgin claims eight panels regrouped and transferred to the Chapel of Saint Geneviève off the ambulatory in the abbey church, six panels in the Victoria and Albert Museum in London and two in the Montreal Museum of Fine Arts. A detail showing Joseph protesting his selection as Mary's betrothed from Saint-Germain (fig. 106) shows the typically short dense figure types favored by the Infancy-Glorification atelier. When compared to the first Magus from the Saint-Julien-du-Sault Herod panel, the High Priest's drapery patterns and gestures are the same. The long fall of mantle over the right shoulder stabilizes the more active display on the left. Both figures maintain extremely rigid stances, emphasized, rather than relieved, by the mechanical gestures of their upraised arms. The bulky folds of material enveloping Herod find their inspiration in the heavy drapery of Joseph (with halo) and the group of suitors crowding behind him. The Saint-Germain-des-Prés figures gather the lower portions of their mantles around their waists producing the same awkward folds as those across Herod's lap.

The broad forehead and symmetrical arch to the brow so typical of the Saint-Julien Magi appear again in the face of the High Priest. This characteristic physiognomy appears also in the panel now in the Museum of Fine Arts, Montreal.[83] The Montreal panel (fig. 107) unites two fragments of scenes in one medallion. A man tending sheep, probably Joachim, is attached to a panel of a priest standing before an altar. The reference is probably to the story of Joachim's expulsion from the Temple because of his sterility. Both the tapered face of Joachim and the more rectangular face of the High Priest appear at Saint-Julien. The Magi display symmetrical brows, wide foreheads and simple straight noses like those of Joachim. However, instead of the markedly triangular outline produced by the narrow chin and slant of the cropped hair, the Magi seem closer to the broader contours of the Priest's head. The two figures of the Detroit Theophilus window seem even closer to the Parisian model. Their open eyes with circular irises produce a similar effect of anxious, doll-like rigidity.

Although the Saint-Germain-des-Prés panels, both in the church and in museums, have undergone radical rearrangements, it seems clear that the Master of the Life of Saint Anne and the Virgin emphasized compositional symmetry rather than a dynamic interplay of figures. In the panels in Paris and Montreal the figures rarely deviate from a vertical alignment. They pivot on highly restricted bases and

---

[82] 1957, 34.

[83] Acquisition no. 29.Dg.4, purchased in 1929. The fourteenth-century border from Rouen, that is presently attached to the Montreal Saint-Germain-des-Prés panel was once a part of the Costessey collection; Maurice Drake, *The Costessey Collection of Stained Glass*, Exeter (1920), 9, no. 58, pl. IV; Lafond, *Year 1200*, III, 408.

approach each other with mechanical gestures. The Saint-Julien-du-Sault Infancy-Glorification atelier clearly favored these same short hesitant figures and a minimum of dramatic content.

This vivid, if somewhat awkward, painting style takes its place among several different artistic currents active in mid-thirteenth-century Paris. Grodecki has stressed that the Master of the Life of Saint Anne and the Virgin worked in an expressively "popular" style as opposed to the sophisticated elegance of the Passion Master of the Sainte-Chapelle or even the Saint Vincent or Relics(?) Masters at Saint-Germain-des-Prés.[84] The Master of the Life of Saint Anne and the Virgin evidently influenced glass painting in Burgundy in a church that also commissioned windows from one of the painters of the Sainte-Chapelle, evidence again that patrons could appreciate a variety of artistic expressions.[85] The style of this Master appears to have had some viability and continued in later Parisian-influenced expressions. Perhaps we see it again in the symmetry, rigid alignment of panels and childlike faces in the Life of the Virgin window from Saint-Sulpice-de-Favières, dated about 1255.[86]

6. THE ISAIAH MASTER ATELIER
(Sainte-Chapelle, Paris; Saint-Julien-du-Sault, Auxerre)

One of the most significant artistic developments of mid-thirteenth-century France has to do with the construction of the Sainte-Chapelle of Paris and its influence on stylistic trends in painting, sculpture and architecture.[87] At Saint-Julien-du-Sault and in the cathedral of Auxerre, a group of windows indicate that an offshoot of the workshop responsible for the Parisian monument traveled to Burgundy very shortly after or perhaps even before the building's dedication in 1248.[88] The Burgundian evidence, then, constitutes one of the first manifestations of the spread of the Sainte-Chapelle glazing style that so deeply influenced several decades of glass painting. Seen in such a context, these windows become important as evidence of a chain of events of political as well as artistic importance.[89]

The impact of the Sainte-Chapelle glass depended to a large measure on the architectural setting of the building. The church was built to evoke the form of a metal reliquary, the lower chapel a wide and stable base and the upper chapel a

[84] At Saint-Germain-des-Prés: Master of the life of Saint Anne, Grodecki, 1957, 33-35, figs. 2, 3, 6, 7; Saint Vincent Master, ibid., 36-37, figs. 10-12, Verdier, 1962-1963, Grodecki, *Vitrail*, 149, fig. 114; Relics Master, Grodecki, 1957, 35-36, figs. 1, 4, 8, 9, idem, 1976, figs. 211-217, *Corpus, France, Recensement* I, 46, pl. III. For the Sainte-Chapelle's Passion Master, see Grodecki, *Corpus, France* I, 92.

[85] See following section on the Isaiah Master atelier.

[86] Françoise Gatouillat, "A Saint-Sulpice-de-Favières, des vitraux témoins de l'art parisien au temps de Saint Louis," *Les Dossiers de l'archéologie* 26 (1978) 50-62; *Corpus, France, Recensement* I, 84-85, fig. 37; Grodecki, *Vitrail*, 163.

[87] See especially, Branner, 1965; ibid., "The Painted Medallions of the Sainte-Chapelle in Paris," *Transactions of the American Philosophical Society*, n.s. 58/2 (1968), 5-42; Grodecki, *Corpus, France* I, 71-309; Dyer-Spencer, 1932.

[88] Much of the following chapter has been published in Raguin (1977). Ideas basic to this study were presented at the 1975 Meeting of the College Art Association: Medieval Art, Session II.

[89] See discussion below.

vision of attenuated space and brilliant light (fig. 108). A veritable cage of glass, the upper chapel has fifteen multi-lancet windows almost fifteen meters high. Grodecki and Caviness have dated the glazing from 1241 to 1248.[90] The rapid, summary treatment of drapery and facial stylization have frequently been compared to contemporaneous manuscript illuminations.[91] Despite the vast program, a single atelier dominated the production: the atelier associated with the artist of the axial window of the Passion. The Passion Master produced nine of the extant windows using a set repertoire of figural types. In the panel of the Ruse of the Gabonites (fig. 109), the crowned figure of Joshua displays a neatly trimmed beard, controlled waves of hair and a fringe of bangs just visible under the base of his flat gold crown. The beardless Gabonite youth reveals a smooth oval-shaped face accented by an unusually large jaw. Making visible his deceit, the youth's hair assumes the backward sweep common to possessed individuals. Quickly sketched vertical folds characterize the short tunics and the hem of Joshua's garments. Joshua's mantle, however, evolves into a series of sharply broken folds that contrast sharply with the verticality of his long tunic.

In the panel of Moses Receiving the Law (fig. 110), the standing figure of Moses repeats the alternation of angular and parallel patterns in his garments. Drapery across the lap of the seated Creator falls loosely from the knees and gathers in a broken fold between the legs.[92] Vertical pleats of material over the chest harmonize with the slinglike drapery pulled taut from shoulder to elbow. In both panels, the delineation of facial traits emphasizes extremely thin lines, a smooth flow from one feature to the next and concern for surface harmony. Every effort has been made to achieve clarity in the compositional format. The figures are most often silhouetted against the deep red or blue of the backgrounds. They relate to each other, and to the sacred text, with calm dispassionate gestures. One receives the impression of a formalized ritual rather than a dramatic sweep of events. In the eloquent dialogue between Joshua and the delegation of Gabonites a psychological rather than a physical space separates the opposing groups. In the Moses panel a ring of clouds surrounding the divinity isolates the figures. The absence of emotion in the faces of the participants increases the solemnity of these ritualized encounters.

Although the Passion Master dominated glazing production, two additional masters and two assistants contributed to the work. These artists differed primarily in their attitudes toward the psychological impact of the figures rather than in principles of drawing. Grodecki has identified the energetic drama of the Judith Master and the emotional tension of the Ezekiel Master, as well as the varying attitudes of the assistants of the Passion Master.[93] The assistant responsible for

[90] Caviness-Grodecki, 1968, 9. The authors have accepted Branner's redating of the beginning of the building to 1241. This would allow seven years for the completion of all the Sainte-Chapelle glass.

[91] Grodecki, *Corpus, France* I, 72, 73, 92. The most frequently cited manuscript is the Psalter of Saint Louis, Paris, Bibl. nat. Ms. lat. 10525; H. Omont, *Psautier de Saint Louis*, Paris, 1905.

[92] The lower part of the Creator's robe is modern.

[93] Grodecki, *Corpus, France* I, 92-93. The Judith Master worked primarily in windows C, Esther, and D, Judith. The Ezekiel Master was responsible

almost all the Isaiah window, as well as scattered panels in other windows, emerges as the most expressive and artistically original offshoot of the dominant atelier. Unfortunately we know little about the composition of the medieval glazing atelier. Most probably, after an apprenticeship in decorative backgrounds and borders, the Isaiah Master began by copying the Master's format only to betray his own personality in the handling of the brush. Thus, while the solutions of the atelier were the same, the feeling behind them differed.

Four panels from the Joshua and Isaiah windows reveal the Master's transformation of his mentor's patterns. For a scene from the opening chapters of Joshua (fig. 111), the Passion Master's figure of the Creator provided the model of the seated king of Jericho interrogating Rahab. The Isaiah Master repeats the arm-sling drapery, pleated folds across the torso, mantle over the shoulder and across the lap and broken folds between the legs balanced by the vertical pleats at the knees. Like the Passion Master's standing Moses, Rahab inclines her head forward, displaying a narrow torso, gesticulating arm and mantle pulled taut from shoulder to elbow in contrast to the complex folds in her lower garments. The faces in the panels of Isaiah's Prophecy of the Birth of Christ (fig. 112), and the Annunciation (fig. 113), like those of the Rahab panel, exhibit the same oval forms relieved by the softly waving locks. The Isaiah Master works closely within the inherited forms basic to the atelier; graceful curve from brow to nose, delicate nostrils, pinched mouth and wide, staring eyes. The figure of Isaiah carrying the promised Messiah (fig. 112) displays the characteristic arm-sling and pleated tunic over the torso. The mantles of Mary and Gabriel, close to the garments of Rahab, show the contrast between angular and vertical folds seen in the Passion Master's drapery of Joshua and Moses (figs. 109 and 110). In the panel of the Martyrdom of Isaiah (fig. 114), the executioners wear short tunics similar to those of the Gabonites (fig. 109). Both the Passion and Isaiah Masters use the same triangular pleats for the skirt, bunched drapery above the waist and three-quarter faces with broad jaws and small features.

The Isaiah Master asserts his own personality through a much heavier grisaille line, greater shading and a more rectilinear composition. A comparison between the Creator (fig. 110) and the King of Jericho (fig. 111) confirms that even when duplicating precise outlines, the pupil rejects the elegant fluidity of his Master's style. A more powerful, darker figure, the Isaiah Master's king revolves around a vertical axis that anchors the oval of the mantle-outlined torso to the pyramidal form of the legs. Compared to the face of Joshua from the Gabonite panel (fig. 109), the king shows a harsher outline as well as more deeply shadowed features. The rigidity of the dress of Isaiah's executioners (fig. 114) contrasts sharply with the graceful fall of the Gabonite's garments (fig. 109). Similarly the uniform flow of the line delineating each leaf in Isaiah's tree is totally alien to the Passion Master's sophisticated variety. The Isaiah Master exaggerates the borrowed facial formulas to produce the

---

for the windows of David, B, and Ezekiel, F. In the Passion Master's atelier, the Jesse Master contributed the Jesse Tree lancet of window J, leaving the left lancet to the Isaiah Master. Assistants also painted panels in windows E, M, N and L.

massive sweep of jaw and tiny displaced mouth seen in the servant to the right in the Jericho panel (fig. 111) and Isaiah's witness (fig. 112). A coarse, almost brutal depiction of character, not only of the common but of the exalted, animates both the faces of the executioners and that of the dying Isaiah (fig. 114), as well as the face of Gabriel from the Annunciation panel (fig. 113).

Throughout the Isaiah Master's panels, a symmetrically ordered arrangement emphasizes a single plane of action. The two executioners function as exterior weight balancing the central tree within which the prophet awaits martyrdom (fig. 114). The insistent verticality of the Jericho panel reinforces the independence of each figure (fig. 111). In a manner similar to the confrontation among Rahab, king and servant, Mary receives Gabriel against a space strictly proportioned by the double arcade (fig. 113). Despite the localizing elements such as sprouting trees and ground-line in the Execution or the drapery on the right and the wall on the left in the Annunciation, the Isaiah Master rigorously isolates his pictorial elements and endows his figures with powerful, but frozen dramatic impact. Even the side trefoil showing Isaiah's Prophecy (fig. 112) attempts a symmetrical composition by stressing the bulk and height of the witness to the left as if the diminished space of the medallion were of no import.[94]

Uncontestedly a product of the Passion Master's tutelage, the Isaiah Master remained aware of the alternative styles of mid-century Paris. Much of the rigidity, planar organizations and spatial isolation so characteristic of the Annunciation panel appears in the Saint Vincent window dated about 1245 from Saint-Germain-des-Prés (fig. 23).[95] This art avoids any indication of depth, emphasizing symmetrical composition and surface patterning. Sharply delineated faces and an expressive, less aristocratic approach link the work of both masters. The boldness of the Isaiah Master's line, however, may relate to an earlier tradition. The style characterized by the painter of the Saint Martin window from Gercy (fig. 10) shows general similarities of drapery patterns in the arms and shoulders. Above all, the Gercy artist favored the same heavy line and energetic sweep of the brush that distinguishes the work of the Isaiah Master.

I am persuaded that the Isaiah Master left work in the royal chapel to accept a commission for windows at Saint-Julien-du-Sault: the Infancy window, the window of Saint Blaise and Saints Peter and Paul, the legend of John the Baptist window and the Passion window.[96] For this enterprise he brought copybooks detailing faces, drapery patterns and medallion formats from the Passion Master's repertoire. We have seen in the discussion of composition and ornament how faithfully the Sainte-Chapelle medallion patterns were reproduced at Saint Julien (text illus. 4). Facial types and drapery patterns are also similar. In the faces of Saint John and the Virgin

---

[94] Note restoration at the lower edge of the robe and to the left of the arm of the witness.

[95] See n. 9 in section 1 above on the Genesis Atelier.

[96] These windows, like all of the Saint-Julien-du-Sault glass, have suffered much damage and equally disastrous restoration campaigns (see Restoration Appendix: Saint-Julien-du-Sault). Enough exists, however, to allow a confident discussion of the origins of the style.

in the Crucifixion medallion from the Passion window (fig. 115), we find the same types elaborated in Isaiah's Prophecy and the Annunciation (figs. 112 and 113). Although reversed, John's face displays the same broad jaw, upward slant in the tiny mouth, short stroke marking the fullness of the lower lip and the beginning of the chin and the narrow nose, all framed by flowing locks and short bangs above a wide forehead. A softer, more feminine type appears in both the face of the Virgin Annunciate and the Virgin at the foot of the Cross (figs. 113 and 115), as well as those of the Virgin and maid servant with doves from Saint-Julien's medallion of the Presentation in the Temple from the Infancy window (fig. 118). Smoothly arched brows frame placid eyes that dominate the elongated well-balanced face. The simple pleats of the head-covering of the woman repeat the flat fold over the crown which is accented by the long looping indentation toward the back of the head.

The sharp breaks and contrapuntal pleating of the mourning Virgin's robe repeat the distinctive folds of Rahab's robe from the Sainte-Chapelle (fig. 111). Like the folds in Simeon's robes (fig. 118), both Burgundian and Parisian drapery patterns emphasize bold strokes of the brush and heavy grisaille in-fill. The figures from both sites display a marked inconsistency in body proportions. The Virgin and Gabriel (fig. 113) are as narrow and rectilinear as the highly restricted figure of Simeon (fig. 118). A much bulkier type appears in Isaiah's witness, whose heavy mantle prefigures the weighty drapery of the Saint-Julien Crucifixion panel. The pattern employed for the drapery of the short belted tunics in the Isaiah Execution panel (fig. 114) reappears in the guards flagellating Christ from the Saint-Julien Passion window (fig. 117). All four figures show strong vertical pleats in the skirts that contrast with the deep indentations at the waist and torso. Above all, the heavily outlined arm, rounded at the shoulder with a fold almost bisecting the upper arm and flowing into the upper forearm shows an identical painterly approach.

With great insistency, the Isaiah Master organizes the Saint-Julien panels according to the same surface symmetry characteristic of his Sainte-Chapelle panels. The unusual bulk of the mourning Virgin and Saint John (fig. 115) balances the central figure of the crucified Christ. In the Flagellation panel (fig. 117) the two guards become the front and back views of the same figure, a concept emphasized by the placement of their legs in front and in back of the medallion border. Two exterior vertical and two interior figures frame the Christ Child in the center of the Presentation panel (fig. 118).[97] This rectilinear format seems particularly close to the composition of the Deposition panel from the Passion window of the Sainte-Chapelle now in the parish church of Twycross, England (fig. 119).[98] Immobile, tall

[97] The symmetrical composition of the panel is in the tradition of symmetrical Presentations, an iconographic type current as early as Carolingian times (Dorothy Shorr, "The Iconographic Development of the Presentation in the Temple," *The Art Bulletin* 28 [1946], 20). The Saint-Julien-du-Sault panel, even in the context of French Gothic examples, exploits this traditional system to treat

the right and left sides as almost mirror images.

[98] Grodecki, *Corpus, France* I, 345–349, pl. 101. The presence of the windows in Twycross has traditionally been attributed to a donation by Sir J. Wathen Waller who acquired the glass through the family of Admiral Howe. Despite the conjectural nature of their precise history, Grodecki states that the windows must have been in Eng-

figures frame the composition while the central figures interact with restrained movements. The mourning Virgin at Twycross is clearly taken from the same basic pattern book that furnished the Saint-Julien Virgin at the side of the Crucified Christ. Drapery is also similar; for example, the mantle that covers Saint John's hand as he holds his book at Twycross and the robe held in a similar gesture by the servant girl with the basket of doves at Saint-Julien.

However one approaches the Saint-Julien-du-Sault glass, the problem of the relationships of the master to atelier appears. Despite identical design motifs, the import of panels differ because of the different artistic personalities executing the work. The figures of Saint Peter and Saint Paul (fig. 120a) from Saint-Julien, for example, show close associations to the Passion Master's Saint John panel (fig. 121) from the John the Evangelist window of the Sainte-Chapelle, now at Twycross. Particularly compelling is the extremely broad sleeve with squarish termination. Despite the repair leads in the Burgundian panel, one can distinguish the swift pull of drapery folds at right angles to the mantle. Even the apparent isolation of the pleats and folds into separately regulated areas seems similar in both figures. The hair, as well, shows the same smooth crown with curling bangs that meld into successive longer clumps at the neck. The Burgundian panel, however, shows more exaggerated facial features, clumsier bodily proportions and a more vigorous disposition of the figure. In general, the Isaiah Master, and his Burgundian work, are characterized by a heightened expressiveness in the faces and a more energetic treatment of the drapery. The face of the guard in the Flagellation panel is an excellent example of the transformation of the Parisian style first seen in the darkened features of the tortured Isaiah (fig. 114).

Draftsmanship in the windows of Saints Peter and Paul and Saint Martin in the cathedral of Auxerre continues this trend. A tracing of the head of a man listening to the sermon of Saint Paul (fig. 123) shows the staring eyes and nose indented at the bridge and enlarged at the tip that ultimately leads back to the model used for the tortured Isaiah.[99] In the Auxerre and the Saint-Julien Flagellation heads, however, the noses curve with greater insistence and terminate in bulbous masses. A more exaggerated arch joins the brow line to the nose, the single stable element

---

land since the first decades of the nineteenth century. The window at Twycross holds only a few of the many panels (perhaps 175?) taken out of the Sainte-Chapelle in 1803 when the building was converted into a storage area for court records (Caviness-Grodecki, 1968, especially 9-10). Additional panels have appeared in the Victoria and Albert Museum, the parish church of Wilton, England, the Philadelphia Museum of Art and other museums and private collections.

[99] Fortunately the narrow walkway passing in front of the Auxerre ambulatory windows has permitted a tactile observation of certain panels, including rubbings of the lead patterns and some tracings. In comparing the tracings from the glass attributed to the Isaiah Master with tracings taken of the Sainte-Chapelle panels during their nineteenth-century restorations (bound in volumes in the Centre de Recherche sur les Monuments Historiques in the Palais de Chaillot), exact correspondences appear in size, cut lines and even the grisaille detailing of features and drapery systems. Since the Auxerre panels of Peter and Paul and Martin stayed scattered in a haphazard order in a number of windows until the David restoration of 1925-1926, there is no possibility that the Sainte-Chapelle tracings could have themselves furnished the models for Auxerre's two Isaiah Master windows.

among almost dislocated features. The silhouetted lips and half-parted mouth of the Auxerre auditor greatly contribute to the forcefulness of the image.

The Miracle of the Tree from the cathedral's Saint Martin window (fig. 127) contains the typical massive figure of the Isaiah Master.[100] Like the witness from the Prophecy panel (fig. 112) Martin wears an extremely heavy mantle whose folds emphasize vertical over diagonal patterning. Both figures gesture with long narrow arms with drapery pulled taut from wrist to shoulder. The heavy applications of grisaille that delineate the folds also define the arm-sling drapery of the companions behind the saint and the arm of Isaiah. The face of the standing figure to Martin's right exhibits striking similarities to the face of the servant to the right in the Jericho panel (fig. 111). In both figures, a tight cap of hair frames an identical slant to the mouth, abbreviated nose, swelling forehead and massive sagging jaw. A tracing of Saint Paul's disciple from the Peter and Paul cycle (fig. 124), like the executioner from the Beheading panel of Saint-Julien's John the Baptist window (fig. 122), shows the continuation of the Sainte-Chapelle youthful facial type but also affirms its greater exaggeration through pulsating contours and more unbalanced features.

The panel from Auxerre showing Nero ordering a servant (fig. 130) confirms beyond a doubt the presence of the Isaiah Master in the cathedral. Both Nero and the King of Jericho from the Sainte-Chapelle (fig. 111) show clusters of scoop folds at the outside of the knees and haphazard broken folds between the legs, complicated in the Burgundian figure by additional pieces of fabric. The narrow pleats of the torso, taut arm-sling, fall of the mantle over the shoulder and loose folds of the sleeve closely link the two figures. Nero's hair style and dark facial features repeat the exact disposition of his Parisian prototype. The short tunic of Nero's servant repeats the distinctive patterning of V-shaped pleats visible in the Saint-Julien Flagellation (fig. 117), but the soft gatherings above the belt follow more closely the drapery at the waist of the Isaiah Master's king. A tracing from the Saint Martin panel of the Miracle of the Resurrected Catechumen (fig. 128) evokes the Passion Master's Gabonite panel (fig. 109) yet points to the Isaiah Master's hand. An emotional figure, the Auxerre man displays the same iconographic type as the first Gabonite. In both heads the hair moves swiftly back from the face to terminate in separate clumps differentiated by heavy grisaille painting. The identical pose served for both figures; three-quarter angle to the head, upraised right arm, bared shoulder,

[100] The style of the Saint Martin window had been connected to the work of the Saint Chéron Master from the cathedral of Chartres (Delaporte and Houvet, 1926, 135-136, repeated by Grodecki, *Vitrail*, 140). Grodecki's most recent evaluation (1978) abandons this idea. He places the Saint Chéron Master in the line of "post-classical" expressions that moved Gothic painting toward the new concepts of the mid-century, thus explaining superficial similarities with the Auxerre glass. Working from about 1220 to 1230 and responsible for the windows of Saints Catherine and Margaret (XXVI), Saint Remi (XXVIII), Saints Simon and Jude (XXXV), Saint Germain (LIV), Saint Pantaléon (XL), Saint Chéron (XLII), many of the upper windows of the transepts and the five lancets under the south rose, the Saint Chéron Master employed a decorative vocabulary and stylistic expression that link him to Parisian manuscript and glass painting toward the second quarter of the thirteenth century. His ability to represent clearly complex narrative, his broad, simplified, almost sketchy rendering of drapery and his preference for definite facial types refigure much of the Sainte-Chapelle glass (Grodecki, *Corpus, France* I, 93, n. 1).

slightly displaced collarbone and parallel lines of the sternum. Like the Saint-Julien glass, the Auxerre figures exhibit a more forceful characterization, heavier application of paint and more awkward stances than the Passion Master's productions. In the deeply shadowed features of Nero's face, the weighty drapery folds of both Nero and servant and the catechumen's impassive acceptance of the gift of life, the Isaiah Master articulated the Parisian systems with a sensitivity all his own.

The axial bay containing the lancets of the Crucifixion and Christ in Majesty was also produced by the Isaiah Master. It thus constitutes our single documented source of large-scale figure painting by an atelier of the Sainte-Chapelle. The procedures are similar to those used by the Apocalypse atelier when moving from a narrative to a hieratic format. Grisaille lines become much bolder and more rigid. Facial details and hair are exaggerated. The transformation can be seen through a comparison of the Virgin Annunciate from the Sainte-Chapelle (fig. 113) with the mourning Virgin from Auxerre's clerestory (fig. 131). The same tall, narrow proportions, inclined head and looped drapery folds confirm an identity of workshop tradition but the larger figure's static monumentality is far removed from the incipient energy of the Sainte-Chapelle image. The clustered segments of the hair and the technique of encircling both arms in taut drapery shown in the mourning Saint John repeat the disposition of Peter and Paul from a Saint-Julien-du-Sault panel (fig. 120a). All of the details, however, are far more exaggerated to insure their legibility from much farther away. These two windows were substituted for the original axial lancets designed by the Apocalypse Master, a decision that realigned the cathedral's iconography to reflect the program of the Sainte-Chapelle.

The theory that the Isaiah Master could have left his Master's tutelage once he had achieved a technical proficiency would explain his limited participation in the Sainte-Chapelle program. His work at Saint-Julien-du-Sault perhaps as early as 1247 would then be his first independent commission. An apprenticeship in the Parisian area would explain the Isaiah Master's sensitivity to the artistic currents of the area, such as the styles of Saint-Germain-des-Prés and Gercy. Likewise, his use of Sainte-Chapelle designs, and yet his gradually heightened expressiveness, could be viewed as testimony of individual growth. Such was the transformation of a Parisian apprentice into a Burgundian Master.

The unique position of the Isaiah Master at Auxerre and Saint-Julien can only be appreciated when seen in the context of the further expansion of the Sainte-Chapelle glazing style. Three cathedrals, Tours, Le Mans and Clermont-Ferrand, present three different responses to the challenge of choir glazing, yet all depend ultimately on the Parisian style. In contrast to the copybook relationship that we have seen at Saint-Julien-du-Sault and Auxerre, these three sites present a very different treatment of figure style, spatial organization and medallion composition, yet all "trail clouds of glory," as it were, from their Parisian birth. In addition, all three cathedrals reflect not only the glazing style of the monument but its architectural forms as well.

Tradition has maintained that the cathedral of Tours owes its choir to direct royal intervention. Here Queen Blanche seems to have instigated the reconstruction of the edifice destroyed in 1233.[101] Typically, the lower portions of the cathedral choir exhibit the same qualities of architectural restraint already evident in the royal abbey of Royaumont.[102] The increasingly elaborate conception of architecture, as enunciated by the Sainte-Chapelle, however, exerted an immediate influence on the work. This new influence produced the striking difference between the open, luxurious treatment of the upper stories and the spare and sober lower areas. The Tours workshop imitated the window tracery of the royal chapel, and, more importantly, adopted the idea of a solid wall of glass. The succession of wide glazed windows terminated by three trilobes in the hemicycle bays shows a clear indebtedness to the Sainte-Chapelle. The glazed triforium at Tours is nothing less than an adaption of the dado of the Parisian model with its repetition of short double-lancet arches topped by a quatrefoil.

Except for the band windows of the bishops of Tours and the canons of Loches, on either side of the hemicycle bays, the windows present a series of colored medallions of narrative cycles from Genesis, the Gospels and saints' lives.[103] Tours has made some attempt, however difficult, to adapt the medallion pattern of the Sainte-Chapelle to the greater distance between clerestory and spectator. The medallions themselves are larger and less complicated and the decorative motifs are simpler.

Papanicolaou's recent analysis of the Tours glass limits the extent to which the Sainte-Chapelle, or even the Parisian area, served as the dominant source for the style, a limitation supported by the local nature of Tours' iconography.[104] She divides the work into three campaigns, of about 1255, about 1265 and about 1270. During the first campaign, an atelier under the direction of a painter responsible for the window of the Passion completed the three axial bays of the chevet clerestory and the standing figures of the triforium hemicycle. Papanicolaou sees the Passion Master as reminiscent of the Sainte-Chapelle's Judith Master but does not believe that he was an active member of the atelier. Rather, the Tours artist absorbed influences from the same artistic milieu. In the detail of the Last Supper medallion (fig. 132), the same general forms of the Parisian style appear: the upper mantle stretched taut

[101] See most recently Branner, 1965, 36-39, figs. 35, 36, and 58; also Francis Salet, *La Cathédrale de Tours*, Paris (1949), 7-10; and Alfred Mussat, *Le Style gothique de l'ouest de la France*, Paris (1963), 164-169. It is interesting to note that the castles of Castille, symbols of the queen, fill the borders in the clerestory windows in bays 5, 11, 12 and 13.

[102] Branner (1965) has been used as the basis for all of the architectural interpretation. See especially 30-39 for Royaumont.

[103] Publications of the glass of Tours have been quite weak and, for the most part, illustrated by drawings. R. Manceau, *Verrières du choeur de l'église metropolitaine de Tours*, Paris (1849); Boissonnot, 1920 and 1932. Grodecki (*Vitrail*, 156,

fig. 112; *Corpus, France* I, 93) has placed the Tours style within the orbit of the Sainte-Chapelle.

[104] 1979. Papanicolaou has produced a very thorough and important survey of glass of the cathedral's choir and related windows in the region. One might suggest, however, that all of the Tours work was the task of a single atelier supporting a series of different painters. (See corresponding definition in Caviness, 1977, 36-37, and Lillich, 1978, 192.) It is clear that to a large extent the basic plan of the windows, the medallion patterns and the facial types and drapery pattern remained constant during the three campaigns. This might be said also of the Sainte-Chapelle itself, which would mean that a single atelier supported three major and several minor masters.

from shoulder to elbow, the quick, calligraphic treatment of the drapery folds and sensitive, delicate faces.

Rapid transformations, however, emerged as the glazing progressed, in general favoring a heightened expressiveness. By the second campaign, Papanicolaou maintains, only assistants of the Passion Master's atelier are present.[105] The Genesis Master, who probably executed the Genesis window in 1255, continued to work in a much more mannered style.[106] Faces are tense, proportions more attenuated and drapery more sharp and angular. Dependence on local tradition, already a factor in the first campaign, becomes more pronounced. This estrangement from Parisian sensibilities culminates in the three western bays of the north clerestory, with the windows of Thomas and Stephen, Denis and Vincent, and Nicholas. A detail of the panel of the unfortunate man and three dowerless daughters (fig. 133) presents remarkably thin arms, dropped waistlines and long, flowing skirts. All of the figures display heads that appear cast from a single mold, a long oval for the faces, brows slanting upward at the nose, tiny mouths and broad lower jaws.[107] The head is characteristically elongated toward the back with the hair flowing up and over the rise. At the sides, long thick curls undulate toward the shoulders. In contrast to the physiognomies of the Sainte-Chapelle narratives, the Tours faces possess a definite dramatic quality. They move from the characteristic dispassion of the Parisian monument to an appearance of deep involvement. Certainly the furrowed brows and the expressive hand gestures of the four Saint Nicholas figures depict a world of anxiety and momentous happening.

The choir of Le Mans, dedicated in 1254, is another mid-century edifice that recalls the Parisian monument in both its architecture and its glass.[108] As Branner has phrased it, "The language of the forms is like a dialect when compared with the ceremonious and measured speech of Jean de Chelles, but it is a dialect of Paris all the same."[109] Like Tours, the triforium is glazed, but here is a complex and varying succession of multi-lancet windows. The windows' diversity of width and tracery creates a correspondence between triforium and clerestory that is repeated on the north and south sides of the choir. Although using wider openings than the Sainte-Chapelle, the Le Mans plan still emphasizes the brilliantly colored effect of a glazed enclosure crowning the lower structure of the edifice.

At Le Mans, no grisaille glass is used, although some attempt at clarity has been made by organizing the triforium panels around narrative programs and reserving the clerestory lancets for a series of standing figures. However, the narrow-

[105] 1979, 173-192. Papanicolaou makes use of the many donor motifs and of much documentary evidence as well as stylistic interpretation to date the activity of the glaziers. She believes that the second campaign included the windows of Saints Peter and Martin, immediately next to the hemicycle bays, the two band windows of the bishops of Tours and the canons of Loches and the four remaining windows on the south: Saint Martial (identified by Papanicolaou as Saint Julien of Le Mans), James, John the Baptist and John the Evangelist, and Eustache.

[106] See Grodecki, *Vitrail*, fig. 112; Papanicolaou, "The Iconography of the Genesis Window of the Cathedral of Tours," *Gesta* 20/1 (1981), 179-189.

[107] Papanicolaou (1979, 103) believes the father's head to be restored.

[108] Branner, 1965, 80-83, and Francis Salet, "La cathédrale du Mans," *Congrès archéologique de France* 119 (1961), 18-58.

[109] Branner, 1965, 81.

ness of the many lancets obligated the artist to place at least two superimposed figures in each schema. Iconographically, such a solution allows the juxtaposition of apostle and prophet, a common typological organization, but practically, the windows are hardly as legible as the great simple presentation of individual figures such as at Bourges, Chartres or Auxerre. The abbreviated narratives of the triforium featuring the lives of the saints and the miracles of the Virgin are most difficult to read from the floor.

Grodecki has suggested that much of the triforium glass and nine of the thirteen clerestory windows (1254-1260) reflect stylistic influence of the Sainte-Chapelle.[110] Papanicolaou does not see any direct connection between the Tours and Le Mans ateliers, but sees both undergoing the same transformation through common regional tendencies.[111] A scene from the life of Saint Julien of Le Mans showing a resurrection of a dead child may typify the strength of the tradition as well as the distance that has intervened (fig. 134). As at Tours, the Le Mans figures have become more elongated and the decorative schema has been simplified. A regimentalized zig-zag punctuated by severely organized double fronds forms the window's border. When compared to the Sainte-Chapelle dispositions, the simplification of the Le Mans windows makes for monotony and the legibility is decreased rather than enhanced. The grisaille lines used to delineate forms are far harsher than at Tours and the compositions of the scenes are flatter and more crowded. The Le Mans artist shows his indebtedness to Parisian sources especially in the bearded facial types, the arm-sling drapery and broken folds of the mantles, but the source is far removed. In comparatively small medallions, the Le Mans artist emphasizes a two-dimensional pattern using leading and heavy grisaille painting to silhouette each element. Indeed, a comparison of the width of the painted lines and the leaded areas shows truly uniform dimensions. The emphasis on deep blues and reds, in imitation of the Parisian model, also contributes to a heavy static effect. The rhythmic interplay that so characterized the Tours glass here gives way to a flat, decorative and static presentation of the pictorial elements.

Recent study has shown that the choir of the cathedral of Clermont-Ferrand is a monument of pivotal significance.[112] Constructed of the dark lava rock of the Auvergne, the cathedral displays an unusually harmonious architectural setting and a dazzling array of medallion windows in the ambulatory and a clerestory of band-window design. The choir was begun about 1248 under the direction of Jean Deschamps and terminated about 1280-1285. The cathedral incorporates the grace and monumentality long associated with the court style and so becomes the first representation of the style in an alien geographical milieu.[113] Although the triforium is a darkened area at Clermont, the impressive height of the vaults, open spaces and repetition of elegant floating arches depend on Parisian architectural traditions.

[110] 1961, 87-88; idem, *Corpus*, France I, 93.
[111] 1979, 229.
[112] Michael T. Davis, unpublished dissertation, "The Cathedral of Clermont-Ferrand: History of Its Construction, 1248-1512," University of Michigan, 1979.
[113] Branner, 1965, 97-101.

The deep radiating chapels of Clermont and the four flat chapels of the choir house forty-two lancets with over ten medallions each. The medallion schema varies from round to quatrefoil to triangular, but all are arranged in a vertical succession, somewhat like beads on a string. However, the sheer dazzle of these walls of glass immediately calls to mind the import of the Sainte-Chapelle interior.[114] An important glazing atelier, exemplified by the window of Saint Bonitus, or Bonnet, an early bishop of Clermont (fig. 135), displays the same elegant proportions and fluid brush-strokes of the Sainte-Chapelle. The folds of the garments are simple and flowing and the figures interrelate with the same ease and dispassionate grace so characteristic of the Parisian work. It is indeed noteworthy that a Parisian painting style of the 1240s could still inspire so close a copy some thirty years later in a monument set in the midst of the Auvergne. Comparing the drapery of the Bonitus panel with that of the Deposition medallion at Twycross, we see that essentially very little has changed. The stances of Saint John and the Clermont-Ferrand Virgin are surprisingly similar. In both panels, a smooth, economic brushstroke details the long drapery folds cloaking the angel, Saint Bonitus and the mourning Virgin. The Auvergnat work, like its Parisian prototype, shows a calm dialogue among the characters, clean spaces behind the figures and a rhythmic interplay of forms. The Clermont Master appears to have differed in emphasizing the concerned physiognomies of his characters and in elongating the figural proportions, trends already evident in the Judith Master of the Sainte-Chapelle and far more exaggerated in the Tours glass.

The book on the development and the expansion on the Sainte-Chapelle style is yet to be written.[115] We understand a little more now of the complexity of the currents that contributed to the climate of mid-century Paris. In some respect, the Sainte-Chapelle may seem like a conservative hiatus before the great innovation of grisaille and colored glass of the second half of the thirteenth century: Saint-Urbain of Troyes, Saint-Père of Chartres and ultimately Saint-Ouen of Rouen.[116] The glass

[114] Emile Mâle ("La peinture sur verre," in A. Michel, *Histoire générale de l'art*, II/1, Paris [1905], 380-385) and du Ranquet (1932, 12; idem, *La Cathédrale de Clermont-Ferrand*, Paris [1928], 95-98) believed that the Clermont windows represented work by royal ateliers. Aubert (*Vitrail*, 164) repeats the assertion that the painters came from the "Domaine Royale," but dates the windows in the late thirteenth and early fourteenth centuries. Grodecki (*Corpus, France* I, 93) cautioned against too strong a link with the Sainte-Chapelle style.

[115] See especially Grodecki, *Vitrail*, 150-156; Françoise Perrot, "Le vitrail au temps de Saint Louis," in *Le Siècle de Saint Louis*, Paris, 1970; Linda Papanicolaou, "Stained Glass from the Cathedral of Tours in the Cloisters Collection and the Impact of the Sainte-Chapelle in the 1240s," *Journal of the Metropolitan Museum of Art* (in press). The glass now housed in two windows of the Chapel of the Virgin in the cathedral of Soissons was produced by artists from the Passion Master's atelier, an observation first put forth by Grodecki (*Corpus, France* I, 93; idem, 1960, 172-173, fig. 7; *Corpus, France, Recensement* I, 170, pl. XXIII). See most recently Madeline Caviness and Virginia Raguin, "Another Dispersed Window from Soissons: A Tree of Jesse in the Sainte-Chapelle Style," *Gesta* 20/1 (1981), 191-198. Unlike the work of the Isaiah Master in Burgundy, the Soissons panels do not reveal a specific hand attributable to a specific Sainte-Chapelle window. See also the north and south roses of Notre-Dame of Paris and the glass of Gassicourt (*New England Collections*, nos. 11b-14). In charting the formation as well as the expansion of the style, the glass of Amiens must be carefully considered (*Corpus, France, Recensement* I, 218-222).

[116] See especially Jean Lafond, "Le vitrail du XIVe siècle en France," in L. Lefrançois-Pillion, *L'Art du XIVe siècle en France*, Paris (1954), 184-238, and Lillich, 1970. For Saint-Urbain see Grodecki ("Les vitraux de Saint-Urbain de Troyes," *Congrès archéologique de France* 113 (1955), 123;

in Burgundy provides essential information in an assessment of dissemination of art forms and workshop systems within this broad picture of one of the most creative periods in French art.

The diffusion of both the Parisian architectural style and the glazing format was so unusually widespread that one must seriously consider that more than aesthetic sensibilities motivated the patrons. Assuredly, the deeply colored multiple medallion style was of striking beauty, yet it has been employed for many sites for which it appears to have been ill suited. The windows of the upper choirs at Le Mans and Tours might have benefited from more attention to clarity and lightness and less of the almost compulsive imitation of Parisian forms.

Given such evidence, one must look elsewhere for some non-aesthetic explanation for the enormous popularity of Saint Louis' monument. The answer must certainly lie in the prestige enjoyed by the king himself. Nowhere has monumental art ever appeared completely divorced from social and political motivations, and the climate of mid-thirteenth-century France was especially conducive to a cohesive union of politics, religion and art. The various patrons who followed the Parisian norms in architecture, manuscript illumination or stained glass were fully aware of the royal context in which they first appeared. This seems particularly true in Burgundy.

The archbishop of Sens, who controlled Saint-Julien as a barony, enjoyed a position of great prestige during the growth of the Capetian monarchy.[117] Guillaume de Champagne, presiding from 1168 to 1176, was the uncle of Philip Augustus, a peer of France, later archbishop of Reims, then Cardinal, and papal legate.[118] Guy de Noyers, his successor, maintained strong ties with the monarchy, assisting at the coronation of Philip Augustus and joining Philip and Isabel in marriage in 1184.[119] Guy established the chapter at Saint-Julien near the episcopal château of Vauguilain.[120] Pierre de Corbeil served as tutor to the future Pope Innocent III, later playing

Vitrail, 165, pl. VIII) who stated that the glass was probably complete for the choir by 1277. Meredith Lillich (1978, 40, n. 8) suggests the dates of 1266 to 1272. Jane Hayward (symposium accompanying the exhibition *Transformations of the Court Style: Gothic Art in Europe 1270-1330*, Brown University, February 1977) suggests that the glass might have been underway at the same time as the church's construction, about 1262, and that much must have been damaged in the fire of 1266. Saint-Père is dated 1270-1315 (Lillich, 1978, 72). Saint-Ouen is dated before 1339 (Lafond, *Corpus, France IV*, 14).

[117] The metropolitan center of Sens once claimed seven suffragen bishops: Chartres, Auxerre, Meaux, Orleans, Troyes, Nevers and Paris itself. The arms of the cathedral chapter thus bore eight crosses and the anagram CHAMPONT. Maximilien Quantin, "Les archevêques de Sens considerés sous le rapport féodal au moyen âge," *Bulletin de la Société des sciences historiques et naturelles de l'Yonne* 4 (1850), 63-77, and R. Fawtier, *The Capetian Kings of France*, London, 1960.

[118] Guillaume also obtained exemption from the "droit de gîte" held by the crown over the town of Saint-Julien-du-Sault. Bouvier, 1911, II, 130; Mellon-Jolly, *Recueil des statuts, ordonnances, et règlements synodaux de l'archidiocèse de Sens*, Sens (1854), 32.

[119] Mellon-Jolly, op. cit., 32-33; Bouvier, 1911, II, 140-150; Geoffroy de Courlon, 1876, 495-501.

[120] In the interests of expediency, Guy gave the chapter the already existing church in Domats, some twenty kilometers to the northwest. M. Quantin, 1868-1873, 282, no. G 1579; Quantin, 1854-1860, II, 452, no. CDXLVI, "Guido Dei gracia Senonensis archepiscopus. . . . Inde est . . . universis, presentibus pariter et futuris, notum fieri volumus quod canonicis quos in ecclesia de Sancto-Petro de Sancto-Juliano-de Saltu instituimus, ad supplementum servitii divini in eadem ecclesia et in ecclesia Sancti-Juliani celebrandi condonavimus ecclesiam de Domaz perpetua possidendam." (Guy, by the grace of God archbishop

a valuable role of mediator between Philip Augustus and the papacy.[121] He also made large purchases of lands around Saint-Julien-du-Sault.[122] The episcopate of Gauthier de Cornut, however, supported extraordinarily close ties between Sens and Paris as well as the construction of the Saint-Julien church. Gauthier began his career as dean of the cathedral of Paris. Resentful of his opposition to the interdict condemning Philip after Queen Ingeborg's repudiation, Pope Honorius II initially refused to confirm Gauthier's selection as archbishop. Gauthier served as royal chaplain for both Philip and his son Louis VIII and he remained in a position of favor throughout the regency, uniting Louis IX and Margaret of Provence in Sens' own cathedral in 1234.[123]

With the arrival of the Crown of Thorns given in 1239 to Saint Louis by the Emperor Baldwin II of Constantinople, Gauthier's influence increased.[124] Baldwin's representatives brought the Crown to Villeneuve-l'Archevêque, about twenty-three kilometers east of Sens and one of Gauthier's prize possessions, where Saint Louis, accompanied by Gauthier and Queen Blanche, went to receive the precious relic. In the "History of the Reception of the Crown of Thorns" written by Gauthier at the command of Saint Louis, the archbishop describes the journey to the gates of Sens, after which Louis, bareheaded and in a simple tunic, walked to the cathedral and placed the relic on the high altar "amid pious exclamations and many tears of joy." Gauthier then instituted a yearly commemoration of the relic's reception.

The building of the westernmost bays of the priory church of Villeneuve-l'Archevêque may be directly linked to the role it played in the ceremony of the Reception of the Crown of Thorns. Branner dates the construction about 1240, and Sauerländer is quite explicit about the early date of the large sculpted portal, shortly after 1242, citing relationships to Parisian sculpture at the close of the 1230s.[125] Strong ties linked the church to Sens and to the archbishop. The priory's founding dates to a 1172 donation by Guillaume de Champagne, and it was dependent on Sens' Augustinian abbey of Saint-Jean. The priory was the most conspicuous religious edifice in the immediate proximity of the archbishop's château, a consider-

---

of Sens, to all who read this now and in the future, we wish it known that we have granted to the canons whom we establish in the church of Saint-Pierre of Saint-Julien-du-Sault, in order to supplement the celebration of the divine service in the said church and in the church of Saint-Julien, the church of Domats, to possess forever.) The château was the most popular of the archbishop's residences and some of its former splendor appears in the extant ruins that stand high on a hill commanding an unforgettable view of Burgundian pastures and the sweep of the Yonne. Bouvier, 1911, II, 142; Tonnelier, 1842, 102; Quantin, 1862, 135; Branner, 1960, 171-172.

[121] Geoffroy de Courlon (1876, 503-511) took special care to describe the elegant speaking style of Pierre and his long intimate discourses with the king.

[122] Tonnelier, 1842, 105; Bouvier, 1911, II, 181.

[123] Geoffroy de Courlon, 1876, 514-523; Bouvier, 1911, II, 200-226.

[124] For specific information on the Crown of Thorns and Gauthier Cornut, see Paul Riant, ed., *Exuviae sacrae constantinopolitanae*, I, Geneva (1877), 45-56, which contains the Latin text of Gauthier's *Historia susceptionis Corone spinee*, while vol. III describes the history of the relic itself. See also Auguste Molinier, *Les Sources d'histoire de France*, III, Paris (1906), 127.

[125] Branner, 1960, 194-195; Sauerländer, 1972, 468-469, pls. 178-179. Jean Vallery-Radot ("L'église Notre-Dame de Villeneuve-l'Archevêque," *Congrès archéologique de France* 113 [1955], 445-456) mentions the reception of the Crown of Thorns but does not make a connection with the patronage of the church.

ation that was also significant in the construction of the collegiate church of Saint-Julien-du-Sault. The portal displays the theme of the Coronation of the Virgin in the tympanum, very similar to the disposition found on Chartres north. Unusual emphasis is placed on the themes of the crown itself and on kingship, however. In the summit of the tympanum, two angels holding a large and elaborate crown hover over the figures of Christ and the Virgin. The three jamb figures to the left, as might be expected, represent the Annunciation flanked by probably the figure of Elizabeth. The two outer figures on the right jamb show two kings, Saul who turns toward David. The inner figure, a bearded man with a shawl over his head may very well be a representation of Aaron, thus an explicit linking of *regnum et sacerdotum.*

The date of the reworking of the west facade and the program of the priory's unusually lavish portal would argue that it was conceived of as a commemorative monument. The rebuilding began immediately after the ceremony of the relic and the sculpture probably kept pace with the architectural campaign. It is conceivable that Gauthier Cornut, who wrote the official account of the reception of the relic, and who instituted a commemorative feast day in his diocese, would have funded and even designed the portal's program. The project would have been carried out even after the archbishop's death in 1241. Gauthier's references to the Canticle of Canticles in the "History" further relate to the Coronation of the Virgin iconography, through which the Virgin and Christ are transformed into the Bride and Bridegroom of the Canticle.[126]

Gauthier began construction on the church of Saint-Julien-du-Sault around this time, strengthening his position through several large purchases of land.[127] The church itself experienced an uneven history of construction, yet it seems fairly certain that the choir was begun about 1235 and that by 1245 the transepts were underway.[128] We have no documents at hand concerning the actual building of the church, but we can surmise from local practice that the construction was directly supervised by a canon from Sens.[129] Gilon Cornut, Gauthier's brother, was chosen to succeed him upon his death in 1241 but was only invested as archbishop in 1244. From all accounts, he followed his brother's example in maintaining as close relations as possible with the monarchy. He participated in the dedication of the Sainte-Chapelle in 1248 and the same year held a provincial council in the city of Paris.[130]

[126] Riant, *Exuviae sacrae constantinopolitanae,* I, Geneva (1877), 47.

[127] Tonnelier, 1842, 105f. In 1223, three years after his appointment to Sens, Gauthier began purchases around Saint-Julien and by 1236 achieved complete dominance of the area. In a country where tradition dies hard, the municipal census of 1789 recorded that over one-half of all the wooded lands of the area belonged to the archbishop. Charles Porée, *Département de l'Yonne, Cahiers de doléances du bailliage de Sens pour les États Généraux de 1789* (2nd ed., 1908, repr. Auxerre, 1927), 332-333.

[128] Branner, 1960, 87-88, fig. 24, pls. 27a and 28b. See also Vallery-Radot, 1958b, 359 and Hautecoeur, 1927, 63-65, 71, pl. 70.

[129] In 1265 the archbishop of Sens confirmed the establishment of a new parish church to serve the inhabitants of Saint-Julien. Jean-Henri, presumably a canon of Sens, left funds for the construction, and Master Stephen, a canon of the cathedral and bailiff for the archbishop supervised the work. See Quantin, 1873, no. 620, 26 April 1265, and Branner, 1960, 4-5.

[130] Geoffroy de Courlon, 1876, 523-529; Bouvier, 1911, II, 226.

The Sainte-Chapelle impressed the Cornut brothers as the visible articulation of the divine protection granted France and her monarchy.[131] The political as well as religious significance of the monument extended to neighboring kingdoms, for Branner has documented Henry III's use of Westminster Abbey as an answer to the French king's claims.[132] The extraordinary lavishness of the interior decoration that created a reliquary "turned outside in" for Edward the Confessor was designed to rival Saint-Louis' reliquary in Paris. Henry also obtained a significant relic of Christ, a Vial of the Holy Blood, which he received with the same mystic reverence exhibited by the French king. In England it was Matthew Paris who fulfilled the same function of official recorder as Gauthier Cornut.

As Henry so clearly perceived it, kingship was the program of the Sainte-Chapelle. In the charter granted Louis by Innocent IV, the pope directly stated "the Lord has crowned you with his crown of thorns."[133] The vast glazing program literally bristles with depictions of coronations, some scriptural, but many apocryphal, such as the coronation of Gideon and the nominations of the chiefs of Juda in the Book of Numbers. In border designs, connecting bosses and mosaic backgrounds, the use of the royal fleur-de-lis and the castles of Castille for the Queen Mother emphasized the link between biblical and contemporary kingship.[134] At Saint-Julien-du-Sault, the window of Saint John the Baptist presents a trellis design inscribing the brilliant yellow lilies, very similar to the background of the Sainte-Chapelle Numbers window. The window of the Infancy of Christ shows the fleur-de-lis in its border and Blanche's castles appear alternating with the lilies in the window of Saints Peter and Paul.[135] The Burgundian windows thus immediately proclaimed their royal as well as Parisian connections.

The same complex reasoning behind the patronage of the Saint-Julien glass program appears again in the cathedral of Auxerre. The construction of the choir of Auxerre had been directly implemented by the energetic bishop Guillaume de Seignelay who funded construction even after being named bishop of Paris in 1220.[136] Under the episcopates of Henri de Villeneuve and Bernard de Sully, most of the glazing had been completed.[137] However, Guy de Mello, appointed bishop in 1247, was not one to allow an opportunity to escape him to flatter his sovereign and commemorate the royal favor he enjoyed through monuments in his newly acquired diocese.

Like the Cornut brothers, Guy was a member of a powerful feudal family. An

[131] Petit-Dutaillis (1964, 378) discusses this concept.

[132] "Westminster Abbey and the French Court Style," *Journal of the Society of Architectural Historians* 23 (1964), 3-18, and idem, 1965, 123-128.

[133] "Quod te Dominus in sua conora spinea . . . coronavit," Innocent, Privileges of the Sainte-Chapelle, 1243, in S. J. Morand, *Histoire de la Sainte-Chapelle royale de Paris*, Paris (1790), pièces justicatives, 2-3.

[134] See especially the windows of Judith (D) and Numbers (M) displaying a trellis design inscribing the lily, the windows of Ezekiel (G) and Exodus (N) showing the castles of Castille, and the window of Esther (C) alternating the lily and castle motifs.

[135] The appearance of the royal insignia led A. J. Havilland-Bushnell (*Storied Windows*, London [1914], 230) to believe that Saint Louis had given the Infancy window to Saint-Julien, an opinion seconded by Rheims (1926, 139-162).

[136] See above, Chap. I, nn. 15 and 16.

[137] Raguin, 1974, 36.

uncle, Dreux de Mello had been "connétable" of France during the reign of Philip Augustus and a notable crusader in 1239. Guillaume de Mello, lord of Saint Bris, was Guy's father. Guy himself first established his reputation as archdeacon of Laon, then bishop of Verdun in 1245 before being named by unanimous vote of the canons two years later to the see of Auxerre.[138] Here was a man of determination and firm political connections in the tradition of Guillaume de Seignelay, renowned for tearing down Auxerre's old Romanesque cathedral simply to let the Gothic "splendor of the new" shine forth in his diocese.[139] Characteristically, one of Guy's first public acts involved his revival of Guillaume's custom of demanding acts of fealty from the lords of the area. Claiming temporal as well as spiritual power from the fifth-century Germain of Auxerre, Guy required that his vassals carry his chair on the day of investiture.[140] He undertook a reconstruction of episcopal châteaux and added a large council chamber to the episcopal palace, currently in use as the reception hall of the Prefecture.[141] Lebeuf reports that the windows contained Guy's coat of arms.[142] I am also convinced that Guy de Mello was the patron of the sculptural program on the west facade, the reliefs of David and Bathsheba: the Judgment of Solomon, seated prophets and sibyls(?), the Seven Liberal Arts, and the stories of Joseph and the Prodigal Son that have long intrigued scholars.[143] The creation of the new axial clerestory lancets and the Martin and Peter and Paul cycles, considerably later than the previous program, reveals an act of patronage tied to Guy's relationship with the monarchy.

Guy enjoyed numerous personal encounters with Saint Louis. The nineteenth-century historian of Burgundy, Courtepée, described the distinguished Guy de Mello as having found great favor with the king and with James Pantaleone, of Troyes, pope as Urban IV in 1261.[144] This assessment was seconded by Petit, who praised the bishop, "pour lequel Saint Louis avait un profond respect."[145] In 1247, after barely taking office, Guy presided at the impressive elevation of the body of Saint Edmund, exiled bishop of Canterbury, witnessed by Louis, Blanche and most of the court.[146] Guy was present at the marriages of Louis' children and in all important

[138] See especially Lebeuf, *Mémoires*, I, 423-448.

[139] *Gesta*, LIX, 475.

[140] Quantin, 1873, nos. 747, 748, 750, 752, 762, and 763, and *Gallia Christiana* XII, *Instrumenta*, nos. 66, 68, 71, 76, 78, 92, and 94 show that Guillaume and Guy demanded multiple acts of homage.

[141] Châteaux at Regennes near Appogny (Quantin, 1862, 107) at Varzy and at Villechaud near Cosne-sur-Loire (ibid., 11).

[142] *Mémoires*, I, 429, also *Gesta*, LXIII, 499-501. Guy had inherited his father's lands and his title around 1260, and immediately established anniversaries for his parent in the cathedral and various parish churches (Lebeuf, *Mémoires*, IV, nos. 195, 197, 198, and Quantin, 1873, no. 594).

[143] A number of charters and information in the *Gesta* provide evidence of Guy's financial resources in a pattern that suggests that he supported a campaign around 1260 and in the late 1260s, dates maintained by Sauerländer (1972, 499-501, pls. 283-287) and Ernest Craven (unpublished dissertation, "The Sculptures of the South Tower Base of the Cathedral of Auxerre: A Rémois Shop in Burgundy," Columbia University, 1963, 114). The program appears to be linked to Guy's studies in classical literature and law, his relationships with the crown and his position as a once neglected but eventually honored younger son. I must reject Denny's suggestion (1976) of Jean de Chalon as patron.

[144] 1847-1848, I, 140-141.

[145] 1884-1894, V, 52-53.

[146] Ernest Petit, "Saint Louis en Bourgogne," *Bulletin de la Société des sciences historiques et naturelles de l'Yonne* 47 (1893), 575-591.

matters, save one, the king consistently settled disputes in Guy's favor. Joinville reports, however, that in this matter of secular enforcement of excommunication penalties, Guy was nonetheless chosen to speak for all the ecclesiastics of the realm.[147] Toward the end of his life, Guy became papal legate for Clement IV during his campaign against Manfred, regent of Sicily.[148] Charles of Anjou, with the rather naive cooperation of his brother Saint Louis marched into Italy with Guy as his spiritual advisor. Due to failing health, Guy refused the grateful pope's offer to make him archbishop of Lyon. In 1269 he succumbed to a last illness shortly after receiving Saint Louis, bound to meet his own death on the tragic Crusade in Tunis.

The Cornut brothers of Sens and Guy de Mello at Auxerre became some of the first medieval personalities to realize the import of Louis' Parisian monument. To assess the significance of these glazing programs, so vividly elder children of the artistic progeny of the Sainte-Chapelle, we must consider them in a wider context. Even beyond their function as aesthetic objects, these monuments are historical documents. They present vivid testimony of that fusion of religious and political sentiment in thirteenth-century France exploited by a saintly king to firmly establish the principle of divine-right monarchy.

7. The Magdalene Master (Semur-en-Auxois)

At Semur-en-Auxois, three windows in the axial chapel relate the story of Mary and Martha using both biblical and legendary sources (see Iconography Appendix: Mary Magdalene).[149] The narrative shows the loss of several important episodes and the panels show some forced rearrangements by restorers.[150] It is evident, however, that a single atelier produced all of the extant glass of this cycle. The use of similar design systems for all three windows has already been discussed under the section on composition and ornament. The painting style of the Magdalene Master is particularly distinctive.

[147] Joinville, *Histoire de Saint Louis*, 1309, in *Historiens et chroniquers du moyen âge*, ed. A. Pauphilet, Bruges (1963), 351. See also Quantin, 1873, lxxix, no. 619, and Lebeuf, *Mémoires*, I, 521.

[148] *Gesta*, LXIII, 501-502. See also Runciman, 1967, 290-293, and Petit-Dutaillis, 1964, 268-272.

[149] De Tervarent (1938) was the first to identify these windows as relating to the story of Mary Magdalene, although he appears to have been mistaken about the exact interpretation of many of the episodes.

[150] Maillard de Chambure, "Histoire et description de l'église Notre-Dame de Semur-en-Auxois," *Mémoires de la commission des antiquités du département de la Côte d'Or* s.1/1 (1832-1833), 72, indicates that the panels now set in four lancets of the axial chapel had been haphazardly divided among windows in two radiating chapels. Fragments of the Saint Peter window even now have been used to complete the Magdalene windows

(I:1 and IV:5, see Iconographic Appendix: Peter). An attempt has been made to identify two roundels in the Krannert Art Museum, Champaign, Ill., as panels from a lost Prodigal Son window at Semur-en-Auxois (Laurie McCarthy, "Two Gothic Stained Glass Rondels," *Bulletin of the Krannert Art Museum* 1/1 [1975], 5-23). There is no extant glass at Semur that corresponds to the iconography or to the style of the Krannert medallions. Jane Hayward, American representative to the international committee of the Corpus Vitrearum Medii Aevi, has studied these panels and has decided not to include them in the survey of medieval stained glass in American collections. For some discussion on the production of deceptive nineteenth-century forgeries, see notes on the Boston Museum panel in *New England Collections*, no. 43; Caviness, 1977, 13-22; Meredith Lillich, review of *The Early Stained Glass of Canterbury Cathedral*, in *Speculum* 54 (1979), 556.

All the medallions show unusually crowded compositions, compressing action into such restricted spaces that it is frequently difficult to distinguish individual figures; for example, in the group of apostles listening to the Magdalene (fig. 136), Vézelay's abbot dispatching envoys (fig. 137) or the Jews comforting Mary and Martha (fig. 138). This sense of crowding is further increased by the tendency for figures to spill over the edges of the border. In the panels of Mary in the wilderness of Provence (fig. 140) and Mary reporting to the apostles (fig. 136), feet, halos and drapery protrude across the circular medallion frame. This effect is also visible in medallions of the first lancet (figs. 137 and 139) where scrolls, heads, hands and drapery float beyond the borders. As compressed as these compositions may seem, the Magdalene Master's drapery patterns are even more charged with tension and stress. Garments bunch rather than flow. Visible in the robes of the seated abbot (fig. 137), or in the striding priest (fig. 140), drapery is portrayed with sharp, broken folds, now swiftly plastered against the body, now shooting away with self-animated violence. The drapery outlining the arm shows the characteristic of a thick grisaille line supported by thinner parallel lines to delineate folds. Deep loops of drapery fall across arms, outline cloaks, and especially, drape over belts. The faces are exaggerated, predominantly oval in form for females with rounded, heavy jaws and large round eyes. The bearded heads, especially visible in the first lancet (figs. 137 and 139), show a greater elongation with a fringe of beard outlining the jaw. Some figures seen in profile, again in the first lancet, have more rounded faces with highly expressive contours.

The overall painting style is one of movement and action, but an action turning inward around each figure, not establishing a dramatic interplay between figures. Grodecki has suggested that this style is associated with the Good Samaritan Master's atelier, active at Bourges from 1205 to 1214.[151] Certainly most of the characteristics of the Magdalene Master can apply to the art of the Good Samaritan Master: crowded compositions, intrusion of figures into the medallion frames, agitated drapery patterns and strongly defined facial types. The Crucifixion panel from the Passion window (fig. 141) is a good example of the Master's style. It is an active exciting portrayal; figures overlap the medallion border and spring in from the sides. The guard offering Christ the sponge may be compared with figures from the first lancet at Semur, the messenger in the short tunic before Vézelay's abbot and the man to the left of the glorified Magdalene (figs. 137 and 139). All three figures show the peculiarly agitated drapery that moves the skirt in harsh lines and thrusts loops of material over the belts. The head of the man next to the Magdalene and the head of the Bourges sponge bearer present the same exaggerated profile of hooked nose, protruding lip and small button-shaped ear.

The use of the heavy grisaille line supported by thin parallel strokes seen in the sleeve of Vézelay's abbot appears in the sleeves of the angels supporting the crown over Christ. All three figures show a similar pattern with broken folds moving

---

[151] *Year 1200*, III, 347; idem, *Vitrail*, 139. See also earlier work on the Good Samaritan Master, idem, 1948.

from both wrist and shoulder and converging into an undulating outline along the lower edge of the extended sleeve. The heavy-jawed face of Vézelay's abbot finds its inspiration in the Bourges Saint John. The deep V-shaped folds in the cloak of the mourning Virgin appear again in the cloak of Mary Magdalene in the second window at Semur (fig. 138). Even the tightly compressed composition of the Bourges Passion medallion echoes the positioning of figures in the Semur trefoil.

The Good Samaritan style also has been linked by Beer to medallions of the Life of John the Baptist from the cathedral of Lausanne.[152] Given Lausanne's nearness to Burgundy, and the position the cathedral holds in the architectural development of the para-Chartrain axis,[153] this thesis merits some consideration. The original location of the window is conjectural, as is its date, the extant panels having been housed in the cathedral's south rose before 1898, then moved to several locations before their present installation in the Musée Historique de l'Ancien Evêché. Beer cites the elongated forms of the bearded male faces and the profile caricature of others as well as the dynamic drapery style as points of affinity between the Bourges and Lausanne Masters. Indeed there are similarities between the elongated faces of the Baptist (fig. 143) and the Crucified Christ, and between the profiles of the guard closest to Herod and the man offering the sponge. Violently agitated drapery might best be found in the detail of the guard from the Lausanne Beheading panel (fig. 142). The Lausanne color is also a very even mixture of pinks, greens, and yellows against a blue ground very much like the even range of color in the Bourges glass.

Grodecki does not support this opinion, preferring to stress Lafond's suggestion that the Lausanne glass shows stronger links to the area of Lyon.[154] The Nativity panel from Clermont-Ferrand (fig. 145) displays some of the Lyonnais characteristics.[155] The use of several parallel lines of grisaille outlining angular V-shaped folds is an artistic technique similar to that of the Lausanne Master. The broad features of the face also seem somewhat related. Nonetheless there appear differences too radical to be accounted for in only a short space of time from the end of the twelfth-century date of the Clermont panels to the 1210 date given by Lafond to the Lausanne Baptist story.[156] The Lausanne figures and drapery are far more dynamic, the compositions more highly charged and the faces more elongated and distorted.

Perhaps a return to the workshop of the Good Samaritan Master will help place these comparisons in perspective. Grodecki traces the atelier's development from work in the cathedral of Poitiers before 1205.[157] Although there are marked differ-

[152] *Corpus, Switzerland* I, 58-72, pls. 40, 41, color pl. 6; also *Year 1200*, I, no. 215, notes by Jane Hayward. Extant work of John the Baptist Master: three medallions catalogued Musée Cantonal d'Archéologie et d'Histoire, Lausanne, nos. 58012, 58014, 58016, and fragments of scenes 58011, 58013.

[153] See especially Bony, 1957-1958, and Chap. I.

[154] Grodecki, 1977, 198, pl. 173; Lafond, "Les vitraux anciens de la cathédrale de Lausanne,"

Congrès archéologique de France 110 (1952), 128-132.

[155] Grodecki, 1977, 192, fig. 168. The two angels are copies, the originals are in the Pitcairn collection, Bryn Athyn, Pa. (Metropolitan Museum of Art, *Medieval Art from Private Collections*, New York, 1968, no. 179).

[156] See above n. 154, *Congrès*, p. 129.

[157] Grodecki, 1948, 104-105; idem, *Vitrail*, 116; idem, 1951, 160-163.

ences in armature systems and fineness of execution, he accepted an "identity of workshop tradition" in the two series. A panel from the Lot window (fig. 144) shows the traits typical of the Good Samaritan Master in the tight arm drapery, elongated male faces, rounder female heads and bold use of paint. The features are unusually heavy, possibly to compensate for the greater distance between spectator and window at Poitiers. The violent drapery patterns and the agitated figure stances seem to be submerged in a more ponderous conception of composition. Grodecki has often referred to the style of this atelier as one in which late Romanesque traditions contribute to produce one of the most noteworthy artists of the early thirteenth century. Grodecki believes the Master's stylistic origins come from the west of France, and Hayward's study of Angevin traditions at this time has brought many similarities to light.[158] However, study of the glass of Poitiers, Bourges, Semur and Lausanne reveals an additional stylistic interaction.

Although these four sites may have different internal relationships, they all betray a common link to an earlier tradition, the art of the Lyonnais. The ultimately Byzantine derivation of this style, evident also in manuscripts and carving, has long been recognized by art historians.[159] The glass of Clermont-Ferrand and Lyon, especially, shows a metallic feeling in the drapery, sharp linear folds and iconographic motifs that can only be due to Byzantine influence.[160] Grodecki dates the earliest glass in this region to the 1160s, but workshops continued into the early thirteenth century.[161] Clermont's Nativity panel (fig. 145) shows a typically Byzantine disposition of reclining Virgin in a mandorla-like bed, with Joseph, the Christ Child, and two hovering angels (copies) occupying isolated compartments at the corners of the panel. The energetic feeling created by the swirling drapery outlines and the angular folds is not far removed from the atmosphere of the Poitiers, Bourges, Lausanne or Semur glass. In the figure of Joseph, especially, the drapery motif, smooth across the knee and pulled back sharply to be anchored by strong downward folds, shares a common source with the drapery patterns over the Vézelay abbot's legs at Semur (fig. 137). The rounded head of the Virgin, with its large staring eyes and heavily modeled head-covering, seems to appear again in Lot's daughter from Poitiers, or in the Magdalene at Semur. Surely the V-shaped pleats in the Virgin's mantle at Bourges and the Magdalene's at Semur seem to derive ultimately from patterns like those over the Clermont Virgin's legs.

Beer suggests that the link between the John the Baptist Master of Lausanne

---

[158] Unpublished dissertation, "The Angevin Style of Glass Painting," Yale University, 1958; Hayward-Grodecki, 1966.

[159] See most recently Grodecki (1977, 187-198), who includes references to Cluny manuscripts, and Walter Cahn, "Autour de la Bible de Lyon. Problèmes du roman tardif dans le centre de la France," *Revue de l'art* 47 (1980), 11-20.

[160] Emile Mâle (in André Michel, *Histoire de l'art* II/1, Paris [1906], 378-380) was one of the first to speak of the Byzantine character of the glass.

[161] The byzantinizing workshops in the cathedral of Lyon (Grodecki, *Vitrail*, 116-117, fig. 87) are dated as late as 1220. See most recently Catherine Brisac, "Les vitraux de l'étage inférieur du choeur de Saint-Jean de Lyon," unpublished dissertation, University of Paris, 1977; idem, "La peinture sur verre à Lyon au XIIe et au début du XIIIe siècle," *Les Dossiers de l'archéologie* 26 (1978), 38-49.

and the Good Samaritan Master at Bourges should not be considered one of atelier. Rather, she sees a general stylistic matrix, extending from Poitiers, to Bourges, north through Burgundy and south through Lyon. The stylistic components available in this area would surely include the Byzantine aspects of Lyonnais art of the late twelfth century.[162]

There appear to be some stronger relationships among the windows discussed, however. The Poitiers glass before 1205 might indeed represent the earlier work of the Good Samaritan atelier, following Grodecki's argument. The stylistic transformation shown in the Bourges windows dated before 1214 might be due in part to the atelier's exposure to the careful painting and Byzantine tendencies of the monuments of Lyon and Clermont-Ferrand. It does seem probable that the Good Samaritan atelier, or one of the painters from this atelier, produced the series at Semur-en-Auxois shortly after 1220. Branner suggests that the construction of Semur's apse was begun in the early 1220s so that it is conceivable that the glass was commissioned about this time.[163] The presence of a window at Semur that duplicates the iconography of the Bourges Mary Magdalene window (fig. 43) would also argue for a close atelier connection.[164] For the work at Lausanne, the connections are more remote. Lafond has dated the Baptist windows about 1210 and Grodecki would place them in the second decade of the thirteenth century.[165] It seems entirely possible that within such a time span, influence from the Good Samaritan's atelier, or from his milieu, could be the factor that transformed an earlier Lyonnais style into the much more dynamic expression visible in the problematic Lausanne panels.

8. NOTRE-DAME OF DIJON

The five lancets beneath the north rose of Notre-Dame of Dijon are all that remain of the Gothic glazing of this impressive building (fig. 5).[166] It appears that the destruction of the original glass owes as much to the efforts of seventeenth- and eighteenth-century officials to modernize the edifice, as it does to the inevitable effects of time and the elements.[167] Even in the five lancets, much restoration and shifting of compositions can be detected, both by the nineteenth-century restorer, Didron, and previous painters.[168] Nonetheless, the strikingly elaborate foliate borders

[162] *Corpus, Switzerland* I, 71-72.

[163] 1960, 66. See also Chap. I.

[164] See Iconography Appendix: Mary Magdalene.

[165] Summarized in Grodecki, 1977, 198. I see no compelling reason to accept Beer's date of after 1219 (*Corpus, Switzerland* I, 72).

[166] No serious study of the Dijon glass has been attempted, a condition perhaps encouraged by the lack of photographic documentation. References to the windows have been made by Vallery-Radot, 1928, 68-70; Oursel, 1938, 81-84; idem, *L'Art de Bourgogne*, Paris (1953), 115-116; Grodecki, *Vitrail*, 140; Viollet-le-Duc, 1875, 401-403, Fyot, 1910, 139-154; and Lafond, 1955, 31.

[167] See Restoration Appendix: Notre-Dame of Dijon. See also account of extensive destruction during the eighteenth-century renovations at Notre-Dame of Paris (Henry Kraus, "Notre-Dame's Vanished Medieval Glass," *Gazette des beaux-arts* 6th ser., 68 [1966], 131-148 and 69 [1967], 65-78).

[168] In some instances, figures appear to have been moved from one lancet to another. There is evidence of the tracing of darkened pieces and insertion of the new glass in the window. Many of the restorations show the characteristic style of Didron's productions that fill the remaining windows in the church.

and backgrounds are clearly original. An examination of the facial style and drapery patterns confirms the initial impression made by the color schema and medallion format; a single atelier was responsible for all the windows, but a second painter of entirely different origins executed the fifth lancet. Neither of these two painting styles seems related to the art of other windows in the Burgundian area.

Although discussed earlier, ornament is so important a clue to localization of the Notre-Dame style that further reference to its foliate patterns is made here. The preference for rinceaux backgrounds over the more common mosaic treatment found at Chartres or Bourges seems a characteristic of the area northeast of Paris and extending as far as Canterbury.[169] It is significant that the artist responsible for the window at Chartres that most brilliantly displays such rich foliate backgrounds, the Saint Eustache Master, has been traced by Grodecki to the Laonnais and to additional work at Saint-Quentin.[170] The color schema of the Saint Eustache window—blue, yellow and green rinceaux against a red background (fig. 147)—is closely paralleled by the fourth lancet at Dijon, with blue, white and green foliage against the red ground (fig. 146). The foliage system of the Eustache window is particularly enhanced by the technique of making rinceaux spring from the borders of the small round medallions at the sides.[171] At Dijon, rich, leafy tendrils also spring from the round and lozenge-shaped medallions of the fourth lancet, contributing to the opulent effect of the interlocked geometric and organic systems.

The painter of the first four lancets at Dijon appears to have derived his style from the same northeastern sources. This connection is further strengthened by the corresponding derivation of architectural forms in Notre-Dame's chevet from the influence of Saint-Yved of Braine, also located in the area northeast of Paris.[172] Dijon's first four lancets, two dedicated to Saint Peter and two dedicated to Saint Andrew, show peculiarities quite distinct from indigenous Parisian, Burgundian or Chartrain expressions. The figures are ample, generously proportioned, and move in well-defined spaces. The details of the panels of the scene of Christ Giving the Keys to Peter (figs. 149 and 153) show the dignified sweep of drapery patterns that sculpt the body as a palpable, three-dimensional form. The mantle around the legs of Christ (fig. 149) follows the curves of the legs, and is lifted up toward the waist in scooplike folds. The tunic falls in generous folds, clearly giving the impression of a body beneath the circular cloth. The billowing fabric that sweeps across the

[169] See especially the detailed summation of these decorative patterns in Caviness, 1977, 44-45. Grodecki (1965, 178) spoke of a conservative trend in monuments of this region that favored the retention of foliage borders and backgrounds into the thirteenth century. Earlier, Viollet-le-Duc (1875, 402) had commented on the "archaic" nature of the Dijon foliage and labeled it an example of the continuation of twelfth-century designs into the 1230s.

[170] Grodecki, 1965. Grodecki also links the Prodigal Son window, the only other example of such curving rinceaux designs at Chartres, to styles at Laon (ibid., 178, n. 28). Caviness (1977, 44) links the richly foliated Joseph window at Chartres to a Canterbury-Sens designer.

[171] A fragment of a window showing the fallen Synagogue in the Pitcairn collection (Caviness, 1977, fig. 157; Metropolitan Museum of Art, *Medieval Art from Private Collections*, New York, 1968, no. 190) from Saint-Remi of Reims(?) shows a fine example of this type of living border, as do many windows in Canterbury, for example, Trinity Chapel N:III, Corona Redemption window, or clerestory N:IX (Caviness, 1977, figs. 167, 169, 137, 127).

[172] Branner, 1960, 56-58.

apostle's arm and floats toward the right side of the medallion and the swinging termination of Christ's mantle are typical of the artist's use of drapery for dramatic effects. The figure of the blacksmith from the donor's panel (fig. 156) although of a slightly more delicate treatment, shows a particularly elegant flow of drapery falling from the shoulders, looping over the belt, and swinging in a rhythmic fashion above the knees. The artist seems to have conceived his figures in large, majestic units, as in the few oval-shaped lines of drapery conveying the image of Sapphira's fallen body from the panel of the death of Ananias and Sapphira (fig. 155). The overall effect of such techniques produces a feeling of calm dignity and an evocation of classicizing schemas.

Faces also continue these classicizing tendencies. The impressive image of the head of Christ from the second lancet (fig. 152) shows a long, straight nose, reminiscent of the long elegant lines of classical sculpture. The large expressionless eyes give a passionless effect to the face which is partially offset by the emphatic brows. The hair moves away from the face in very carefully drawn clumps, each defined through a large amount of grisaille infill. If the repair lead is discounted, one can see that the form of the head is an unusually square-jawed one, with the beard directly in line with the line of the ear. The face of Sapphira (fig. 155) exhibits the same long nose and unexpressive mouth line as the head of Christ.

The compositions are centered, and frequently tend toward a symmetrical format, such as the image of the demons strangling the inhabitants of Nicea in their baths (fig. 148). When not precisely symmetrical, the compositions nevertheless take on a rectilinear format, producing a very stable balance of the pictorial elements.

That monuments in the northeast relate to the first Dijon style is clear, but such influences must be qualified. These monuments belong to what has loosely been described as the classicizing style, which includes works such as Nicholas of Verdun's Klosterneuburg altarpiece, the Ingeborg Psalter, the Visitation group of the cathedral of Reims and a series of stained glass productions at Paris, Saint-Quentin, Laon, Troyes, Orbais, Braine and Soissons.[173] This development has re-

[173] KLOSTERNEUBURG ALTARPIECE: dated 1181 (Otto Demus, "Nicholas of Verdun," *Encyclopedia of World Art* 10, London, 1965, cols. 634-640). INGEBORG PSALTER: dated 1195-1213 (Florens Deuchler, *Der Ingeborpsalter*, Berlin [1967]). REIMS SCULPTURE: dated 1230-1233 (Sauerländer, 1974, 54-55, figs. 202-203, 485, color pl. p. 55). NOTRE-DAME OF PARIS: west rose about 1220, contemporary with the architecture (Lafond, *Corpus, France* I, 23-34, pls. 2-3, color pl. 1). SAINT-QUENTIN: windows in the chapel of the Virgin: Life of the Virgin and Infancy of Christ, about 1220 (Grodecki, 1965, 180-188, figs. 110-118; *Corpus, France, Recensement* I, 166-167). LAON: windows in the chevet, Legend of Theophilus and Saint Stephen, Passion, Typological Infancy Cycle, about 1210-1215. East and north roses about 1200-1205 (Grodecki, *Vitrail*, 118-119, n. 11, figs. 88, 91, 95; A. Florival and E. Midoux, *Les Vitraux de la cathédrale de Laon*, Paris [1882-1891]; *Corpus, France, Recensement* I, 162-167, figs. 87, 88, pl. 12). TROYES: windows in the axial chapel, two windows of the Life of the Virgin, two windows of the Public Life of Christ. A Tree of Jesse now in the second ambulatory chapel on the north was probably originally included in this group. Dated about 1215-1220 (Lafond, 1955, 31, 35-43, figs. pp. 35 and 43). ORBAIS: window of Crucifixion with Ecclesia and Synagoga over porch in south transept, about 1220 (Grodecki, *Vitrail*, 118; Lafond, 1955, 26). BRAINE: panels from rose of Saint Yved now in upper choir (north) of the cathedral of Soissons, about 1220 (*Corpus, France, Recensement* I, 171, fig. 95). SOISSONS: hemicycle of choir, four windows: Jesse Tree, panels *in situ* and in the Pitcairn collection, Bryn Athyn, Pa.; Last Judgment; Creation and Fall; Life and Glorification of the Virgin. Ambulatory: Martyrdom of

ceived recent attention through the exhibition at the Metropolitan Museum of Art, "The Year 1200," and through subsequent publications, notably Caviness' work on Canterbury.[174] The effect of these monuments, their date from the 1170s through the 1230s, their rather widespread dissemination, and above all, their coexistence with several different styles (for example, the varied sculpture workshops at Reims or the distinctive glazing ateliers of Bourges or Chartres) all of this makes us extremely cautious about localizing too rigidly the styles of this period.[175] It seems that even as early as 1200 workshops had become sufficiently mobile to travel to widespread locations and to cooperate with workshops of different areas in the execution of a single coherent program.

This process is particularly evident at Bourges, as has been shown by the detailed analysis of Grodecki, which isolates three distinct and extremely high quality workshops: that of the Good Samaritan Master, that of the Relics of Saint Stephen Master and that of the Master of the New Alliance window.[176] We are concerned with this third workshop, which was also responsible for the Last Judgment window and three less important windows in the first radiating chapel to the north, depicting the legends of Saint Denis, Saints Peter and Paul and Saint Martin.[177] Grodecki now dates the Bourges campaign at 1205-1214, making the New Alliance atelier contemporaneous with that of the Saint Eustache Master of Chartres. He has already cited similar "northern" tendencies in the work of the two ateliers, without seeing any workshop relationships.

A comparison of the figure of Moses indicating the Brazen Serpent from the New Alliance window (fig. 150) and the figure of Christ handing the keys to Peter from the second Dijon lancet (fig. 149) indicates striking similarities. One notices immediately the similar undulating silhouette of back and legs produced by the taut pull of the mantle. Small, delicately drawn pleats enrich the area about the hips, while the lower mantle exhibits bolder oval-shaped folds and a double roll with deep

---

Saints Crépin and Crépinien, Corcoran Art Gallery, D.C., and one original panel in first chapel to the south of the axial chapel; Relics of Saints Crépin and Crépinien, first radiating chapel to the south of the axial chapel; Life of Saints Nicaise and Eutropia, divided between the Louvre and the Isabella Stewart Gardner Museum, Boston. All dated about 1212-1220 (Louis Grodecki, "Un vitrail démembré de la cathédrale de Soissons," *Gazette des beaux-arts* 42 [1953], 169-176; idem, *Vitrail*, 123, fig. 92; idem, 1960; Philippe Verdier, "Stained Glass from the Cathedral of Soissons," *The Corcoran Gallery of Art Bulletin* 10 [1958], 4-22; *Year 1200*, I, no. 213; *Corpus, France, Recensement* I, 169-172, figs. 93-94, pl. 13). Four panels from a legend of Saint Blaise in the Musée Marmottan, Paris, appear related to the Soissons glass but cannot be linked with certainty to the cathedral (Grodecki, 1960, 173-175).

[174] Including review by Willibald Sauerländer, *The Art Bulletin* 53 (1971), 505-516; Caviness, 1977, especially 49-58, 151-155.

[175] Caviness (1977, 153) suggests that we must begin to think in larger terms of common artistic soil, stating, "By this time—perhaps approaching 1200 and extending into the thirteenth century—there was more clearly a single artistic province, which included Canterbury as a northern outpost, and which extended throughout much of northeastern France." Recently Catherine Brisac has identified this northern style in three windows of the cathedral of Lyon; the windows of the Infancy and Saint Stephen of about 1215-1220, and the window of Saint John the Baptist, after 1226 ("La peinture sur verre à Lyon au XIIe et au début du XIIIe siècle," *Les Dossiers de l'archéologie* 26 [1978], 46-49, 5 figs.). Such discoveries reinforce the concept of a wide-spread artistic province and the itinerant nature of thirteenth-century glazing workshops.

[176] 1948; idem, *Year 1200* III, 339-359.

[177] 1948, 87-90, figs. 19d,e; idem, *Year 1200* III, 347-349, figs. 3, 12-14.

indentations at the edge. Similar drapery appears in the axial chapel windows of the cathedral of Troyes. A medallion of the Purification from the Infancy with Typological Subjects window (fig. 154), recognized by Lafond as belonging to the classicizing style group, shows the same scoop folds and flying drapery as the Giving of the Keys medallion (fig. 153).[178] The drapery flowing over the head and arms of the Virgin Mary as she presents the Christ Child exhibits the same sweep of independent cloth that so dramatically flows across the apostle's arm in the Dijon panel. Indeed both Dijon and Troyes panels use the drapery as an impressive space filler, allowing the compositions to remain essentially ordered in a "Poussinist" mode of stable verticals and horizontals. The classicizing tendencies of the drafting style of Villard de Honnecourt may also help to qualify the Dijon accomplishment. The particularly fluid treatment of the tunic of the blacksmith (fig. 156) seems a corollary to Villard's sketch of soldiers carrying a bow and spear (fig. 157).[179] The loosely gathered short tunic of the soldier falls in the same natural folds over the belt, and even swings to the side in an action similar to that of the Dijon figure.

Although the "classicizing style" exhibited an extremely long life in French styles of art, I would tend to place the Dijon windows at the far end of the style's development, most probably around the mid-1230s. This dating would correspond well with Branner's belief that the transept and the eastern bays of the nave were under construction by 1230.[180] The Dijon glass shows a progressive simplification and altering of the early style of the Master of the New Alliance window of Bourges or the Troyes axial chapel atelier. This can be seen by a comparison with the Tree of Jesse window attributed to the area of Troyes, and now in the Victoria and Albert Museum, London (fig. 151).[181] The Jesse Tree prophet in this illustration shows a much more pronounced flattening of forms, especially in the schematicized surface detailing of the mantle over the knee. The sharply defined pleats of the skirt are far more diagrammatic than the more fluid and natural fall of material in the Bourges figure of Moses (fig. 150). The gesture of the upraised hand and the fall of the sleeve folds in both the Jesse Tree prophet and the figure of Christ from Dijon (fig. 152) are extremely close.

Further similarities between the Victoria and Albert panel and the Dijon style can be seen in a comparison of the sway of the lower tunic and the oval-shaped mantle folds, and the flying drapery to the right. The Jesse Tree prophet's head is quite different from the Dijon head of the preaching Christ, relying on oval forms that create a more active, dynamic effect. The Dijon Christ retains the rectilinear "classical format" evident in the head of the Virgin from the Purification panel from Troyes Cathedral (fig. 154). The insistently straight nose appears to place the Dijon

[178] 1955, 36, 41-42.

[179] Paris, Bibl. nat. Ms. fr. 19093 fol. 25v. probably around 1235; cf. H. Hahnloser, *Villard de Honnecourt, Kritische Gesamtausgabe des Bauhüttenbuches*, Vienna, 1935.

[180] 1960, 132.

[181] Grodecki (*Vitrail*, 140, fig. 110) dates the glass around 1225, "d'une qualité semblable à celle des vitraux de Troyes mais de provenance inconnue." Bernard Rackham (*Victoria and Albert Museum, Department of Ceramics: A Guide to the Collections of Stained Glass*, London [1936], nos. 5, 6-1881, pp. 32-33, fig. 4) also sees a Troyes provenance.

style firmly within the orbit of the classicizing style. At present, it does not seem possible to link the atelier that produced the first four Dijon lancets to any other production, either in Burgundy or in the contributing areas discussed. It does seem quite certain, however, that this particularly impressive style was part of an extremely complex development. Dijon thus figures as yet another document for our understanding of one of the finest expressions in glass painting of the late twelfth and early thirteenth centuries.

The style of the fifth lancet at Dijon is best exemplified by figures from the first, third and fourth medallions: Andrew Adoring the Cross (figs. 158 and 159), Andrew's Crucifixion (fig. 160) and Andrew's Exorcism of a boy (fig. 161). Through comparison of tracings taken from all five lancets it is clear that the smaller figures of the fifth lancet come from an entirely different stylistic tradition than that of their classicizing counterparts. The tracing of the executioner stripping off his cloak (fig. 158) and the photo of the executioner to the upper right of the cross (fig. 159) illustrate this vivid change. Features are far more exaggerated and anatomy more crudely handled than in the figures of the first painter. The heads are particularly striking in that they are extremely large in proportion to the bodies. Large rounded eyes and similarly arched brows balance broad, curved noses. The foreheads are low, the jaws almost deformed and the hair coarsely drawn. In comparison to the classical heads of the first atelier, the rustic, vigorous nature of these creations becomes even more apparent. The drapery of the Fifth Lancet style is similarly unsophisticated, emphasizing heavily shaded, broad indentations around the waist and in the folds of the garment being pulled over the head.

Of particular importance is the anatomy of the guard's torso, repeated in the body of Saint Andrew being stretched on the cross (fig. 160). An undulating curve outlines the stomach area above which a conical shape serves to separate the ribs. This detailing is very close to that found in the body of Christ in the Bourges Crucifixion panel by the Good Samaritan Master (fig. 141).[182] Indeed, close inspection (unfortunately impossible in a black and white photograph) reveals that the figure of the Crucified Andrew from the third medallion uses the same dots around each nipple and short curved lines to show the indentation of the sternum.

Although the compositions have been altered by extensive restorations, it is clear that the small size of the figures has contributed to much more isolation among the narrative elements. In the Crucifixion of Andrew the little figures seem to dangle at the extremities of the medallion. Indeed, the medallions almost seem less important than the decorative patterns that form their setting. All told, the general appearance of the Fifth Lancet style associates it with painting styles at the beginning of the century. We seem here to be dealing with a very late manifestation of the Romanesque tradition on French soil, although clearly other areas such as Strasbourg and Cologne retained the more highly charged and decorative expression until late

---

[182] Grodecki, 1948; idem, *Year 1200*, III, 343-347, figs. 2, 7-11, 14; idem, *Vitrail*, 139, figs. 104, 106.

in the thirteenth century. One might suggest that the Fifth Lancet peculiarities indicate that the painter might have been more accustomed to working in manuscripts. His penchant for small figures and detailed, expressionistic faces coupled with his general insensitivity to visual impact in the narrative would argue that he was more attuned to demands of smaller-scale painting.[183]

[183] See various interpretations of the relationship of glass and manuscript painting: the Petronella Master of Canterbury (Caviness, 1977, 77-82, figs. 151-160), a series of panels from Troyes (Louis Grodecki, "Problèmes de la peinture en Champagne pendant la seconde moitié du dou- zième siècle," *Romanesque and Gothic Art: Studies in Western Art* [Acts of the Twentieth International Congress of the History of Art, I] Princeton [1963], 129-141, and idem, 1977, 140-147, figs. 118-125) and panels from Clermont-Ferrand (ibid., 190-194, figs. 163-168).

IV. Auxerre 57:15-23, Saint Lawrence window, tortures

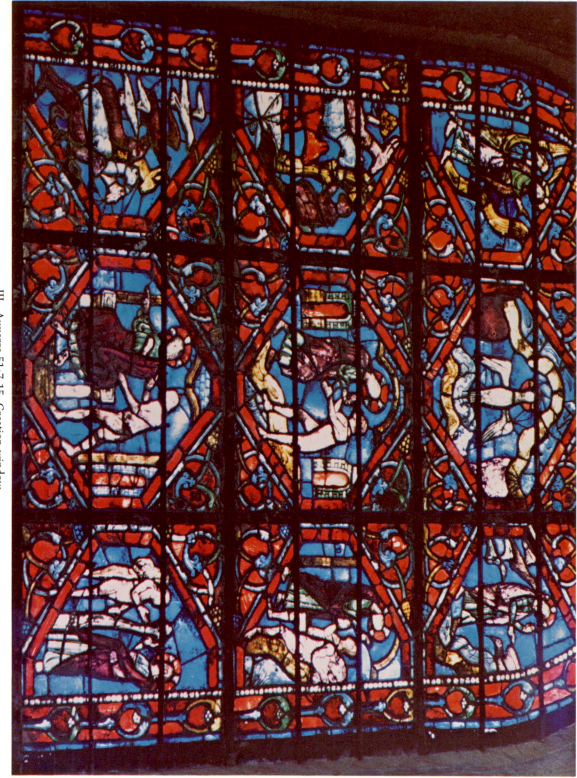

III. Auxerre 51:7-15, Creation window

II. Auxerre 68:1-6, Apocalypse window

I. Auxerre 67:7-10, Saint Nicholas window, selection of Nicholas as bishop

V

ICONOGRAPHY OF THE WINDOWS

*By setting off the ceiling panels and walls with a variety of
kinds of work and a variety of pigments, you have shown the
beholders something of the likeness of the paradise of God,
burgeoning with all kinds of flowers, verdant with grass and
foliage; cherishing the souls of the saints with halos according
to their merit. (Theophilus, On Divers Arts)[1]*

Given the length the analysis of the style of the Burgundian ateliers has required,
the analysis here of the iconography of the windows will be quite brief. The reader
is directed to the iconographic appendices where reconstructed programs of the axial
chapel and the upper choir of Auxerre cathedral are outlined. Saints and biblical
personages appearing in the glass of Auxerre, Notre-Dame of Dijon and Semur-en-
Auxois are arranged alphabetically. Since the local devotional practices and references
to depictions in other French glass cycles are cited at length in these appendices,
they will not be repeated here. This chapter serves primarily to draw attention to
broad iconographic questions such as decisions concerning programs and unusual
Burgundian themes.

The cathedral of Auxerre contains thirty-nine windows in the ambulatory and
axial chapel with evidence remaining from thirty-five separate thirteenth-century
ensembles. The upper choir contains fifteen double-lancet windows surmounted by
roses all containing some original glass. Despite the damage caused by the Huguenot
attack of 1567, and the subsequent restoration programs that have often grouped
two or even three narrative programs in a single lancet, the extent of the original
program is still evident to the modern viewer. Because of the decision to regroup
the panels, subsequent restorers were discouraged from any wholesale recreation
of presumed iconographic details, a decision which preserved the integrity of the
program.[2]

Confronted with the wealth of saints' lives and biblical subjects in a Gothic
building that has retained its original glazing as well as Auxerre, the spectator is
quite literally enveloped by the "Economy of Salvation." Tall, impressive figures
in the upper choir radiate a correspondence between the Old and New Testaments
and frame images of Eternity in the eastern bays.[3] On the lower level, in shining

---

[1] Theophilus, 1963, 79; Prologue to the Third
Book: The Art of the Metalworker.

[2] Only in the case of the David and Saint
Mammès windows did the glass painter Vessière
expand the story from a few extant panels to create

two full windows. The rather brutal effects of the
harsh modern panels effectively discouraged any
further attempts.

[3] This type of program in the upper windows
of the building can be traced to the glass of Augs-

splendor, exemplars of Christian action demonstrate the path leading to that upper realm. The narrative windows, although devoted to specific themes, frequently show striking similarities. Sometimes it seems as if the iconographic means used to depict certain actions were as widespread as western Christianity. Iconographic systems transformed specific truths relating to a single individual at a particular time and place into ritual manifestations of one significant truth, that the life of the Christian reflected the life of Christ. Such depictions were the visible embodiments of the words of Paul, "With Christ I am nailed to the cross. It is now no longer I that live but Christ lives in me" (Galatians 2:19-20). The essential characteristics of Christ's life—miracle-making, passion, triumphant death—lie at the heart of medieval hagiography.

The depiction of Saint Lawrence at Auxerre (fig. 44, pl. IV) provides an example. Three times Lawrence is led before his enemy, and three times he is condemned to the severest of tortures. He is stripped, beaten and burned, each time the compositions varying slightly to lead the viewer from one episode to the next. The scenes of torture are arranged in the central medallions, while prison guards, the officiating tyrant and Christian witnesses form compositional as well as ideological frames at the side. The window culminates in a half-length bust of Christ, visual seal of the belief that the saint's actions are accepted by Christ who rewards such fidelity with eternal life. The other windows in the ambulatory present variations on these themes, particularly the Margaret, Catherine and Samson windows.

The universality of the systems is attested to by the striking similarity between the iconography of the Saint Catherine window (fig. 51) and that of the Saint Margaret window from the church of Saint Margaret, Ardagger, Austria (fig. 52).[4] Like the Auxerre presentations, the Austrian glass silhouettes the figures to emphasize clear iconographic readability. The medallion showing the beheading of Margaret uses precisely the same formula as the beheading of the empress in Auxerre's Catherine window. The female bodies fall at precisely the same angle to the left, balanced by an image of a persecutor on the right. The interchangeability of the schemas is further demonstrated by the similarity of the torture of Saint Margaret and the torture of the empress in the Catherine window.[5] Both figures are placed in the center of the composition, their hands raised above their heads while the torturers are silhouetted to the right and to the left in symmetrical order. Similarities in hagiography also encouraged common workshop approaches. Auxerre's Saint James window is quite similar in conception to the Saint Andrew cycle (figs. 24 and 32). The two apostles' lives followed common hagiographical types, a factor that seems to have contributed to the parallels in the visualizations of them in the cathedral's program.[6] The medallions are of approximately the same diamond

burg Cathedral of about 1100 (Grodecki, 1977, 50-51).

[4] Grodecki (1977, 232-236, fig. 202, cat. no. 30) treats the glass as an example of the late flowering Romanesque, dated between 1226 and 1241.

[5] This same image was used for representations of Saint Agatha in the glass of Gercy (*Corpus, France, Recensement* I, pl. XIV) and in the cathedral of Clermont-Ferrand (du Ranquet, 1932, 243-256).

[6] See descriptions in the *Golden Legend* (369-377 and 7-16) that emphasize the far-flung mis-

shape and both windows can be attributed to later production of the Genesis atelier.

The choices made at Auxerre among iconographic subjects appear to reflect local traditions. Almost all of the saints had relics housed in the cathedral or were the object of local devotion.[7] In keeping with tradition, the patron saint of the cathedral was represented frequently. The image of Saint Stephen appears in the north bay of the hemicycle and in a side window of the axial chapel, and an account of his relics in the ambulatory. Auxerre's Relics window shows iconography made traditional in the windows of Châlons-sur-Marne and Bourges.[8] Very possibly the narrative included the saint's life and martyrdom, lost with the lower portions of the window. In many instances Auxerre's treatment of widely known saints such as Eustache and Martin follows systems used at Chartres and presumably part of a "common" currency available to the glass painter. Many of the episodes, especially Eustache witnessing the loss of his sons, his expulsion from the ship (fig. 39) or his reunion with Theobista not only incorporate similar compositional devices but almost the same dramatic energy. The cycle of Peter and Paul must have originally occupied two lancets, since even after the Huguenot destruction enough panels remain to fill an entire window and leave several panels for insertion into other bays. The cycle, then, could afford to be particularly detailed, in some instances presenting rarely depicted episodes, such as the death of Ananias and Sapphira or Peter's vision of the unclean beasts. Such iconographic thoroughness is typical of Auxerre's program, which also shows two full windows of Saint Nicholas, one devoted to his life and another depicting some of the most prominent miracles ascribed to his intercession after death. The events of Genesis unfold in two windows, with a second account of the Fall juxtaposed with scenes from Exodus.

Auxerre's tendency to elaborate many themes would make a full-window treatment of an Ascension-Pentecost (fig. 78) a logical possibility. In general, the panels in each of the Auxerre narratives do not seem to have suffered radical internal rearrangement altering their iconographic content. This series of seated apostles, angels and a standing Christ would have no meaning outside an Ascension-Pentecost function. Indeed the loss of more glass relating to an Ascension theme would seem the natural result of the loss of lower parts of the window. The apportioning of one figure per panel, actually, constitutes the only iconographic novelty for such a window. Representations of the Ascension and Pentecost were quite common in manuscript and in glass sources, but for the most part, the witnesses to Christ's ascent and the apostles gathered to receive the Holy Spirit were grouped together, as in the twelfth-century panel from Clermont-Ferrand, or the typological window from Canterbury.[9] The representation from Saint-Père-de-Chartres from the win-

---

sions and numerous miracles of both apostles.

[7] Lafond (1955, 46-47) recognized that the decoration of the upper choir windows of Troyes was most frequently inspired by the relics possessed by the cathedral, especially those that had been obtained from Constantinople by bishop Garnier de Trainel during his ministration to the Fourth Crusade.

[8] The cathedral of Bourges is also under the patronage of Saint Stephen.

[9] See Ascension and Pentecost miniatures from Parisian manuscripts related to the Apocalypse atelier's style: Evangeliary of the Sainte-Chapelle, Paris, Bibl. nat. Ms. lat. 8892, fol. 10v., and the Christiana Psalter, Copenhagen Gl. Kgl. S 1606-4 fol. 20v. (Branner, 1977, figs. 105 and 118). The

dow of the Passion stretches the event over an entire register, creating a horizontal effect.[10] All of the scenes of the Saint-Père window, however, are designed according to this three-medallion format, and the figures still overlap each other as in the Clermont-Ferrand and Canterbury examples.

Another unique contribution of Auxerre is its detailed depiction of the Apocalypse (pl. II). The Auxerre cycle relates more closely to manuscript than to glazing traditions. The impressive Apocalypse window of Bourges organizes a series of quadrilobed medallions that frame three monumental representations of the Son of Man in a hieratic presentation of the Second Coming. The Auxerre version, even in its fragmentary state, is a sequential narrative, unfolding as if pages in a book. Even the organization of individual scenes seems most related to the manuscripts. For example, the Rider on the White Horse (fig. 67) repeats the iconographic essentials of an illustration from the Paris Apocalypse (fig. 68).[11] John appears to the left, an angel appears from a cloud, and the rider moves majestically to the right brandishing his bow. The crowning incidents are slightly different but still place the action in the upper left of the composition. The inclusion of the scenes of John's life at the end of the series (thereby surviving the Huguenot destruction) may be the strongest link between an early group of Apocalypse illustrations and the glass. This peculiarity distinguishes what James identified as the first family group.[12] The depiction of the poison episode: Aristodemus' orders, the death of the prisoners and John drinking the cup can be seen in the Paris manuscript (fig. 71) as well as in the Auxerre glass (fig. 70).[13] Design motifs also seem similar, even when the iconographic context differs, to witness the angel surrounded by a mandorla from the Oxford Apocalypse (fig. 69) and the Woman Clothed with the Sun from Auxerre.[14] Both glass and manuscript include images of the Evangelist to the right.

The precise relationship between the manuscript cycles and the glass must await further elucidation. The English origin of the manuscripts as well as their relatively late date effectively remove them as models for the Auxerre glass. The sources of this series have yet to be explained. The loss, then, of so many scenes through the Huguenot destruction seems particularly tragic. Originally containing sixteen circular medallions arranged in clusters of four, plus a medallion in the summit, the Auxerre cycle dates as one of the earliest examples in this "new wave" of thirteenth-century Apocalypse narratives.

Le Mans medallions of these themes are grouped with scenes of the Dormition and Coronation of the Virgin (Grodecki, 1961, 86). Clermont-Ferrand is dated 1160-1170 (Grodecki, 1977, 192, 281, fig. 165). Canterbury is dated about 1200 (Caviness, 1977, 115-116, fig. 137).

[10] Dated toward 1315 (Lillich, 1978, 145-155, pl. 48).

[11] Paris, Bibl. nat. Ms. fr. 403, fol. 7v.

[12] Montague Rhodes James, *The Apocalypse in Art*, London (1931), 47-50.

[13] Paris, Bibl. nat. Ms. fr. 403, fol. 44v. The Auxerre glass also follows the tradition for the poison episode common in windows relating to John's life. At Chartres (Delaporte and Houvet, 1926, pl. XI) the events, including the crushing of the snakes in a mortar are contained in a single quatrefoil. In the Saint-Chapelle (*Corpus, France* I, 192, pls. 46-47) a servant prepares the poison in a similar manner and John drinks from the cup. The Sainte-Chapelle's original west rose of the Apocalypse is now replaced by a Renaissance window of the same theme. Grodecki, *Corpus, France* I, 81, 310-328; idem, *La Sainte-Chapelle*, Paris (1976), 56.

[14] Oxford, Bodeleian, D.4.17, fol. 6v.

The easternmost windows of the lower church, like the hemicycle of the choir, received some of the most important theological statements. Today the eastern wall of Auxerre's axial chapel contains a Tree of Jesse, Life of the Virgin and Theophilus Legend that seem logical reconstructions of an original program that very probably followed precedents established in the 1140s at Saint-Denis.[15] Suger had placed a Tree of Jesse and an Infancy window in the axial chapel, and provided a neighboring chapel with a Typological Passion. These themes appear to have become standard subjects. At Troyes, the axial chapel contains two windows of the Life of the Virgin and two of the Public Life of Christ to which Lafond adds the Tree of Jesse now in a side chapel.[16] The flat chevet of Laon shows the windows of Theophilus, the Passion and a Typological Infancy cycle.[17] Similar programs appear at Saint-Quentin.[18] The axial chapel at Le Mans was provided with windows of the Passion, Life and Miracles of the Virgin (including a Theophilus Legend), a Jesse Tree and other subjects relating to Christ as Redeemer and Mary as mediatrix.[19]

The Renaissance windows installed after the Huguenot attack showed little relation to the medieval tradition but presented the story of Job, the Three Kings and the Seven Sons of Saint Felicity.[20] Following the loss of the windows during the Franco-Prussian war, Leprévost and Steinheil replaced the Theophilus window in the right bay (after augmenting it with new panels), created a new Tree of Jesse around the seven original panels for the left and made a new Life of the Virgin for the center. The images of the Virgin and Child and Saint Stephen, each with their donor portraits, probably remained in their original positions. The juxtaposition of grisaille in the side windows and fully saturated glass in the eastern wall is comparable to the presumed organization of the Chapel of the Virgin at Saint-Germain-des-Prés dating slightly later than Auxerre.[21]

In assessing the import of Auxerre's program, one must realize that Auxerre is a cathedral; a corporate structure existing for a large secular population directed by a body of canons under the influence of a bishop. Its program inevitably reflects an amalgam of devotional attitudes. Recent research has begun to define the difference in approaches toward cathedral, monastic and collegiate programs. The programs of Canterbury Cathedral (a peculiarly English foundation fusing monastery and cathedral) and those of the abbey church of Saint-Père of Chartres and Saint-Ouen of Rouen show tightly organized and highly erudite themes, all intimately connected to the particular concerns of the monks at each foundation.[22] In all three cases the programs were laid out at a specific date and subsequent campaigns main-

---

[15] Louis Grodecki, "Les vitraux de St. Denis: L'Enfance du Christ," in *De Artibus Opuscula XL: Essays in Honor of Erwin Panofsky.* Ed. Millard Meiss, New York (1961), 177-185; idem, 1976, 71-92. See also the similar themes in the west windows of Chartres, of about 1150-1155: Passion, Life of Christ and Jesse Tree (Delaporte and Houvet, 1926, pls. I-IX).

[16] 1955, 35-43.

[17] Grodecki, *Vitrail,* 118-119.

[18] Grodecki, 1965, 180-188.

[19] Grodecki, *Vitrail,* 155. Grodecki also suggests that the original glass of the axial chapel at Bourges must have possessed windows relating to the Incarnation, such as a Childhood of Christ, Life of the Virgin and perhaps a Tree of Jesse (*Year 1200,* III, 340).

[20] Lebeuf, 1723, pièce justicative, LVII; Guilhermy, Auxerre, fol. 692; de Lasteyrie, 1857, 189.

[21] Grodecki, 1957, 34.

[22] Caviness, 1977, 106; Lillich, 1978, 80-82, 190; Lafond, *Corpus, France* IV, 16-18.

tained the integrity of the original programs. This does not seem to have been the case for secular cathedrals, where donors seem to have had considerable influence on the decisions affecting the subjects of the windows they supported. The narrative windows of the lower portions of the cathedrals appear to be the one most dependent on donor cooperation, in part explaining the apparent lack of system among the extraordinary array of Chartres' saints' lives and biblical narratives.[23]

The upper windows of cathedrals, where narratives were seldom employed, frequently displayed more evidence of ecclesiastical control. Chartres, for example, achieves coherence through four major iconographic ensembles: Marian themes in the choir clerestory hemicycle, the Old Testament in the north transept (corresponding to the sculptural decoration), the Last Judgment in the west rose and the Apocalypse in the south rose.[24] The cathedral of Tours presents a complex didactic statement in its choir clerestory and triforium.[25] The windows of Auxerre's upper choir, as well, may be seen to display careful iconographic planning. Ten of the fifteen double-lancet windows pair prophets and apostles in the familiar juxtaposition of Old and New Testament figures. Saints James, Peter, Matthew and John are identified by inscriptions, while Saint Paul seems recognizable by facial type. Nine of the ten Old Testament personages carry legible inscriptions: Moses, Aaron, Habacuc, Malachias, Abdias, Daniel, Isaias, Amos and Ezekiel. In bays 18 and 20, to the north and south of the axial bay, the patron saints of the church occupy positions of honor (figs. 86 and 89). Saint Stephen stands to the immediate right of Christ with Saint Germain, the greatest bishop saint of the cathedral, at his side. On the south, Saint Lawrence, traditionally linked with Saint Stephen,[26] is accompanied by Saint Amâtre, Germain's immediate predecessor. Thus the choir inserts Auxerre's own particular concerns into the universal system of typological exposition. The two great bishop-confessors of Auxerre are linked to Christianity's two greatest deacon-martyrs. Present not only through images in glass but through the relics guarded on the cathedral's altars, these four saintly ecclesiastics continue the line of prophets and apostles in the preceding bays. They succeed in "time" as well as "place," forming Auxerre's historical present in the plan of divine revelation.

An understanding of the concepts embodied by Auxerre's original axial bay confirms that this was a program of theological subtlety. Before 1250 the program was centered around two different images of Christ, one framed by a mandorla and surrounded by the tetramorph and the other holding a cruciform staff, blessed by the Dove of the Holy Spirit and flanked by the Virgin and Saint John, windows

[23] Delaporte and Houvet (1926, 133) believed the choice of subjects was left up to the donors. This appears to be borne out by the fact that many corporations frequently show their activities below the narratives of their patrons: the innkeepers below Saint Lubin (ibid., pl. CLXXV), the carpenter and coopers below Noah (ibid., pl. CLXXIX).

[24] Ibid., 431, 464-471, 493, 519.

[25] Papanicolaou, 1979, 199-222. The program

is based on a scholastic reinterpretation of Saint Augustine's concept of the Celestial Jerusalem including the powers of church and state and the early history of mankind.

[26] See the account of the discovery of Stephen's relics (*Golden Legend*, 411-412). Lawrence withdrew to one side of the sepulcher so that the body of Saint Stephen could be laid in the same tomb.

now relegated to the two westernmost bays of the choir (figs. 82 and 84). Their meaning has as yet not been satisfactorily explained. Undoubtedly long-standing local traditions motivated much of Auxerre's iconography, as evident in the devotional practices associated with the images displayed in the ambulatory narratives. The complexity of such traditions is attested to by the much discussed twelfth-century fresco of the mounted Christ in the vault of the crypt. An image of great power but enigmatic theology, the painting appears to fuse aspects of Christ's Entrance into Jerusalem with Christ of the Apocalypse.[27] The juxtaposition of several images of Christ in the thirteenth-century glass could then relate to earlier traditions, possibly even the lost Romanesque glazing.[28] The traditions may even go farther back.

The memory of the importance of Auxerre's school of biblical studies during the Carolingian period,[29] which produced a commentary on the Apocalypse by Haymon of Auxerre, might have had a subtle influence on the choir program as well as the Apocalypse narrative in the ambulatory. Carolingian formats such as those shown in the Christ in Majesty from the Vivian Bible (fig. 83), juxtaposing prophets and evangelists around a mandorla framed Christ, suggest Auxerre's disposition (figs. 82 and 84).[30] The four evangelists appear like antique authors at their writing desks and bust-length portraits of the four prophets, Ezekiel and Daniel at the sides, Isaiah above, and Jeremiah below the figure of Christ. The four animals hover close to the mandorla. The presentation is a fusion of Old and New Testament revelations. The four great prophets are thus linked to the four evangelists, a juxtaposition that enjoyed great popularity even throughout thirteenth-century programs.[31] The tetramorph provides the link. Ezekiel saw the four animals around the fiery chariot (Ezekiel 1:5-10) and John witnessed the "living things" surrounding the Son of Man of the Second Coming (Apocalypse 4:7-8).[32] The Auxerre axial bay repeats the stern frontality of the Carolingian image, as Christ is enthroned on the rainbow, framed by the mandorla and the four symbolic animals. The prophets appear ac-

[27] See Chap. II, n. 28.

[28] The representation of the Trinity in the "Throne of Grace" formula in the axial bay of the clerestory at La Trinité, Vendôme, is similar to the mid-twelfth-century example at Saint-Denis, and may possibly relate to an earlier program of glazing. See Meredith Lillich, "The Choir Clerestory Windows of La Trinité at Vendôme: Dating and Patronage," *Journal of the Society of Architectural Historians* 35 (1973), 240.

[29] See Chap. II, n. 6.

[30] Paris, Bibl. nat. Ms. lat. 1, fol. 329v., produced by the lay-abbot of Saint-Martin of Tours, Count Vivian (843-851) for Charles the Bald. John Beckwith, *Early Medieval Art*, New York (1964), 52-59, figs. 47, 49; André Grabar and Carl Nordenfalk, *Early Medieval Painting*, New York (1957), 148. For greater detail on the school of

Tours, see Wilhelm Koehler, *Die Karolingischen Miniaturen* I, *Die Schule von Tours*, Berlin (1930-1933).

[31] The most impressive example of this concept is undoubtedly the four evangelists riding on the shoulders of the four prophets in the lancets beneath the south rose of Chartres (Grodecki, *Vitrail*, 129, pl. XIV; idem, 1978, p. 58, fig. 29; Delaporte and Houvet, 1926, pls. CIC-CCII).

[32] See Ursula Nilgen, "Evangelisten und Evangelistensymbole," in *Lexikon der Christlichen Ikonographie* I, Rome (1968), col. 696-713, esp. 706-707; Wilhelm Neuss, *Das Buch Ezechiel in Theologie und Kunst bis zum Ende XII. Jahrhunderts*, Munster in Westf. (1912), esp. 248-253; Frederick van der Meer, *Maiestas Domini, Theophanies de l'Apocalypse dans l'art chrétien*, Rome (1938).

companied by their New Testament equivalents in the bays of the choir that radiate from this central image.

The unusual, but authentic, inscription BARTHOLOMEUS on the banderole across Christ's chest has prompted scholarly comment. A nineteenth-century historian, Daudin, speculated that a rigorous school of biblical exegesis existed at Auxerre during the thirteenth century.[33] The inscription would be a sophisticated play on the Hebrew words meaning "filius suspendentis aquas." Lafond assumed that the glass painter left his signature in a gesture similar to the prominent identification of Gislebertus in the tympanum of the cathedral of Autun.[34]

Forming a visual and theological complement to this impressive image was the lancet to the left, Christ flanked by Mary and John, now in the westernmost choir bay to the north. The window is an iconographic rarity: Mary acclaims Christ by her gestures, she does not mourn; John shows a peculiar long physiognomy and beard, perhaps indicating that the image refers to John the Baptist rather than the Evangelist.[35] This identification would then explain the prominent Dove of the Holy Spirit in the window's summit. The personification of the Sun and Moon are traditional to the Crucifixion, but the central image of Christ triumphant with cruciform staff follows the tradition of Resurrections. I would suggest that we are dealing with a conflation of temporal events, as opposed to the conflation of eschatological events in the companion lancet. The image of Christ between the Virgin and Saint John evokes the Messiah announced at the Baptism in the Jordan, the suffering Christ of the Crucifixion, and the Christ whose victory over death is shown in the Resurrection.[36] Christ, and above all, His humanity, is thus manifest through time. In the image to the right, faith alone reveals the divinity of Christ, beyond the limitations of time or place. Auxerre's axial bay reconciles an ancient tradition of Christ as Supreme Judge, Lord of Creation with the new Gothic sensibility toward the human nature of the second person of the Trinity.[37]

This unique presentation among glazing programs of the period was perhaps too idiosyncratic to remain unchallenged. The present axial lancets of the Crucifixion and Christ in Majesty were commissioned shortly after 1250 very probably by the new bishop, Guy de Mello.[38] This substitution brought the Auxerre program more into accord with the Passion-oriented iconography of the Sainte-Chapelle. The central window of the Sainte-Chapelle was dedicated to the Passion, as was the central

---

[33] E. Daudin, "Une verrière de la cathédrale d'Auxerre," *Annuaire statistique et monumental du département de l'Yonne* 36 (1870-1872), 193-196.

[34] Lafond, 1958a, 64; Denis Grivot and George Zarnecki, *Gislebertus, sculpteur d'Autun*, Paris (1960), esp. 13-14. A far more modest signature is found at the bottom of one of the Joseph windows in the cathedral of Rouen (Ritter, 1926, pl. XIV).

[35] It should be noted that the Vivian Bible presents John as a bearded figure. John is also bearded in the Apocalypse manuscripts cited here.

[36] There is no way of determining whether the nineteenth-century Sacrifice of Abraham in the lower part of the window bears any relationship to the original program. The theme clearly stresses the concept of a suffering Messiah.

[37] One of the most easily recognizable shifts from a Romanesque to a Gothic sculptural program was the substitution of the suffering Messiah of a Last Judgment for the Divine Presence of the apocalyptic vision. See especially, Mâle, 1923, 369-380, and Sauerländer, 1972, 27-32.

[38] The most important windows of a cathedral

window of Saint-Julien-du-Sault. Although the presentation of a Crucifixion in the easternmost windows of the building was a common disposition that may be traced back to the late-twelfth-century program of Saint-Remi of Reims,[39] the coincidence of the Parisian style and the radical reorganization of the program would argue for a clear attempt to imitate the royal chapel.[40]

Like the hemicycle lancets, the roses of the hemicycle bays display unusual iconographic juxtapositions.[41] The inclusion of both the combat of Virtues and Vices and the Liberal Arts is unique in thirteenth-century glass programs. To the north, eight Virtues triumph over eight corresponding Vices. In the central rose, above the images of Christ, John the Baptist, symbols of the evangelists and three angels surround the image of the Lamb of God. To the south, seven Liberal Arts supplemented by Philosophy, the culmination of worldly knowledge, represent the sublimation of the secular world to the realm of divine grace. The roses of the twelve remaining windows show some decorative infill, but also commemorate the prophets Jeremias, Malachias, Job, Micheas, Habacuc, Elias and Daniel.

The pictorial cycles in the lower level of the choir repeat typological expositions in perhaps a broader sense. Many of the Old Testament personages prefigure Christian heroes, as David prefigures Christ in the sculptural program of the facade. The Creation (51) perhaps parallels the creation of the Christian Church, through the lives and miracles of Peter and Paul (57 and 58). The lives of the patriarchs, Moses (56) and Noah, Abraham and Lot (52) typify the lives of the apostles, Andrew (55) and James (70) and the early Christian saints, Stephen (70), Lawrence (57), Nicholas (67 and 71), Martin (66), Mammès (50) and the saints of local tradition, Eloi (71), Bris (74) and Germain (67). Eustache's experiences (66) of early favor, then life of persecution and bondage, form a telling parallel with the story of the change of fortunes of Joseph in the Old Testament (53). Auxerre includes the parable of the Prodigal Son, which may serve as exemplar for two Old Testament and two New Testament penitents: David (49) and Samson (56), and Mary Magdalene (73) and Mary of Egypt (72).

Auxerre possesses a window of the Tree of Jesse, a traditional visualization of the translation of the Old Law into the New Dispensation through the coming of Christ. Mary's position as mankind's intercessor is commemorated in the Legend of Theophilus (63). One thus finds the Old Law transformed into the New through the Jesse Tree, the confirmation of the Early Church through the outpouring of the

---

program, the hemicycle glass was frequently the gift of the most prestigious donor. For example, the axial window of the Tree of Jesse in the cathedral of Soissons was offered by Philip Augustus (Grodecki, 1965, 188).

[39] Dated 1180-1185, the Virgin and Child appears in the axial bay of the clerestory and the Crucifixion immediately below in the tribune (Grodecki, 1977, 133-138, figs. 113, 114). The Saint-Remi program inspired the program of the cathedral of Reims and that of Saint-Père of Chartres (Lillich, 1978, 93).

[40] Sites linked to the Sainte-Chapelle program show the same emphasis on the Passion. Troyes Cathedral's central window of about 1245 is dedicated to the Passion (Grodecki, *Vitrail*, 143) as is the axial window of Tours, dated 1255 (Papanicolaou, 1979, 33-37, 203, pls. 15-19).

[41] Auxerre's hemicycle roses have received particular attention beginning with early studies in the nineteenth century. Cahier and Martin, 1841-1844, planche d'étude, XVII; Westlake, *A History of Design in Painted Glass*, London (1881), pl. 50a and b; Mâle, 1923, 82ff.

Spirit at Pentecost (57 and 72), and the final culmination of the epic of salvation in the Apocalypse (68).

Auxerre's extraordinary emphasis on Old Testament themes, Creation (pl. III), Noah, Abraham and Lot, Moses and a Second Genesis cycle, David, Joseph and Samson, deserves special note.[42] Only the Sainte-Chapelle displays a wider variety. The portal sculpture also stressed Old Testament subjects, showing a Creation cycle on the left, the Joseph story in the central portal, David and Bathsheba to the right and a large relief of the Judgment of Solomon. The cathedral should be viewed as a whole since the sculptural programs, including the much later south portal of Saint Stephen and north portal of Saint Germain, repeat many of the themes depicted in the glass.[43]

The original glass of the choir's hemicycle presented a conflation of theological themes portraying the Dual Nature of Christ and the relation of the winning of salvation in time to its manifestation throughout eternity.[44] I am reluctant to see the program solely as a typological ordering, although the general mode of thought enabled almost any subject to be interpreted in a typological argument.[45] Rather, we should be aware of the various levels of religious imagery. The glass and sculpture certainly display an aesthetically arresting group of narratives, engaging even on a secular level. They can be seen as moral fables, encouraging emulation among the faithful, or as typological systems stressing the continuity of the Old and New Testaments in an unbroken manifestation of Divine Providence. For the more learned the great theological questions of the Nature of God, Man's Fall and Redemption, Death and Immortality are incorporated into the very fabric of the edifice, just as medieval man saw them incorporated into the fabric of existence.

In closing, it is essential to note that certain of Auxerre's windows refer to specifically Burgundian themes, themes also present at other glazing sites. Chief among them is the legend of Saint Mary Magdalene. This legend is almost a textbook example of medieval hagiographic methods.[46] The "historical" Magdalene appears to be a conflation of three women mentioned in the New Testament, the repentant sinner who washed Christ's feet with her tears (Luke 7:36-47), Mary of Bethany,

[42] See introd. by Sydney Cockerell to M. R. James, *A Book of Old Testament Illustrations of the Middle of the Thirteenth Century*, Cambridge (1927), 33.

[43] Sauerländer, 1972, 499-501, pls. 282-287; C. Enlart., "La sculpture des portails de la cathédral d'Auxerre du XIIIe à la fin du XIVe siècle," *Congrès archéologique de France* 74 (1907), 599-626; E. Daudin, "La cathédrale d'Auxerre; sculptures des portails," *Annuaire statistique et monumental du département de l'Yonne.* 36 (1870-1872), 161-192, and ibid., 37 (1873), 3-39; Paul Deschamps, *La Cathédrale d'Auxerre*, Paris (1948), for illustrations; Porée, 1926, 44-76, most recently, Folke Nordström, *The Auxerre Reliefs*, Uppsala (1974).

[44] See Jan van der Meulen ("Chartres: Die Weltschopfung in Historische Sicht," *Francia* 5 [1977], 81-126), who identifies a Creation scene in the left portal of the west facade, linking it to the archivolts of the north transept portal. Van der Meulen's work brings to light the importance of the relationship of all parts of a medieval building and adds much to our appreciation of the complexity of medieval programs.

[45] See especially, Beryl Smalley, *The Study of the Bible in the Middle Ages*, Notre Dame Press, Indiana (1978).

[46] See especially Réau, 1955-1959, III/2, 846-859 and V. Saxer, *La Légende de Marie Madeleine*, Paris (1955).

the sister of Martha and Lazarus (Luke 11:39) and Mary Magdalene who first saw the risen Christ (John 20:1-18).[47] Mary Magdalene is also identified by Luke as "Mary, who is called the Magdalene, from whom seven devils had gone out" (Luke 8:2), allowing for the elaboration of her career as penitent in the wilderness of Provence. This aspect of Mary's persona is connected to the similar actions of Mary of Egypt, who in turn, reflects the great emphasis the early church in the east placed on the hermetic life of physical abnegation.

Outside of Burgundy, during the first half of the thirteenth century, only the Chartres window comes at all close to duplicating the extraordinary attention given to the Magdalene's adventures at Auxerre and at Semur-en-Auxois. Bourges does not represent any scene outside the biblical sources (fig. 43), a decision probably reflecting the lack of local investment in the confirmation of her relics on Burgundian soil. Both Auxerre and Semur support the legends made popular by the shrine of the Magdalene in the abbey of Vézelay. Auxerre shows her activities in Provence and her death, the lower portions of the window presumably being dedicated to the biblical narrative. Semur, I believe, contains the most complete of all the cycles, depicting her early life, sojurn in Provence, miracles, and death (including that of Martha) and then the translation of her relics by the monks of Vézelay.

In the later part of the century, very possibly into the 1280s, three windows in the cathedral of Clermont-Ferrand were dedicated to the saint. The first window contains the biblical events, ending with Christ's appearance to Mary after His resurrection. The central window recounts the journey to Marseilles, pilgrimage of the provincial leader and the story of Saint Maximien. The third lancet concludes with Mary's retreat into the wilderness and the events surrounding her death.[48] The Clermont cycle is very close to the 1289 date of the discovery that the body of the Magdalene still remained in Provence. Only when the Clermont glass is firmly dated can its relationship, if any, to the Burgundian-Provençal controversy be determined.

Saint Andrew is featured in the windows of Auxerre, Troyes and Notre-Dame of Dijon, reflecting his popularity in the region. The cult of Andrew at Auxerre was established early and continued throughout the Middle Ages. Andrew's position for the whole of Burgundy, as well as Auxerre, seems to be connected to an early legend. The ducal house of Burgundy regarded Andrew as its patron saint since the apostle was believed to have carried the gospel to Scythia, the ancestral home of the Burgundian tribes.[49] The patronage of Andrew, as well as that of Saint George, supported the well-known expansionist policies of the Burgundian house. Saint Andrew is recognizable by his cross as one of the six apostles sculpted for the abbey of Rougemont and one of the saints and apostles featured in the five windows of the facade of the abbey of the Madeleine of Vézelay.[50]

---

[47] This identification already appeared in the Gospel of John (John 11:2).

[48] The final two medallions showing the translation of relics to Vézelay are twentieth-century restorations.

[49] Réau, 1955-1959, III/1, 76-84; *Golden Leg-*

end, 8.

[50] Pierre Quarré, "Les statues de l'atelier de Rougemont," *Year 1200*, III, 580, 582. The other statues at Vézelay can be identified as Mary Magdalene, John the Evangelist, Peter, Paul and Lazarus(?).

The iconography of the three Andrew glass cycles does not seem to be related to any sources outside Burgundy itself. Indeed, the three sites exhibit extremely close interdependencies in their iconographic narrative, although the painting styles of the windows derive from very different sources. Certain key scenes, the exorcism of a child showing a demon leaping from the child's mouth and Andrew's reception by the Niceans at the city gate, are hagiographic types than can be found also in the narratives of the miracles of Saint Martin of Tours or other saints. The resurrection of the young man from his bed is actually very similar to the scenes of Saint Peter resurrecting Tabitha. The demons strangling the inhabitants of Nicea in their tublike bath (fig. 148) and Andrew's subsequent exorcism of the evil spirits in the form of dogs, who poke their heads up from coffinlike boxes (fig. 24), are unmistakably of local origin. Such divergence of iconographic and stylistic models encourages us to look more closely at the complexity of the artistic product. Such a repetition of exact compositions would imply that the model was a visual, not a written, one, no matter how popular or available hagiographic texts concerning Saint Andrew might have been. Such a visual source could be conceived as a handbook of designs in the possession of the atelier. That these handbooks might be ultimately connected to a single manuscript source is possible, but in the case of the Burgundian Andrew cycle, no evidence has been found to support this. One is also faced again with the possibility that the glass cycles themselves might have served as modes of transmission for the iconography.

VI

CONCLUSION

*An art historian, then, is a humanist whose "primary material"
consists of those records which have come down to us in the
forms of works of art.* (Erwin Panofsky)[1]

Perhaps the most general conclusion reached from a study of thirteenth-century
glazing programs in Burgundy is that it confirms the importance of Paris as the
major influence of its time. In Lafond's words, "the real center was Paris, the seat
of the Royal court and the world-famous university, a place where the glass painters'
ovens need never be put out."[2] This assessment of artistic activity corresponds with
that of historians of political movements and social relationships: Paris is seen to be
a crucial area for innovations in education, for the rights of the bourgeoisie and for
concepts of modern nationhood. Here it is shown that where glazing and manuscript
illumination are concerned, five of the eight Burgundian ateliers show some relationship with traditions in the capital. In two cases, the Saint-Germain-lès-Corbeil
atelier and the Isaiah Master's atelier, it has been possible to identify the same
workshop tradition in windows in Burgundy and in the capital. The Genesis and
Infancy of Christ—Glorification of the Virgin ateliers show the influence of Parisian
work from the abbey of Gercy and the abbey of Saint-Germain-des-Prés. The
Apocalypse atelier has been identified with Parisian painting styles. The manuscripts,
as well, were part of this development. Branner has noted that in the early years
of the century the better manuscripts were still produced by regional centers.[3] Only
the younger and presumably less artistically mature painters migrated to the capital.
By 1220 the pattern had altered encouraging the finest illuminators to shift their
locales. This development thus parallels the eclipse by Paris, by the third decade of
the thirteenth century, of regional centers, such as that of the Poitou, the Laonnais
or the Lyonnais.

Analysis of the Burgundian programs contributes also to our knowledge of the
composition and working habits of the medieval glazing atelier. It bears out Caviness'
definition of the "workshop" as a group of artists sharing the same model books.[4]
For each new artistic expression there seems to have been a correspondingly indi-

---

[1] "The History of Art as a Humanistic Disci-
pline," in *Meaning in the Visual Arts*, New York
(1955), 10, originally published in *The Meaning
of the Humanities*, ed. T. M. Green, Princeton
(1940), 89-118.
[2] "The Stained Glass Decoration of Lincoln

Cathedral in the Thirteenth Century," *Archaeological Journal* 103 (1946), 153.
[3] "Manuscript Painting in Paris around 1200,"
Year 1200, III, 173-185.
[4] 1977, 36.

vidual set of medallion patterns and decorative motifs. Each workshop seems to have maintained a repertoire of ornamental systems as well as figural types that were differently incorporated according to the personality of the executing artist. Thus it is possible to see the Genesis atelier as a single unit despite its inclusion of a Genesis Master and a Genesis Inheritor, as well as individual assistants whose hands I have not tried here to isolate.

The ability of medieval artists to cooperate with each other, even to the extent of sharing designs or working on the same window, is also borne out by the study of Burgundian programs. The Saint Margaret window at Saint-Julien-du-Sault was most likely designed by the Isaiah Master's atelier since it uses a curved armature and repeats a pattern from the Sainte-Chapelle. The figures, however, are undisputably products of the atelier of Auxerre's Apocalypse Master, which even then appears to have modified its painting style to bring it closer to the grace and calligraphic swiftness of the Isaiah Master's oeuvre.

The individual modifications undergone by many of the ateliers at Auxerre also confirm this sense of cooperative interaction. The borrowings among the later windows of the Genesis group and the windows of the Saint Eustache Master's atelier sometimes make precise assessment of individual responsibilities difficult. The ateliers of both the Isaiah Master and the Saint-Germain-lès-Corbeil Master made significant changes when working at Auxerre. The Isaiah Master no longer used curved ironwork as a support system although medallion effects similar to those of the Sainte-Chapelle and Saint-Julien-du-Sault were maintained. The Saint-Germain-lès-Corbeil atelier elaborated its figural compositions and background settings in order to harmonize them with the narrative formats already in use in the cathedral.

Modifications in response to the demands of placement and program demonstrate the sensitivity of the medieval atelier and its essential role in the iconographic import of the project. A shift from small- to large-scale figure painting is documented in the ateliers of both the Apocalypse and Isaiah Masters, a change that emphasizes the hieratic character of the presentation by exaggerating the features and by a bolder and more two-dimensional use of line.

That model books traveled from place to place with the atelier is clear from the fact that the size, cut lines and even the drawing of heads and drapery traced from the windows at Auxerre are identical to those taken from the Sainte-Chapelle. The use of cartoons for so many of the Sainte-Chapelle panels assures that exact-size drawings were employed by the glazing ateliers.[5] Since such cartoons existed as drawings on chalked boards, they were certainly not carried from place to place. Model books were. When an artist began work at a new site he had to transfer the reduced designs in the model book to exact-size drawings, inevitably leading to stylistic transformations. The copying of models by an assistant for later use after

[5] *Corpus, France* I, 91. For additional observations on the use of cartoons see Meredith Lillich, "A Stained Glass Apostle from Sées Cathedral (Normandy) in the Victoria and Albert Museum," *The Burlington Magazine* 119 (1977), 497-500, and idem, 1978, 49, note 9, for Saint-Père of Chartres and other sites.

the break-up of the atelier would seem a logical step in the transmission of the craft.

It must be emphasized that these workshops did, indeed, travel. For example, the Saint-Germain-lès-Corbeil atelier produced windows at four different sites—Saint-Germain, Troyes, Semur-en-Auxois and Auxerre—during a time span of no more than fifteen years. It should not seem at all unusual to find churches geographically close sharing ateliers. Branner has suggested that the most logical method of engaging an architect was to employ one who had recently completed a particular building that had been seen and approved by the patron.[6] In all probability the artists of these windows were hired in the same manner. The method of apportioning the work among the ateliers is hard to determine. Certainly it depended on a variety of factors: the health or longevity of the dominant master, his ability to work in the specific situation required, the availability of funds and perhaps even the competition among several patrons.

Analysis of the windows supports the growing consensus that the medieval atelier enjoyed a much greater variety of representational resources than previously supposed.[7] The origins of stylistic inspiration, figural design and iconographic systems were often quite far apart. The Apocalypse atelier employed an iconographic guide that comes from an entirely different source from that of its painting style. The Andrew cycles at Auxerre, Troyes and Notre-Dame of Dijon share identical iconographic motifs but incorporate these stylistically in completely different ways.

This study also makes it possible to date the many campaigns. Previous opinion put Auxerre's windows in the first third of the thirteenth century and attributed the patronage to Henri de Villeneuve who was buried in the choir in 1234. There is a representation of an Agnus Dei in the rose of the axial bay of the choir and Lebeuf noted that the reverse of Henri's episcopal seal carried the same image.[8] Lafond pointed out that the Agnus Dei serves primarily as a symbol of Christ, not as an identification of the bishop, but he still attributed the glass to Henri's episcopate, following de Lasteyrie, Bonneau and Fourrey.[9] Grodecki, noting the stylistic diversity among many of the windows, stated that only some of the glass might be dated to Henri's episcopate.[10]

Indeed, only two of the ateliers began work before Henri's death. The Genesis atelier, responsible for fifteen of the thirty-two ambulatory windows, started work during the closing years of the choir's construction about 1233 and continued through 1244. Another atelier, under the direction of the Eustache Master, probably arrived at the same time. The atelier associated with the windows of Saint-Germain-lès-Corbeil, which produced the Auxerre windows of the Life of Saint Nicholas and the

[6] 1960, 5.

[7] See also Lillich (1978, esp. 147-156) for the Passion window of Saint-Père de Chartres, and Caviness (1977, esp. 120-138) for the design sources of Canterbury's typological windows. Both authors present a wide variety of material that served to determine the ultimate composition of a window.

[8] *Mémoires*, I, 402.

[9] The tradition ascribing the work to Henri's patronage was so well established in the nineteenth century that during Vessière's restoration the lower portion of the axial lancet of Christ in Majesty was provided with an image of the bishop based on designs by Steinheil. Lafond, 1958a, 60; de Lasteyrie, 1858; Bonneau, 1885, 296; Fourrey, 1929, 6.

[10] *Vitrail*, 140.

Relics of Stephen, probably arrived five years later, about 1237. A fourth atelier began with the windows of the Apocalypse and Saint Eloi in the ambulatory and then expanded to produce all of the large standing figures in the upper choir and the axial chapel, probably working from 1235 to 1245. The windows of Saint Martin and Saints Peter and Paul and the present axial bay of the choir were produced by the atelier of the Isaiah Master of the Sainte-Chapelle shortly after 1250.

Auxerre's glass was completed some fifteen years after the building itself but the other Burgundian campaigns seem to have been carried out closer to the dates of actual construction. One might add that this cathedral was unusual in that the major portion of its initial expenses were paid for by the bishop. Perhaps its canons were pressed to finish the work and the glazing of the windows could be the most easily postponed. Through a comparison with examples of the so-called "late-classicizing style" the glass in the five lancets below the north rose of Notre-Dame of Dijon appears to have been produced in the mid-1230s, a date that corresponds to the construction of the transepts. Glass at Semur-en-Auxois can be dated to the early 1220s for the Magdalene Master and about 1228 for the window of Saint Peter. Confirming Lafond's studies are the dates of 1245-1250 for the glass of Saint-Julien-du-Sault and shortly after 1250 for that of Saint-Fargeau.[11]

There are no written records concerning individual donors of the windows, and except for the figures below the images of Saint Stephen and the Virgin and Child of the axial chapel, they are not depicted in the windows themselves. The inscription HVRRICVS PRESBITER appears to refer to one of the priests of the cathedral, but he is not recorded elsewhere. Branner was careful to point out that bishops were normally not the prime instigators for building campaigns.[12] We sometimes learn of individuals, secular, like Louis IX, or religious, like Guy de Mello or Gauthier Cornut, but more frequently the patrons of a religious edifice were the members of the religious communities whose livelihood and daily activities were so closely tied to these monuments. The actions of these corporate bodies are far less documented than those of prominent churchmen and nobles. For the cathedral of Auxerre, most of the windows probably depend on the actions of the cathedral chapter, of which certain members asserted a more active interest than others—perhaps the individuals pictured in donor positions in the glass of the Lady Chapel.

The engagement of an atelier from the Sainte-Chapelle, as documented for four windows in Saint-Julien-du-Sault and windows in the ambulatory and clerestory of Auxerre, has been ascribed to the motives of patronage that combined admiration for the beauty of the work, availability of workmen and a keen understanding of the association of this style with the personality of France's saintly king, Louis IX. Such instances are rare, but serve to show that the medieval patron was strongly influenced by the context of the model. A work of art that became a "prime object" in many artistic undertakings did not always display aesthetic or technical perfection. Its significance, and perhaps its easily assimilable characteristics, encouraged its

[11] 1958b, 368; idem, 1948, 127.   [12] 1960, 4-5, 39.

replication.[13] It was not the individual quality of the painting style of the Sainte-Chapelle that was so important but the conception of the chapel as a unified whole, an interior space that engulfed the spectator in glowing color and light. The summary painting style, restricted use of iconographic models and limited repertoire of figural types all supported this harmonious effect—an effect which transformed the building into a symbol of France's preeminence as leader of western Christendom under Saint Louis and contributed to the swift dissemination of this style in architecture and stained glass.

Finally, a word about quality. Some of the windows rank among the most impressive works of art of their time. Viewers have, indeed, been sensitive to the extraordinary effect of glass in its setting, but it is important to single out the execution of individual panels. The Auxerre windows of Saint Eustache and Saint Lawrence, or the Passion window of Saint-Germain-lès-Corbeil, display artistic determination of a supremely high order. Each window is conceived in accordance with the demands of the narrative, achieving a technical interaction between composition of individual panels and medallion format. We experience power in dramatic characterization supported by great sophistication in painting style. Here, clearly, is "primary material" not only of significance but of beauty.

[13] The extraordinary vaulting of Saint-Philibert of Tournus (Kenneth J. Conant, *Carolingian and Romanesque Architecture*, New York [1978], 141-146) or the complex iconography of Suger's windows of Moses and Allegories of Saint Paul (Grodecki, 1976, 93-102, idem, "Vitraux allégoriques de Saint-Denis," *Art de France* I [1961], 19-46) were far too idiosyncratic to allow multiple replication.

Appendices

Appendix One

Summary of the Restoration Campaigns of
the Cathedral of Saint-Etienne of Auxerre and of its Glass

(Based primarily on unpublished documents in the national archives of the Commission des Monuments Historiques de France: Dossier 1566bis, la Cathédrale d'Auxerre.)

1567	(Sept. 27) Destruction by Huguenots; clerestory glass loses lower portions, ambulatory legends truncated.
1570	(May 3) Chauvin, mason of Auxerre, engaged to fill many windows with masonry (Archives de l'Yonne, E 489, III/1st series).
1572-1593	Restoration directed by Pigal, glass painter of Auxerre; clerestory figures reglazed and repainted in lower portions, ambulatory glass regrouped in smaller number of windows, many windows shortened by masonry infill. Renaissance glass placed in axial chapel (61, 62, 63) and ambulatory (69); remaining windows filled with clear glass (Lebeuf, 1723, pièce justicative LVII).
1790-1802	Revolutionary period, no deliberate damage to glass, but neglect causes deterioration.
1806	Consul General of the Department authorizes 6,000 francs for maintenance of the cathedral.
1805-1810	(?) Releading (?) of many panels by Touquet, glass painter of Auxerre.
1841-1844	Cahier and Martin's drawings of hemicycle glass (1841-1844 planche d'étude XVII).
1848	Storm damages ambulatory glass.
1854, 1858, 1864	Visits of François de Guilhermy: panel by panel description. (Guilhermy, Auxerre).
1856	Minister of the Interior commissions Viollet-le-Duc to ascertain artistic merit of the cathedral.
1863	Piéplu, architect of the Monuments Historiques prepares estimate of restoration costs for cathedral: glass, masonry, and covering.
1866	Joseph Veissière, glass painter from Seignelay, awarded contract for restoration of glass. Works with brother using designs of Steinheil.
1866-1875	Restoration of ambulatory and clerestory windows.
1870	Cathedral hit by artillery shells, which struck east windows of axial chapel and damaged the Renaissance glass. Virgin and Child also damaged.
1874	Veissière creates windows of David (49) and Saint Mammès (50) around remaining thirteenth-century panels.
1879	Steinheil and Leprévost awarded contract for reglazing of the axial chapel: new window of the Life of the Virgin (62), Tree of Jesse (61) incorporates seven original panels, Legend of Theophilus (63) at least one-third original.

1885	Bonneau publishes description of cathedral glass.
1924	A. David estimates costs of restoring ambulatory windows.
1925-1927	David cleans and releads ambulatory glass. He regroups disparate panels for legends of Saint Martin, Saints Peter and Paul, Saint Bris, Saint Vincent, Relics of Saint Stephen, Saint Germain, Apocalypse, Saint Eloi and Ascension-Pentecost after suggestions made by Bonneau and transmitted by Fourrey.
1929	Fourrey publishes review of ambulatory windows in new placement.
1930	David restores window of Noah, Abraham and Lot.
1930-1939	Photographs of ambulatory glass by Robert Metcalf; copies in the Dayton Art Institute, Dayton, Ohio.
1939-1950	Windows taken down during war: releading and some repainting by R. Moreau, glass painter of Auxerre. Panel by panel photographic record taken for Monuments Historiques.

Appendix Two

Summary of the Restoration Campaigns of the Church of Saint-Pierre of Saint-Julien-du-Sault and of its Glass

(Based primarily on unpublished documents in the national archives of the Commission des Monuments Historiques de France: Dossier 1578, Saint-Julien-du-Sault.)

1337-1453	Severe damage to church during the Hundred Years' War.
1536-1557	Archepiscopate of Cardinal Louis de Bourbon at Sens. Restoration of the upper parts of the choir and vaults, vaults of the ambulatory nave side-aisle vaults (Tonnelier, 1842, 109; Vallery-Radot, 1958b, 358-365).
1773	Chapter suppressed and Saint-Pierre becomes a parish church (Quantin, 1868, 168).
1837	(Nov. 8) Evaluation by sub-prefect of Joigny concerning historical monuments in his district. Statement that Saint-Pierre of Saint-Julien-du-Sault was "a medieval monument in the Gothic style and its windows would be most precious if they had not been so often repaired by inept hands" (Forestier, 1959, II, 462).
1841	Saint-Julien-du-Sault classified as a "monument historique."
1844	Joseph Vessière at work releading the ambulatory windows.
1846	Viollet-le-Duc surveys the glass and comments on its "great beauty."
1850	(June 9) Letter from Girard, dean of the church, relates that the Vessière restoration had been interrupted with only four out of ten windows repaired.
1864	(Sept.) Visit of François de Guilhermy noting windows in the same position as today (Guilhermy, Saint-Julien-du-Sault).
1868	Maximilien Quantin publishes brief description naming subject of the windows that corresponds closely to Guilhermy's notes (Quantin, 1868, 167-168).
1880	Leprévost and Steinheil begin new restoration campaign.
1885	Leprévost signs agreement to continue campaign with the younger Steinheil after the death of Steinheil's father.
1890	(June 23) Paul Boeswillwald, chief architect of the Commission des Monuments Historiques de France, reports on the completion of ten windows out of fourteen.
1901	(Jan. 18) Four remaining windows, Theophilus, Infancy-Glorification and two Late Gothic windows appear in bill from Steinheil.
1904	(June 13) Letter from the supervising architect, Louzier, on the inventory of Leprévost's Parisian studio after the glass painter's death. Fragments from the Late Gothic and Renaissance periods had been kept in the shop and not put back in the church. Louzier believed the fragments deserved releading and returned them to Saint-Julien-du-Sault. In all probability,

the panels of Saint-Julien-du-Sault glass found in museums and private collections and the copies placed in the church emanated from Leprévost's shop.

1914   Havilland-Bushnell (*Storied Windows*, London [1914], 230-234) publishes description of glass, linking it to Parisian traditions, and suggests Saint Louis and Robert d'Artois as donors.

1926   Iconographic description of glass by Gabrielle Rheims (1926).

1939-1950   Windows taken down during war. Restoration and releading begun in 1945 by G. David. Panel by panel photographs taken for the Monuments Historiques.

1950   (Nov. 23) Masons replace windows in church under direction of Jean Trouvelot, architect.

Summary of the Restoration Campaigns of the Church of Notre-Dame of Dijon and of its Glass

(Based primarily on unpublished documents in the national archives of the Commission des Monuments Historiques de France: Dossiers 357-359, Notre-Dame de Dijon.)

1651	During the civil discord following the Thirty Years' War, canon shot from the château by supporters of the prince of Condé breaks three windows and damaged several others. Glazier Jean de Prades engaged to rework the windows using white glass. The colored glass was to be relegated to borders of no more than "quatre pouces" (Fyot, 1910, 139).
1688	Boulmier, master glazier (maître-vitrier) of Dijon, proposes to take out the old glass in two windows facing the altar and replace it with white glass, as he had done for some chapels (Fyot, 1910, 140).
1688	(Apr. 4) Storm damages south rose and Boulmier proposes to replace it with white glass (ibid.).
1838	Replacement of windows destroyed during the revolution by "windows without figures" (ibid.).
1851	Watercolor drawings of five thirteenth-century lancets made by T. Joliment (3rd and 4th lancets published in Oursel, 1938, p. 83).
1863	(Mar. 6) Statement of actions necessary for restoration of Notre-Dame: purchase for destruction of the house "Mallebranche" and shops surrounding church—repair of supports and buttresses—repair of tower.
1863	(Dec. 31) Paul Boeswillwald, Inspecting Architect for the Monuments Historiques, surveys church. Restoration begins.
1865	(Aug. 17) Report on restoration campaign, published in *Mémoires de la commission des antiquités de la Côte d'Or* 7 (1865-1869), 27-38. Viollet-le-Duc voices concern over possible destruction of valuable buildings of a later date in an attempt to clear the area around Notre-Dame. He warns that a choir filled with white glass will give too harsh an illumination to the interior.
1865	(approximately) Viollet-le-Duc makes drawings of foliage in border designs of the 5th lancet under the north rose (published in Viollet-le-Duc, 1875, 402-403, fig. 12).
1873	(or shortly before this date) Didron restores the thirteenth-century glass under the north rose.
1874	Decision to fill the windows with stained glass of the thirteenth-century style. The windows of Chartres and the ancient panels at Notre-Dame are to be taken as models.
1875	(Dec. 1) Minister of Instruction Publique des Cultes et de Beaux-Arts states that the church has been opened for services. All parts of the church are repaired, with the exception of the porch and the west facade.

1880-1885	Restoration of the facade with new sculpture.
1896	(May 20) Didron speaks of fifteen years of work, with the modern windows nearly complete, stating, "The project comprising the windows of the choir, the chapels, and the arms of the transepts, as well as the windows of the side aisles of the nave had been approved after the restoration of the old windows located in the lancets underneath the roses (*sic*) of the transept." The architect Laisne supervises the installation.
1897	Completion of the modern windows (Fyot, 1910, 154-160).
1939	The five lancets under the north rose taken down during World War II (not photographed for Monuments Historiques inventory).
1945	(June 9) Bill for restoration and reinstallation of the thirteenth-century glass.

Appendix Four

Reconstruction of the Program of the Axial Chapel of Auxerre

THE POWER OF THE VIRGIN'S INTERCESSION

(L: = Left; C: = Center; R: = Right; N: = North; S: = South)

East Wall (MH 248 924)

L: 61   Jesse Tree.

C: 62   Life of the Virgin or Infancy of Christ (lost).

R: 63   Legend of Theophilus.

Side Walls

N: 59   Virgin and Child with donor in grisaille frame SCA MARIA: HVRRICVS PRES-
BITER (MH 248 923).

   60   Grisaille (MH 60-N-182).

S: 64   Grisaille (MH 60-N-183).

   65   Stephen and donor in grisaille frame S. STEPHANVS EPISCOP: DEI: IN: HO-
NORE: ILLVD: FECIT (MH 248 925).

Appendix Five

Reconstruction of the Hemicycle Program of the Choir of Auxerre

CHRIST MANIFEST IN TIME AND CHRIST THE ETERNAL JUDGE

(L: = Left; C: = Center; R: = Right)

L: 18a Germain, fifth bishop of Auxerre (MH 229 054—MH 229 055).

18b Stephen, deacon martyr and patron saint of the cathedral (MH 229 054—MH 229 055).

Rose: Virtues and Vices (MH 229 056—MH 229 059).
Entire bay 53-N-819.

C: 19a Christ holding cruciform staff, with Sol and Luna, the dove of the Holy Spirit and the Virgin and John the Baptist (a conflation of the Baptism, Crucifixion and Resurrection) (MH 229 013—MH 229 016).

19b Christ seated and holding banderole with the inscription BARTOLOMEVS. Mandorla and four symbols of the evangelists surround Christ (a conflation of the vision of Ezekiel and the Apocalypse) (MH 229 050—MH 229 053).

Rose: symbols of the four evangelists (or animals of the Apocalypse), three censing angels, John the Baptist, Lamb of God in the center (MH 229 068—MH 229 072).

R: 20a Lawrence, deacon martyr LAVRENCIVS (MH 229 073—MH 229 075).

20b Amâtre, fourth bishop of Auxerre AMATOR (MH 229 073—MH 229 075).

Rose: Seven Liberal Arts and Philosophy (MH 229 076—MH 229 079).
Entire bay 53-N-358.

18 Virtues and Vices (MH 229 056—MH 229 059).
Chastity CASTITAS, seated, holding book and palm (hand with portions of books and palm old): Luxury LUXURIA, standing woman holding a mirror (mirror modern, large portions of body old, some inscription old).

Humility HUMILITAS, seated woman holding shield with dove (first part of inscription, upper portions of body, parts of shield old): Drunkenness EBRIETAS, figure drinks from a cup (modern, but large portions of body, old). Originally complementing Sobriety.

Patience PACIENCIA, frontal, seated woman holding a shield with the Lamb of God (large part old): Despair DESPERACIO, figure thrusts sword into chest (most of robe and inscription old).

Justice IVISTICIA, seated woman holding staff and book (heavily restored): Sorrow DOLOR, seated figure tearing hair (large portions of robes old).

Concord CONCORDIA, seated woman worships cross (very heavily restored): Discord DISCORDIA, two men struggling (heavily restored).

Wisdom SAPIENTIA, seated woman holding a book (portions of the robe old): Stupidity TULTICIA, a fool with club and disheveled garments raising stone to mouth (falsely restored as a cup; almost completely modern).

Sobriety SOBRIETAS, seated woman holding book and drinking from a small cup (modern, rest of figure also heavily restored): Pride SUPERBIA, warrior in long tunic and holding banner falling from horse (foot, portions of horse, robe, old). Originally complementing Humility.

Charity LARGITAS, seated woman gives clothes to tiny figure (almost completely modern): Avarice AVARICIA, seated woman puts money in chest (portions of inscription and body old).

Cahier and Martin (1841-1844, planche d'étude XVII) noted the same figures, except that the positions of Pride and Drunkenness were interchanged. Some confusion must have resulted from the multiple restoration campaigns. Compare with the west rose of Notre-Dame of Paris (Lafond, *Corpus, France* I, 23-34) and the Virtues and Vices on either side of the Infancy window in Lyon (Bégule, 1880, 131-138) to explain some of the inconsistencies in the Auxerre cycle. The Lyon cycle has yet to be adequately published with restorations noted. PATIENTIA appears at Lyon as the counterpart of IRA, represented as a man piercing himself with a sword. Although the suicide is labeled DESPERATIO at Auxerre, the juxtaposition with PATIENTIA is the same. Justice was probably not a part of the original program, and the modern inscription is a misinterpretation of the remains of LAETITIA. In 1841, Cahier and Martin noted only the letters TITA. In Lyon, DOLOR faces LAETITIA, depicted as a woman with a crown, her hands set wide, not unlike the Auxerre representation of Justice. Joy thus conquers Sorrow.

For iconography, see Mâle, 1923, 99-131. For iconographic treatment with emphasis on development up to the early thirteenth century, see Adolf Katzenellenbogen, *Allegories of the Virtues and Vices in Mediaeval Art*, London (1939, Norton ed. 1964).

20 Liberal Arts (MH 229 076—MH 229 079).
Philosophy PHILOXOPHIA, seated young man holding book (almost completely modern).

Geometry GEOMETRIA, seated, frontal woman with large compass (large portion of robe old, head probably traced from old glass).

Arithmetic (falsely placed inscription DIALETICA), seated woman turned to the side and gesturing with hands (upper portions of body old).

Astronomy AVSTRONOMIA, seated woman turned to the side and pointing to the stars (heavily restored).

Grammar GRAMMATICA, seated woman holding a book in one hand and a switch in the other; seated student with bare torso (large portions of Grammar's body old).

Dialectic (falsely placed inscription ALIMETICM) seated woman turned to the side, counting off points of argument with her fingers; a large serpent winding around her waist (major portions old).

Rhetoric RETORICA, frontal, seated woman holding book and staff (head, portions of drapery old).

Music MUSICA, seated woman turning to the side to ring a set of bells with a hammer (lower portions of robes old).

The Auxerre rose belongs to the late twelfth- and thirteenth-century tradition that progressively subordinated the Liberal Arts to Philosophy (A. Katzenellenbogen, "The Representation of the Seven Liberal Arts," *Twelfth-Century Europe and the Foundations of Modern Society*, University of Wisconsin [1961], 42-45). Compare the glass cycle to the sculptural representation of the Liberal Arts and Philosophy on the jamb socles of the right portal of the cathedral. Standing in the spandrels between the gables, Philosophy wears a crown, Grammar instructs two pupils, Dialectic wears a snake around her waist, and Rhetoric makes a gesture of argumentation. The Quadrivium appears on the left jamb: probably Arithmetic and Geometry followed by Music and Astronomy. Representations of the Liberal Arts in sculpture and glass were much more common around 1200 and Auxerre's program is a rare mid-century exception. The Auxerre sculpture should be dated about 1260, the product of a Rémois workshop (Sauerländer, 1972, 500, pl. 285). See also Mâle, 1923, 75-93; Katzenellenbogen, *The Sculptural Programs of Chartres Cathedral*, New York (1959), 15-22, and Cahier and Martin, 1841-1844, planche d'étude XVII.

Liberal Arts cycles in twelfth- and thirteenth-century French glass:

Laon, north rose (Grodecki, *Vitrail*, 118, fig. 91; *Corpus, France, Recensement* I, 163, fig. 88), Saint-Yved of Braine, now at Soissons (Grodecki, 1960, 171, note 24; *Corpus, France, Recensement* I, 171, fig. 95), panels from rose, Picardy or Champagne, Pitcairn collection, Bryn Athyn, Pennsylvania (Metropolitan Museum of Art, *Medieval Art from Private Collections*, New York, 1968, nos. 186, 187).

Appendix Six

Iconography of the Narrative Cycles
(alphabetically by subject)

WINDOWS OF THE CATHEDRAL OF AUXERRE, NOTRE-DAME OF DIJON,
NOTRE-DAME OF SEMUR-EN-AUXOIS

(All numbers used refer to the current numerical listing of the Monuments Historiques for window and for panel. Cliché numbers for photographs of individual panels or groups of panels are indicated to the right in the diagrams. The number below the window refers to the entire window photographed *in situ*. An x within a panel indicates that the panel is modern.)

ANDREW

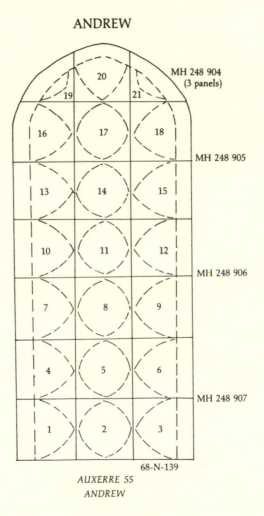

AUXERRE 55
ANDREW

AUXERRE 55 ANDREW

1. The aged but wanton Nicholas implores Andrew's help. ANDREAS.
2. Andrew exorcises a child of a demon. ANDREAS.
3. Demons trample over the bodies of their victims.
4. Three men with supplicating gestures, inhabitants of Nicea.
5. Andrew and a disciple exorcise the demons who have taken the form of dogs.

6. Two demons strangle a man and a woman in their bath.
7. Andrew baptizes the grateful Niceans.
8. Resurrection of a young man who had been killed by the demons that Andrew had banished from Nicea.
9. Andrew commands two demons to depart.
10. Andrew confronts a young man greeting him with flowers.
11. A large group of people with flowers leaving the city gate.
12. Three men (very heavily restored).
13. Andrew arrested by two soldiers.
14. Three soldiers kneel down before Andrew, the city in background.
15. Christians sleep while an angel protects them with rays from his hand.
16. Aegeus orders guard to arrest Andrew.
17. Andrew thrust into prison by guard.
18. Two guards beat Andrew with clubs.
20. Andrew on X-shaped cross (almost completely modern).

The cult of Saint Andrew enjoyed great antiquity at Auxerre, where Bishop Palladius, 623-659, dedicated a small church in a Benedictine monastic complex to Andrew (Louis, 1952, 19; J. Mabillon, *De re diplomatica*, Paris [1681], 465; *Gesta*, XXI, 341). Guillaume de Toucy, 1167-1181, dedicated an altar in the cathedral's crypt to the saint (Lebeuf, *Mémoires* I, 337; Bouchard, 1979, 89-90). Andrew is mentioned in the early thirteenth-century missal from Auxerre (Leroquais, 1924, II, 87). The early fourteenth-century voussoires of the cathedral's central portal show three scenes from Andrew's life (Porée, 1926, 65-66). The 1420 list of relics mentions Andrew twice (Lebeuf, *Mémoires* IV, 240). Two Burgundian cycles show strong iconographic similarities to Auxerre: Troyes and Notre-Dame of Dijon.

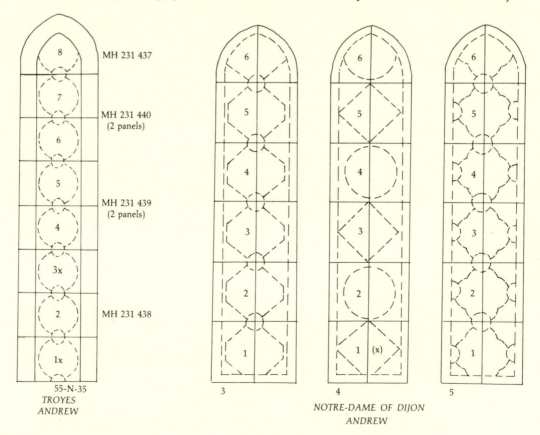

55-N-35
TROYES
ANDREW

NOTRE-DAME OF DIJON
ANDREW

Fourth bay in chapel of Saint Nicholas.

2. Two demons expelled by Andrew.
4. Andrew resurrects a young man who had been killed by the demons fleeing Nicea; parents at the head of the bed.
5. A man presents a possessed child; Andrew causes demon to leap from the child's mouth.
6. Andrew greeted at the gate of a city by a couple with flowers.
7. Andrew exorcises demons who have taken the form of dogs.
8. Andrew baptizes the Niceans.

Not only the subject matter but the composition of the panels closely parallel the dispositions at Auxerre. The remaining two panels in the window are modern (Lafond, 1955, 30-31). A window in the same chapel, executed about 1250 under the influence of the Sainte-Chapelle narrates the saint's martyrdom.

Notre-Dame of Dijon

Andrew Third, fourth and fifth lancets under north rose, erroneously identified as Saint Bartholomew and Saint Benigne: Oursel, 1938, 81-84; Vallery Radot, 1928, 68-70. Reference to similar panels at Auxerre and Troyes are indicated by A or T followed by the panel number.

3:1 Signature of donors, blacksmiths; two men at forge.
3:2 Signature of donors, welders; two persons and grill work.
3:3 Two demons strangle inhabitants of Nicea in their bath. A 55:6.
3:4 Demons strike and trample victims. A 55:3.
3:5 Resurrection of young man killed by demons. A 55:8, T 4.
3:6 Healing of a sick person.

4:1 Standing man (heavily restored) greets two men (modern).
4:2 Andrew exorcises demons in the form of dogs. A 55:5, T 7.
4:3 Andrew received by the inhabitants of Nicea. A 55:10 and 11, T 6.
4:4 He baptizes two people in a font. A 55:7 and 8.
4:5 A kneeling man and companions supplicate the saint.
4:6 Andrew, with book, greeted by two persons outside a city. The narrative of Andrew's death was produced by another artist and occupies the fifth lancet.

5:1 Andrew adoring his cross; Executioner stripping off clothes (some excellent figures, but panel completely reworked).
5:2 Andrew approached by a suppliant.
5:3 Andrew attached to cross by three guards.
5:4 Andrew exorcises demon in child. A 55:2, T 5
5:5 Andrew met at city gate by crowd; one man carries a flower. A 55:10, T 6
5:6 Andrew approaches a building housing several demons.

The Auxerre, Troyes and Notre-Dame of Dijon panels follow the *Golden Legend* (7-16) where the legend of Saint Andrew shows many similarities to that of Saint Bartholomew (ibid., 479-485). The windows of Saint Andrew at Chartres (Delaporte and Houvet, 1926, 290-296, fig. 30, pl. XC) and at Tours (Grodecki, *Vitrail*, 156, fig. 120) have no particular relationship to the Burgundian programs.

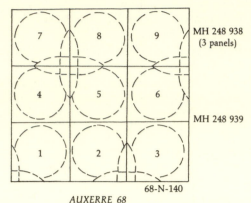

AUXERRE 68
JOHN THE EVANGELIST AND THE APOCALYPSE

Auxerre 68 Apocalypse

1. John observing an angel who points to the rain of hail, fire and blood caused by the sound of the first trumpet.
2. Son of Man seated on a cloud and holding a sickle; angel observes.
3. Rider on the White Horse; angel crowns rider; John observes.
4. Son of Man enthroned surrounded by seven angels with trumpets.
5. Woman clothed with the sun revealed to John by an angel. S:IO:HES.
6. Son of Man sitting on the Lamb whose forefeet hold the book with the seven seals; John observes.
7. Aristodemus orders poisons prepared from crushed serpents; the poison tried on three condemned prisoners.
8. Aristodemus watches John drink from the cup. S:IO:HES. } in single medallion
9. John resurrects the three prisoners. S:IO:HES. before 1927

51:1 Fourth horseman and the mouth of hell. (Described by Guilhermy, Auxerre, fol. 694, but primarily modern; see drawing p. 139.

During the episcopate of Gaudri, 918-933, John's relics appear in the cathedral's records (*Gesta*, XLIV, 375). Guillaume de Toucy, 1167-1181, included John in the dedication of the high altar of the Romanesque church (Lebeuf, *Mémoires* I, 337), and the early fourteenth-century voussoirs of the central portal show three scenes from the life of the Evangelist.

The life of John was a popular theme in thirteenth-century French glass cycles: Chartres (Delaporte and Houvet, 1926, 160-164, fig. 9, pls. X-XII); Bourges (Cahier and Martin, 1841-1844, 270-276, pl. XVB); Troyes (Lafond, 1955, 46; Cahier and Martin, 1841-1844, planche d'étude XIIID); Angers (Farcy, 1910, 158-159; Hayward-Grodecki 1966, 30-31); Tours (Boissonnot, 1920, 120-122, pl. XIV, 1932, 32-33, pl. XIV; Papanicolaou, 1979, 115-121, pls. 81-87, and radiating chapel, 117, fig. 20); Sainte-Chapelle (Grodecki, *Corpus France* I, 185-194, pls. 46-48); Saint-Pierre of Saint-Julien-du-Sault (Lafond, 1958b, 365-366; Rheims, 1926, 153-154). At Lyon (Bégule, 1880, 110-115) panels show an angel dictating the Apocalypse and the vision of the Son of Man surrounded by the seven candles. Only Bourges (Cahier and Martin, 1841-1844, 220-231, pl. VII; Grodecki, 1948, pl. 20 a & b; Mâle, 1923, fig. 102) appears to have dedicated an entire window to the narrative of the Apocalypse.

The Auxerre union of the life of the Evangelist with a detailed account of the Apocalyptic vision therefore must be related to manuscript painting, where the scenes of John's life frequently introduced the sequence of biblical illustrations. The Auxerre habit of depicting John writing or listening is also continued throughout many of the manuscript cycles. (L. Delisle and P. Meyer, *L'Apocalypse en français au XIIIe siècle*, Paris, 1901, 93-96; M. R. James, *The Apocalypse in Latin*, Oxford, 1927. Especially Paris, Bibl. nat. fr. 403, Oxford, Bodleian Auct. D4.17, and New York Morgan 524. See also P. Brieger, *English Art*, 1216-1307, Oxford, 2nd ed. 1968, 159-170. Consider also the lingering influence of the Carolingian commentary on the Apocalypse by Haymon of Auxerre, which had already inspired a twelfth-century German manuscript (Oxford, Bodleian 352, in M. R. James, *The Apocalypse in Art*, London, 1931, 41).

ASCENSION-PENTECOST

MH 248 917

AUXERRE 57
ASCENSION-PENTECOST

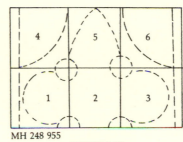

MH 248 955

AUXERRE 72
ASCENSION-PENTECOST

Auxerre 57 Ascension-Pentecost

3-8   Four side medallions, each with a seated apostle turning toward the center of the window: 3, 5, 6, 8. Two central medallions, each with an apostle seated frontally: 4, 7.

Auxerre 72 Ascension-Pentecost

1-6   Two medallions showing a seated apostle turned to the side: 2, 6 (reset incorrectly in the center and to the right). Three side medallions of attendant angels turning toward the center: 1, 3, 4. Heavily restored medallion showing Christ standing in a frontal pose and blessing: 5.

The apostles all hold books. Peter, 57:6, is distinguished by a large set of keys, and John, 72:6, by his youthful, beardless face. Rays descending from above touch the heads of most of the apostles. One is inevitably led to suggest that this window refers to the apostles receiving the Holy Spirit and witnessing the Ascension. So elaborate a treatment of these themes is unusual in glass of the thirteenth century, but relates to the central motif the twelfth-century tympanum at nearby Vézelay. (A. Katzenellenbogen, "The Central Tympanum of Vézelay, its Encyclopedic Meaning and its Relation to the First Crusade," *The Art Bulletin* 26 [1944], 141-151; Michael D. Taylor, "The Pentecost at Vézelay," *Gesta* 19 [1980] 9-15.) The devotion evidenced by Guillaume de Seignelay to the memory of the apostles (Lebeuf, *Mémoires*, I, 379; Bouchard, 1979, 136) may have been significant in the choice of theme.

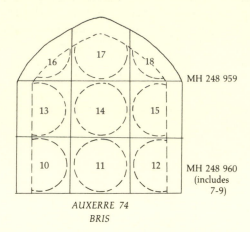

AUXERRE 74
BRIS

AUXERRE 74 BRIS (Prix or Priscus)

17. Half-length figure of Christ holding an orb and blessing.
13. A peasant guarding a flock makes a gesture of exclamation.
14. Two peasants show well to a priest and a cleric who remove the dismembered relics of Saint Bris and his companions.
15. The priest carries the head of Saint Bris into a church; he is flanked by a cleric and an attendant.
10. A woman and two men witness the translation of relics.
11. The relics in a cart guided by a man sitting on the carthorse.
12. A cleric precedes a priest into a church.

The identity of this saint was first discovered by Fourrey ("Note sur une verrière de la cathédrale d'Auxerre," *Bulletin de la Société des sciences historiques et naturelles de l'Yonne* 81 (1927) 99-103. Bris was a local saint martyred under Aurelian in 274 (Réau, 1955-1959, III/3, 1122). The bodies of Bris and his companion were thrown into a well at Coucy-les-Saints (now Saints). A disciple named Cot retrieved Saint Bris' head and was on his way to Lyon when he himself was martyred, the relic remaining where he fell. In the fifth century Saint Germain had a monastery built at Coucy-les-Saints while the resting place of the saint's head became the site of the church and later town of Saint Bris (Quantin, 1868, 15-16; Héric, *Miracula sancti Germani Episcopi Autissiodorensis*, I, 1, xvi, in Duru, 1850-1863, II, 122; *Acta Sanctorum*, May vol. 6; May 26, pp. 366-367). Bishop Hugues de Noyers, 1183-1206, received rent from the town of Saint Bris (*Gesta*, LVIII, 448; Bouchard, 1979, 108). Guillaume de Seignelay, 1207-1220, honored the saint's feast day by transferring the feast of Saint Alexander from November 13 to November 14, leaving Saint Bris with a day of his own (Bouchard, 1979, 136). Bishop Guy de Mello, 1247-1269, was lord of Saint Bris, tracing his title back to the 1103 donation made by the counts of Auxerre to Dreux de Mello (Lucien Prieur, "L'église de Saint-Bris-le-Vineux," *Congrès archéologique de France* 116 [1958], 170).

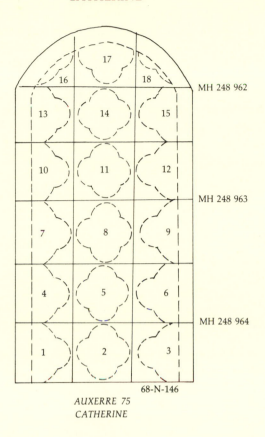

MH 248 962

MH 248 963

MH 248 964

68-N-146

AUXERRE 75
CATHERINE

AUXERRE 75 CATHERINE

1. The Emperor Maxentius seated under arcade and making a gesture of command. MAXE/NE/IVS.
2. A group of men are beheaded (panel in poor condition). This could refer to the martyrdom of the fifty pagan philosophers converted by Catherine's arguments.
3. Seated philosophers (inscription PHILOSOPHI modern).
4. Catherine thrust into prison by a club-wielding guard; Maxentius watches.
5. Catherine in prison visited by Christ and an angel. KATERINA.
6. Catherine led from prison by guard and presented to Maxentius. KATERINA.
7. Catherine tied to columns and beaten by two guards with whips. KATERINA.
8. Catherine between two wheels. Two angels appear from above and destroy the wheels killing the pagans below. KATERINA.
9. The empress confesses her conversion to Maxentius. REGI.
10. Empress flanked by two guards who lead her to her torture.
11. Empress tied to central post flanked by guards who tear her breasts with pincers.
12. Half-naked, crouching empress stabbed with a lance by a standing guard.
13. Catherine, flanked by guards, brought forward. KATERINA.
14. Guard seizes Catherine's hair and prepares to strike with a sword. KATERINA.
15. Catherine's body, wrapped in shroud, placed in tomb by two angels. KATERINA.

17. Two crouching persons receive oil flowing from Catherine's tomb. OLEUM.

Catherine appears in the only extant thirteenth-century mural decoration of the upper cathedral, a fresco in the present treasury off the south ambulatory. The narrative occupies four registers: Catherine preaching, disputing with the sages and then beheaded, placed in tomb and administered to by six angels, her soul rising to heaven in a mandorla held by two angels (Paul Deschamps and Marc Thibout, *La Peinture murale en France*, Paris [1963], 113, fig. 34, dated toward 1270). The 1420 list of relics at Auxerre records those of Saint Catherine (Lebeuf, *Mémoires*, IV, 241). Cahier and Martin (1875, 73-77, pl. IV) show state after Vessière's restorations.

Catherine cycles in twelfth- and thirteenth-century French glass:

Angers (Farcy, 1910, 148-149; Hayward-Grodecki, 1966, 17-20); Rouen (Ritter, 1926, 8, 38); Chartres, Margaret and Catherine in the same window (Delaporte and Houvet, 1926, 254-260, fig. 25, pls. LXVIII-LXIX); Saint-Père of Chartres (Lillich, 1978, 145-146, pls. 79-81); Fécamp (Lafond, "Les vitraux de l'abbaye de la Trinité de Fécamp, chap. XLVIII of *l'Abbaye benedictine de Fécamp, ouvrage scientifique du XIIIe centenaire*, Fécamp [1961], III, 99-101, notes pp. 254-255, pl. opp. p. 100); Coutance, legend doubtful, almost entirely nineteenth-century restorations (Lafond in Daage, 1933, 88); east window of Dol (Lillich, 1978, 145-146).

The identity of Catherine's persecutor seems to be somewhat ambivalent. Some (Timmers, 1947, 950) place Catherine's death in 306 or 307 during the reign of Maximian, co-emperor with Diocletian from 286-310. This was argued for Auxerre (Bonneau, 1885, 343; Porée, 1926, 99). The Golden Legend speaks of the Emperor Maxentius 306-312 (*Jacobi a Voragine, Legenda Aurea*, ed. Th. Graesse, Leipzig, 1850, chap. CLXXII; *Golden Legend*, 708-716). Delaporte, Ritter and Hayward identify the tyrant as Maxentius. The inscriptions in the Catherine window at Angers read MASENCIUS or MACENCIUS, similar to the inscription at Auxerre MAXE/NE/IVS (Hayward-Grodecki, 1966, 17-20; Fourrey, 1929, 101). Although Maxentius is not recorded as ordering religious persecutions of Christians on anything like the scale of Diocletian and Maximian, his name might have been associated with anti-Christian actions since he was defeated at the Battle of the Milvian Bridge by the first Christian emperor, Constantine.

CREATION AND FALL

Auxerre 51 Creation and Fall

17. Seated Creator places the lights in the firmament.
13. Creator walks, followed by an angel, and separates the waters from the land.
14. Spirit of God in the form of a dove hovers over the waters.
15. Creation of the birds and fishes.
10. Creation of the animals; seated ape faces cow, horse and deer. (The parallel of ape and Adam, in panel 8, must have been intended as a commentary on man's baser nature and as a premonition of the Fall. [H. W. Janson, *Apes and Ape Lore in the Middle Ages and the Renaissance*, London (1952), especially "The Ape and the Fall of Man," 107-144.])
11. God forms Adam from the dust of the earth.
12. Eve taken from Adam's side.
7. Animals present themselves to be named.
8. Seated Creator indicates animals to a seated Adam.
9. God forbids Adam and Eve to eat of the tree.

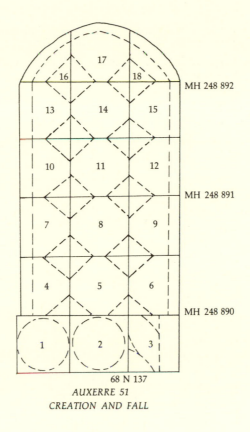

MH 248 892

MH 248 891

MH 248 890

68 N 137

AUXERRE 51
CREATION AND FALL

4. Demon tempts Eve while Adam watches.
5. God confronts Adam and Eve as they cover themselves with leaves.
6. Adam works the ground; Eve holds Cain and Abel in arms.

AUXERRE 56 GENESIS AND EXODUS (Creation panels) (see p. 157)

7. God forbids Adam and Eve to eat of the tree.
8. Eve, urged by serpent, eats fruit while Adam watches.
9. Adam and Eve cover their nakedness with leaves while God confronts them.
4. Angel with fiery sword expells Adam and Eve from Paradise.
5. God confronts Adam and Eve dressed in animal skins.
6. Eve spinning, Adam digging the ground.

Early fourteenth-century reliefs narrating Genesis from the Creation to the flood appear on the dadoes on either side of the left portal of the cathedral's facade.

The unusual arrangement of narrative starting at the top of the window appears to have been popular in Genesis-Creation scenes. The Good Samaritan windows of Chartres (Delaporte and Houvet, 1926, pl. XIX-XX), Sens (Bégule, 1929, 52-54; Grodecki, *Vitrail*, fig. 101) and Bourges (Grodecki, 1948, 91, n. 2, pl. 18a) are all expositions of the Creation, Fall and Redemption and begin at the top. Despite its extremely fragmentary conservation, the Creation window from the Sainte-Chapelle (Grodecki, *Corpus, France*, I, 94-106, pls. 14-18) probably read in the conventional bottom to top format. The Tours Creation cycle also starts from the bottom with the creation of the earth and sky and ends with the death of Tubalcain at the top. Additional Genesis scenes were once located in the transept (Boissonnot, 1920, 103-105, 144-146, pl. IV, 1932, 24-28, pl. IV; Papanicolaou, 1979, 65-89, pls. 49-55,

105-107). Some sites appear to have allowed variation in the direction of the narrative, such as Poitiers (Grodecki, 1951). At Canterbury (Caviness, 1977, 102) all read from top to bottom, a treatment that Caviness labels as "bookish." The Creation windows, however, are unique at Auxerre. Consideration should include manuscript traditions where Genesis initials frequently placed the Creation scenes of the "I" of "Incipit" in a top to bottom order.

Additional Creation cycles in twelfth- and thirteenth-century French glass:

Soissons, in top to bottom order (*Corpus, France, Recensement* I, 171, pl. 13); Amiens (ibid., 220); Aignières, church of Saint-Vaast (ibid., 217, fig. 121).

DAVID

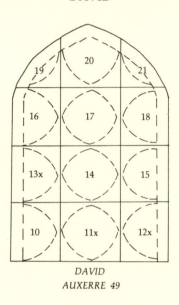

DAVID
AUXERRE 49

AUXERRE 49 DAVID

> Seven extant panels in top of window; remaining panels produced by Vessière in 1874.
> 10. Emissaries of Saul search for David in his bed, but find a statue placed as decoy.
> 14. Two groups of mounted warriors face each other; the battle of Gelboe.
> 15. Saul thrusts his sword into his heart. SAVLE.
> 16. Oxen bring the Ark of the Covenant to the house of Amminadab; Oza attempts to hold up the leaning side and is struck down.
> 17. David playing harp followed by two men playing viols.
> 18. Absalom, caught in the branches of a tree, is pierced by Joab's lance.
> 20. Seated king, probably David.

All seven panels were noted in the nineteenth century (Guilhermy, Auxerre, fol. 688).

David and Bathsheba appear in the jamb socles of the cathedral's right doorway. Sauerländer (1972, 499-501, pls. 283, 285) and Ernest Wayne Craven ("The Iconography of the David and Bathsheba Cycle at the Cathedral of Auxerre," *Journal of the Society of Architectural Historians* 34 [1975], 226-237) date the work about 1260, the product of a Rémois workshop. They characterize the iconography as unusual but consistent with the treatment of David as a prototype of Christ, separating Bathsheba (the Church) from Uriah (the Old Law). Denny (1976, 25-30, figs. 2-3) believes that the sculpture refers to the marriage of Jean de Chalon to Alix, countess of Auxerre, in 1268 and is a direct result of Jean's patronage.

David cycles in twelfth- and thirteenth-century French glass:

Sainte-Chapelle (Grodecki, *Corpus*, France I, 275-292, pls. 77-82)

ELOI

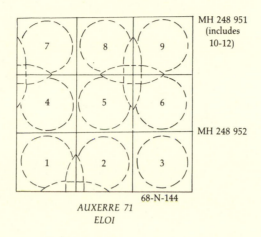

MH 248 951
(includes
10-12)

MH 248 952

68-N-144

AUXERRE 71
ELOI

AUXERRE 71 ELOI

1. Eloi receives the king's order for a golden throne; the gold is weighed by an assistant.
2. Eloi works at his forge observed by the king. S:ELOIGIUS.
3. A man leads two horses before a building.
4. Clovis II supervises weighing of gold pieces before Eloi. REX CLODOVEUS.
5. Consecration of Eloi as bishop of Noyon.
6. Eloi pinches the nose of the demon.
7. Eloi and Ouen kneel before consecrating bishop. SANCTUS AUDOIN S: ELIGIUS.
8. Procession of bishop and two acolytes with aspergil and holy water bucket.
9. Death of saint; soul transported by two angels (heavily restored).

Eloi was named treasurer by two French kings, Clothaire II and Dagobert I. In 640 Clovis II named him bishop of Noyon. Without inscriptions it is hazardous to name a specific royal figure, and identifications vary for panels at Auxerre, Le Mans and Angers. The two weighing episodes, 71:1 and 4, must surely refer to the miraculous construction of two precious objects (thrones or crowns) from the material set aside for one.

Although closely associated with the French monarchy and honored throughout France (Réau, 1955-1959, III/1, 422-427), Eloi was venerated particularly by Henri de Villeneuve, 1220-1234. Henri augmented the solemnity of Eloi's feast at Auxerre, a practice that continued for several centuries. Henri's devotion may be related to the bishop's place of birth, Villeneuve, where Eloi once had a church dedicated to him (Lebeuf, *Mémoires*, I, 401-402). For the cult at Noyon see Charles Seymour, Jr., *Notre-Dame of Noyon in the Twelfth Century*, New York (1968), 23-25, 38-39, 46-48.

Eloi cycles in twelfth- and thirteenth-century French glass:

Angers (Farcy, 1910, 163-165; Hayward-Grodecki, 1966, 35-36); Le Mans (Hucher, 1864, unpaginated; Grodecki, 1961, 77).

EUSTACHE

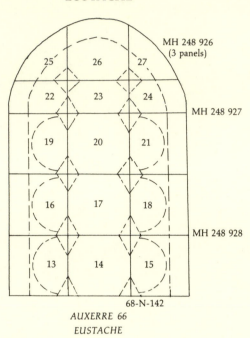

AUXERRE 66
EUSTACHE

AUXERRE 66 EUSTACHE

13. Two rustics lean on staffs and witness Eustache's distress.
14. Eustache, in the middle of a river, sees a wolf and a lion flee with his two sons.
15. Two witnesses to the scene stand with helpless gestures.
16. Eustache's wife and two small sons under architectural frame.
17. Eustache forced from ship; wife and sons watch from ship.
18. Two men with flowing mantles and gestures of lamentation.
19. Two standing figures, possibly the Emperor Trajan sending a messenger to search for Eustache or receiving Eustache's renewed service.
20. Seated Eustache recognized by his wife and his two grown sons.
21. Eustache in battle in the service of the emperor.
23. Small figure working bellows.
26. Eustache and family thrust into iron bull to be roasted when Eustache refuses to sacrifice to idols.

The author of the *Gesta* biography of Hugues de Noyers (+ 1206) was in all probability a cathedral canon named Eustache who wrote during the episcopate of Guillaume de Seignelay, between 1207 and 1220 (Auguste Molinier, *Les Sources d'histoire de France*, I/2 Paris, 1902, no. 1385, pp. 93-95; Duru, 1850-1863, I, 512; Bouchard, 1979, 99). This is the only reference to an Eustache in the thirteenth-century records, and it is tempting to see a connection between the Auxerre window and Hugues' biographer. Eustache was also the patron saint of hunters (Delaporte and Houvet, 1926, 398) making him a popular figure.

For iconography, see Réau, 1955-1959, III/1, 468-471, and Thomas J. Heffernan, "An Analysis of the Narrative Motifs in the Legend of St. Eustace," *Medievalia et Humanistica*, n.s. 6 (1975), 63-89.

Eustache cycles in twelfth- and thirteenth-century French glass:

Sens (Bégule, 1929, 48-49, fig. 56, pl. XVI); Chartres (Delaporte and Houvet, 1926, 398-404, fig. 51, pls. CLXVII-CLXXIV, color pls. XVII-XVIII; Grodecki, *Vitrail*, 129, fig. 93; idem, 1965); Saint-Pierre of Dreux (Grodecki, 1953, 54-55, no. 16; idem, 1962, nos. 146-147); Le Mans (Hucher, 1864, unpaginated; A. Ledru, *La Cathédrale du Mans*, Le Mans [1929], 77; Grodecki, 1961, 86); Tours (Boissonnot, 1920, 122-123, pl. XV, 1932, 43-44, pl. XV; Papanicolaou, 1979, 126-128, pls. 94-98).

GERMAIN OF AUXERRE

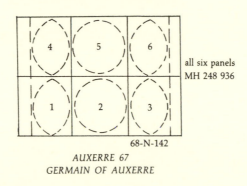

all six panels
MH 248 936

68-N-142

AUXERRE 67
GERMAIN OF AUXERRE

AUXERRE 67 GERMAIN OF AUXERRE

1. Germain on horse or mule accosted by a man; possibly the horse thief or the servant of Leporius asking alms. S. GERMANUS.
2. Germain accompanied by a cleric cures a person presented by two supplicating men; probably the exorcism of a man whose demon caused him to steal a tax collector's revenues (head of possessed modern). Sometimes labeled as the healing of the son of Elaphius, lord of the region. ???? ANUS.
3. Germain and cleric confront a group of soldiers lying dead; a horse. Generally accepted as Germain stopping Eocharis, king of the Alans. GERMAN.
4. Resurrection of the son of Volusian; parents at head of the bed.
5. Germain standing in front of a church labeled VERGIAUS. He prevents the collapse of the church at Varzy. GERMANUS.
6. Two clerics holding candles follow a cleric with a bowl; probably a procession to honor the translation of Germain's body from Ravenna to Auxerre.
66:12 Germain blessing a half-naked man (panel almost entirely modern including inscription) (see p. 152).

Germain, fifth and greatest bishop of Auxerre, succeeded Amâtre in 418, and both bishops appear in opposite bays in the hemicycle of the choir's clerestory. Tradition asserted that Germain had been temporal lord of Auxerre before becoming bishop, a concept exploited particularly by Guillaume de Seignelay, 1206-1220, when insisting that the counts of Auxerre offer him fealty and carry the episcopal chair into the cathedral for his investiture (Lebeuf, *Mémoires*, I, 369; Bouchard, 1979, 127-135; *Gallia Christiana*, XII, ed. Congregation of Saint Maur, OSB, Paris [1770], Instrumenta, nos. 66 and 68; Quantin, 1873, 744, 746). Although Germain's life appears in several general works (Gregory of Tours, *Historia francorum*, X, xli, in Duru, 1850-1863, I, 121-122; Bede, *Historia ecclesiastica*, I, xvii-xxi, in Duru, 1850-1863, I, 189-196; *Golden Legend*, 396-400) two local accounts appear to have inspired Auxerre's cycle. Constance, a priest of Lyon wrote about 475 (*Vita sancti Germani, Autissiodorensis Episcopi*, in Duru, 1850-1863, I, 47-99, and *Acta sanctorum*, July vol. 7:

July 31, pp. 202-221) followed in the ninth century by Héric, a monk of Saint-Germain of Auxerre (*Vita et miracula sancti Germani Episcopi Autissiodorensis*, in Duru, 1850-1863, II, 1-189 and *Acta sanctorum, ibid.*, pp. 221-287). The *Gesta* account (*Gesta*, VII, 315-321) uses the Constance and Héric narratives as almost exclusive sources. All of the events identified in the Auxerre window appear in the accounts of Constance and Héric, except for the miracle of the church of Varzy, which figures prominently in the *Gesta* (317-318). Varzy was the site of an episcopal château (*Gesta*, LXIII, 500; Lebeuf, *Mémoires*, I, 429), which might explain the mention of its church in the *Gesta* and in the window.

The site of Germain's tomb quickly became a place of pilgrimage and between 493 and 545, Clothilde, wife of Clovis I, rebuilt the abbey church of Saint-Germain (Héric in Duru, 1850-1865, II, 133; Louis, 1952, 60-98; Mortet, 1911-1929, II, 74-78). The cathedral, however, appears to have been in continual possession of Germain's shroud. Tradition assigned the still extant cloth to the actions of Empress Placidia who wrapped Germain's body in precious fabric when she sent it back to Auxerre after his death in Ravenna (Challe and Quantin in Lebeuf, *Mémoires*, I, 73). Later historians however (Louis, 1952, 39-40) believe that the relic may be one of the sumptuous fabrics given by Charles the Bald during the 859 translation of Germain's relics (Quantin, 1854-1860, I, 69). The reliquary containing the shroud, sometimes called the tunic, is mentioned in the ninth, tenth and fifteenth centuries (Lebeuf, *Mémoires*, I, 191; *Gesta*, XLIV, 375; Lebeuf, *Mémoires*, IV, 241). For the present state of the reliquary, see J. Taralon and M. Devallon, *Les Tresors des églises de France*, Paris (1965), no. 810.

Germain is named in the dedication of Carolingian and Romanesque altars (*Gesta*, XL, 359; Lebeuf, *Mémoires*, I, 337; Bouchard, 1979, 89-90). The early thirteenth-century Auxerre missal mentions Germain in both the sanctoral and the calendar (Leroquais, 1924, II, 87). The tympanum of the cathedral's north portal depicts Germain's life, funeral procession and miracles, forming a late-fifteenth-century pendant to Stephen's life on the south.

Germain cycles in twelfth- and thirteenth-century French glass:

Chartres (Delaporte and Houvet, 1926, 370-375, fig. 43, pls. CXLVI-CXLVII) shows the life of the saint, including Auxerre's stories of the tax collector and the horse thief.

JAMES

Auxerre 70 James

10. James repulses three demons sent by the magician Hermogenes.
11. Demons report back to the seated magician.
12. Three Pharisees, who had commissioned Hermogenes, witness failure.
13. Hermogenes kneels before James to beg his protection.
14. James gives Hermogenes his staff as protection against the demons.
15. Hermogenes holding staff.
16. Hermogenes casts books of magic into the sea.
17. Hermogenes and his disciple Philetus repent at James' feet.
18. James baptizes Hermogenes and Philetus.
19. James has rope placed around neck and is led before Herod Agrippa.
20. James stands before the seated Herod.
21. James led to prison by a guard.
22. Herod orders James to be beheaded; the scribe Josias holds the rope around James' neck.

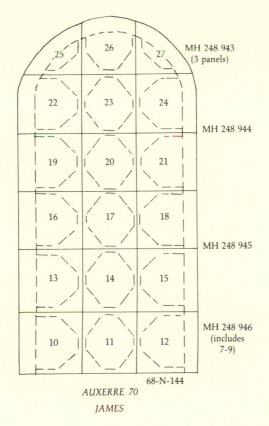

MH 248 943
(3 panels)

MH 248 944

MH 248 945

MH 248 946
(includes
7-9)

68-N-144

AUXERRE 70

JAMES

23. Josias kneels to ask for baptism. James baptizes him (and two followers?) with water in a vase.
24. Executioner with drawn sword and James.
26. James beheaded.

Auxerre's narrative parallels the text of the *Golden Legend* (368-371). James the Greater was one of the most popular saints of the twelfth and thirteenth centuries, due primarily to the discovery of his relics at Compostella and subsequent development of pilgrimages to his shrine (Kenneth Conant, *Carolingian and Romanesque Architecture*, New York [rev. ed., 1978], 157-162, nn. 157-159, map p. 20; Y. Bottineau, *Les Chemins de Saint-Jacques*, Paris and Grenoble, 1964). Auxerre served as a gathering place for pilgrims since it was the last major city before the important pilgrimage stop of Vézelay.

In the 1420 list of relics, James is mentioned immediately following Peter and Paul, preeminent as founders, and Andrew, particularly venerated in Burgundy (Lebeuf, *Mémoires*, IV, 240). In the voussoirs of the cathedral's central portal, from the early fourteenth century, Saint James lectures Hermogenes and Philetus and then delivers the latter from an evil spirit.

James cycles in twelfth- and thirteenth-century French glass:

Chartres (Delaporte and Houvet, 1926, 307-313, fig. 33, pls. CI-CV, color pls. V and XI); Bourges (Cahier and Martin, 1841-1844, 271-272, pl. XVA); Tours choir window and radiating chapel window originally from the church of Saint-Julien of Tours (Boissonnot, 1920, 118-120, 139, pl. XIII, 1932, 39-40, pl. XIII; Papanicolaou, 1979, 115-121, pls. 81-87, fig. 20).

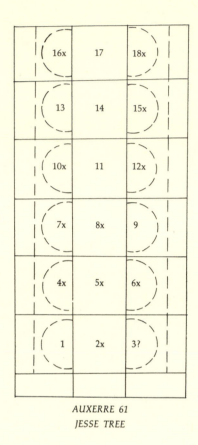

AUXERRE 61
JESSE TREE

Auxerre 61 Jesse Tree

1, 3 (?), 9, 13 standing prophets from side panels.
11, 14, seated kings from center panels.
17 seated Virgin, center panel.

Seven extant panels remained in the nineteenth century (Guilhermy, Auxerre, fol. 693v.). Steinheil and Leprévost set old panels in a reconstructed Jesse Tree in 1879, but only six of the seven listed by Guilhermy can be identified with certainty.

Jesse Trees in twelfth- and thirteenth-century French glass:

Saint Denis (Grodecki, 1976, 71-80, pl. VI, figs. 33-65); Chartres (Delaporte and Houvet, 1926, 143-149, pls. I-III, color pl. I); Soissons (Grodecki, "Un vitrail démembré de la cathédrale de Soissons," *Gazette des beaux-arts* 42 [1953], 169-176; *Corpus, France, Recensement* I, 171, pl. 13); Troyes (Lafond, 1955, 42-43, fig. p. 43); Troyes(?) now in Victoria and Albert Museum, London (B. Rackham, *Victoria and Albert Museum, Department of Ceramics: A Guide to the Collections of Stained Glass*, London, [1936], nos. 5, 6—1881, pp. 32-33, fig. 4; Grodecki, *Vitrail*, 140, fig. 110); Tours (Boissonnot, 1920, 111-113, pl. IX, 1932, 33-35, pl. IX; Papanicolaou, 1979, 44-45, pls. 26-31); Angers (Farcy, 1910, 164); Le Mans (Grodecki, 1961, 78, 87); Beauvais (Leblond, 1926, 64; *Corpus, France, Recensement* I, 178, pl. 14); Aignières, church of Saint-Vaast (*Corpus, France, Recensement* I, 217;

Cothren in *New England Collections*, 22-23); panels in Oise style in the Worcester Art Museum and the Metropolitan Museum of Art, New York (Cothren, ibid.); Saint-Germain-lès-Corbeil (*Year 1200*, I, No. 219; Perrot, 1975); Gercy (Perrot, ibid.); Sainte-Chapelle (Grodecki, *Corpus, France* I, 172-184, pls. 42-44); Amiens (*Corpus, France, Recensement* I, 220-222); Baye, chapel in castle (Grodecki, 1978, 50, fig. 8).

For development of the iconography, see Arthur Watson, *The Early Iconography of the Tree of Jesse*, Oxford and London, 1934, and Madeline Caviness, "The Canterbury Jesse Window," *Year 1200* III, 373-398.

JOSEPH

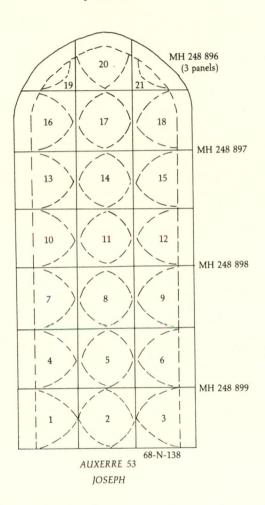

AUXERRE 53
JOSEPH

AUXERRE 53 JOSEPH
    For the most part, the scenes read from right to left.

3. Joseph stripped of his cloak by his brothers.
2. Joseph's brothers thrust him into a well.
1. Brothers present the bloody cloak to a seated Jacob.
6. Group of brothers surrounding the half-naked Joseph.
5. Three brothers bargain with a mounted Ismaelite.
4. Joseph, on horse, led to Egypt by mounted Ismaelite.

9. Joseph entrusted with keys of authority by Potiphar.

8. Chief butler cast into prison.

7. Pharaoh orders servant to remove chief baker.

11. Potiphar's wife reaches out to Joseph; in second image, Joseph flees leaving cloak in her hands.

10. Potiphar's wife shows cloak to her husband while Joseph watches.

12. Joseph interprets the dreams of the chief butler and chief baker while in prison.

15. Chief butler led from prison by guard.

14. Pharaoh's dream of the seven fat and seven lean kine, seven full and seven lean ears of grain.

13. Chief butler handing cup to Pharaoh at table.

18. Joseph led from prison by guard.

17. Joseph presented to Pharaoh; he interprets dream.

16. Four men witness scene. One holds pieces of gold.

20. Joseph in triumphal chariot drawn by two oxen. Two men petition him, possibly his brothers.

The story of Joseph is featured on the left socle of the central portal of the cathedral. The program is unusually extensive and includes references to pagan antiquity through a figure of Hercules and a satyr. These references continue on the same side of the door jamb with a figure of a sleeping cupid (Erwin Panofsky, *Renaissances and Renascences in Western Art*, New York [1969], 91-96, figs. 61, 62, 64). Sauerländer (1972, 501, pl. 286) dates the cycles toward 1270. Denny (1976, 23-34) believes that the theme refers to Jean de Chalon in the role of a younger but ultimately successful brother.

Joseph cycles in twelfth- and thirteenth-century French glass:

Poitiers, two complex windows (Auber, 1849, 361-364; Grodecki, 1948, 105, pl. 22 d/e; idem, 1951, 152ff.); Rouen, two complex windows (Ritter, 1926, 395-398, fig. 50, pls. CLXII-CLXVI, color pls. XIV-XVI); Bourges (Cahier and Martin, 1841-1844, 240-244, pl. X); Sainte-Chapelle, including two panels now housed in the Cluny Museum, Paris (Grodecki, *Corpus, France* I, 104, 105, 123, 337-338, pls. 14, 15, 18, 20, 21); Tours (Papanicolaou, 1979, 129-134, pls. 99-101); Chartres (Delaporte and Houvet, 1926, pls. CXIX-CXXII).

LAWRENCE

AUXERRE 57 LAWRENCE

9. Decius orders Lawrence tortured so that he might reveal the hiding place of the church treasures.

10. Lawrence between two guards.

11. Lawrence stripped by two guards.

12. Decius witnesses beating; demon whispers in his ear.

13. Lawrence stretched horizontally; three guards beat him with clubs.

14. Lawrence dressed as deacon led off to prison, probably by the prefect Valerian.

15. Lawrence's hands tied as he is led from prison by a guard.

16. Lawrence beaten a second time.

17. The seated Decius watches the torture.

18. Decius, standing, accompanied by a servant.

19. In prison, Lawrence baptizes two persons.

20. Lawrence, his hands bound, led away by two guards.

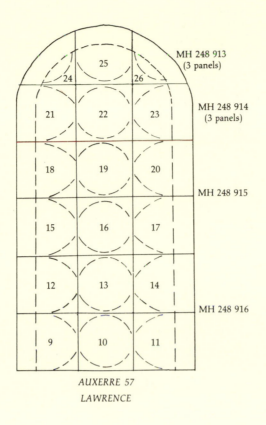

MH 248 913
(3 panels)

MH 248 914
(3 panels)

MH 248 915

MH 248 916

AUXERRE 57
LAWRENCE

21. A guard and a man in a long cloak witness the torture.
22. Lawrence on the grill; two guards stir the fire with long poles.
23. Decius and guard survey the scene of Lawrence's death.
25. Half-length portrait of Christ blessing.

Lawrence was linked to another deacon martyr, Saint Stephen, the patron saint of the cathedral (*Golden Legend*, 411-412), and both figure in the hemicycle glass of the choir clerestory; Saint Lawrence and Saint Amâtre to the right, Saint Stephen and Saint Germain to the left. In the mid-ninth century, the abbots of Saint-Germain of Auxerre dedicated one of the four lateral oratories of the crypt to Lawrence (Louis, 1952, 60-62). During the episcopate of Gaudri, 918-933, relics of Saint Lawrence appear in the cathedral records (*Gesta*, LXIV, 375). Bishop Guillaume de Toucy, 1167-1181, included Saint Lawrence in the dedication of the high altar of the Romanesque cathedral (Lebeuf, *Mémoires*, I, 337; Bouchard, 1979, 89-90). The 1420 list of relics contains two entries for the bones of Saint Lawrence (Lebeuf, *Mémoires*, IV, 241-242).

Lawrence cycles in twelfth- and thirteenth-century French glass:

Poitiers (Grodecki, 1977, 71, 74-76; idem, *Vitrail*, 98, fig. 67; idem, 1951, 148-149); Angers (Farcy, 1910, 163-165; Hayward-Grodecki, 1966, 39-41); Bourges (Cahier and Martin, 1841-1844, 265-268, pl. XIV); Rouen, three deacon martyrs in one window, Lawrence, Stephen, and Vincent (Ritter, 1926, 50, pl. XXVII); Chartres, only fragments remaining (Delaporte and Houvet, 1926, 377-381, fig. 45 and 46, pls. CXLVIII-CXLIX); Mantes-Gassicourt, in window with saints Stephen and Vincent (*Corpus, France, Recensement* I, 132).

Appendix Six

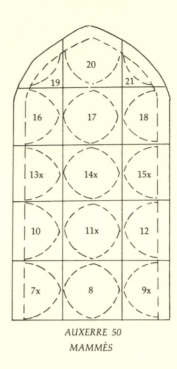

AUXERRE 50
MAMMÈS

Auxerre 50 Mammès

8. Guided by an angel, Mammès builds a house far from civilization.
10. Animals flock to hear Mammès read the scripture.
12. Christ appears to the saint.
16. Pagan priests kneel before an idol in the form of a nude statue.
17. Two guards thrust Mammès into a fiery furnace. S. MAMMES.
18. Mammès in prayer before a book on an altar. S. MAMMES.
20. Mammès and king seated under arcades.

Remaining twelve panels painted in 1874 by Veissière.

Mammès was a Cappadocian hermit who made cheese from the milk of wild animals and distributed it to the poor. He refused to sacrifice to pagan idols and was martyred by the Emperor Aurelian, 270-275 (*Acta sanctorum*, Aug. vol. 3: Aug. 17, pp. 423-446).

The Auxerre window appears to be the first appearance of Mammès in Western art (Réau, 1955-1959, III/2, 866-868). In the fourth century Bishop Urscinus of Sens reputedly brought back relics of Mammès after a voyage to Cappadocia (Jean Taralon and M. Devallon, *Les Trésors des églises de France*, Paris [1965], 264) and a large group of Mammès's relics arrived at Langres in the eleventh century (Réau, *ibid.*; *Bibliotheca Hagiographica Latina*, II, Brussels [1900-1910], 772; *Acta sanctorum, ibid.*, p. 434). Despite the presence of Mammès' relics in Burgundy, the saint may have been confused with Saint Martinus or Mamertinus, the second abbot of the monastery of Saint-Marien at Auxerre (*Golden Legend*, 226-228; Louis, 1952, 16-17; *Gesta*, XIX-XX, 329 and 339). For the appearance of Mammès in the sixteenth century and additional iconography, see J. Beaudoin Ross, "Jean Cousin the Elder and the Creation of the Tapestries of Saint Mamas," *The Art Bulletin* 60 (1978), 28-34.

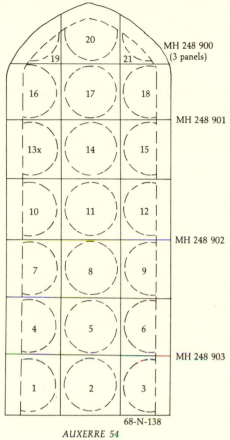

AUXERRE 54

MARGARET OF ANTIOCH

AUXERRE 54 MARGARET OF ANTIOCH

1. The prefect Olybrius, repulsed in his offer of marriage, condemns Margaret to torture. OLIMBR.
2. Margaret thrust into prison; Olybrius watches.
3. Margaret tied to column while two guards beat her; Olybrius watches.
4. In prison, Margaret uses a bunch of sticks to strike a crouching demon.
5. Still within the prison wall, Margaret tramples the demon underfoot.
6. A dragon's enormous head confronts Margaret in prison.
7. Margaret led by a guard before Olybrius. S. MARGARETA HOLIBRIUS.
8. Two guards flank Margaret as she stands in the midst of a fire (figure of Margaret and water quenching flames modern).
9. Four witnesses to the scenes of torture.
10. Olybrius under arcade giving orders.
11. Margaret in tub of water flanked by two guards with jugs.
12. Group of people representing the five thousand who were converted when the tub miraculously broke.
13. Architecture (a modern reconstruction with some old fragments).

14. Five thousand new converts beheaded by two guards with swords.
15. Single guard beheading the converts.
16. Olybrius under arcade giving orders (modern).
17. Margaret beheaded by two guards with swords.
18. Three men with helpless gestures watching the scenes.
20. Margaret's soul in mandorla supported by two angels.

The iconography is rather traditional (*Golden Legend*, 351-354). The present inscriptions were visible in the nineteenth century (Guilhermy, Auxerre, fol. 690-690v.) although they were omitted from the published drawing of the window (Cahier and Martin, 1875, 67-73, pl. IV). Auxerre's 1420 list of relics includes those of Saint Margaret in a palmwood box (Lebeuf, *Mémoires*, IV, 241).

Margaret cycles in twelfth- and thirteenth-century French glass:

Chartres, in the same window with Saint Catherine (Delaporte and Houvet, 1926, 254-260, fig. 25, pls. LXVIII-LXIX); Saint-Pierre of Saint-Julien-du-Sault (Rheims, 1926, 150-151; Lafond, 1958b, 365); Clermont-Ferrand (du Ranquet, 1932, 223-241).

MARTIN

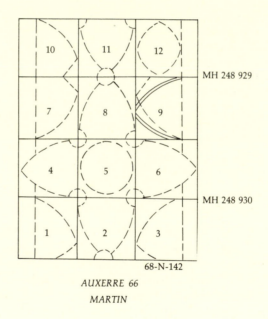

AUXERRE 66

MARTIN

AUXERRE 66 MARTIN

1. Martin recuscitates the catechumen who died before his baptism.
2. Martin says mass and is miraculously clothed by a hand reaching down from heaven; a cleric attends him.
3. Martin under a doorway attended by a follower.
4. Two robbers capture Martin on his way across the Alps and tie him to a tree.
5. Martin lies on his deathbed; an angel at his head, a demon at his feet.
6. Martin causes a tree to reverse direction and crush hostile pagans.
7. Martin exorcises the slave of Tetradius.
8. Martin blesses his kneeling mother while his obdurate father watches.

9. Martin converses with another bishop, possibly Hilary of Poitiers. (Double line in diagram indicates form before 1925-1927 restorations.)
10. Martin gives orders to a mason.
11. Church built by two laborers.

Despite widespread veneration throughout France (Mâle, 1923, 330-333; *Golden Legend*, 663-674; Papanicolaou, 1979, 47-61), Martin had a particularly close relationship with Auxerre. Bishop Palladius, 623-659, dedicated a church to Martin in a large Benedictine monastery outside the city (Louis, 1952, 19). During the Norman invasions at the end of the ninth century, the body of Saint Martin was transferred to the monastery of Saint-Germain at Auxerre. The monks exerted themselves in an unsuccessful attempt to prevent the return of the precious relic to Tours (Louis, 1952, 60-62). Guillaume de Toucy, 1167-1181, set up a perpetual fund for the altar of Saint Martin in the cathedral and ordered greater solemnity for the celebration of his feast (Lebeuf, *Mémoires*, I, 337). The 1420 list of relics records that Auxerre possessed ''a large part of the mantle of Saint Martin of Tours as well as relics of his bones'' (Lebeuf, *Mémoires*, IV, 241).

Martin cycles in twelfth- and thirteenth-century French glass:

Chartres (Delaporte and Houvet, 1926, 241-247, fig. 23, pls. LIX-LXII); Bourges (Cahier and Martin, 1841-1844, 251-254, pl. XIIA); Angers (Farcy, 1910, 169-171; Hayward-Grodecki, 1966, 23-26); Le Mans (Hucher, 1864, unpaginated; A. Ledru, *La cathédrale du Mans*, Le Mans [1929], 77; Grodecki, 1961, 84); Tours, choir lancets and dispersed cycle now in windows of radiating chapel (Boissonnot, 1920, 113-115, pl. X, 1932, 35-36, 56-58, pl. X; Papanicolaou, 1979, 47-61, pls. 38-43, figs. 7, 24); Beauvais? (*Corpus, France, Recensement* I, 178; Lafond, in Leblond, 1926, 64, did not accept this identification); Gercy (see p. 42).

MARY OF EGYPT

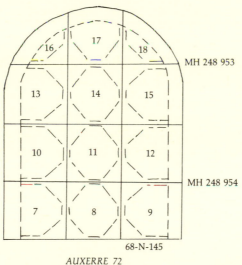

MH 248 953

MH 248 954

68-N-145

AUXERRE 72
MARY OF EGYPT

AUXERRE 72 MARY OF EGYPT

7. Mary buys bread from shopkeeper.
8. Mary walking in desert holding the loaves.
9. Mary stops and prays at the banks of the Jordan.

10. Zosimas meets the penitent who is dressed in animal skins.
11. Mary receives communion from Zosimas. S. ZOSIMAS.
12. Mary lies down to die with her hands folded across her chest.
13. A lion digs a grave for the saint.
14. Zosimas and the lion place Mary in her grave.
15. Mary's soul in a mandorla carried by two angels.
17. An angel waving a censer (heavily restored).

Mary of Egypt was frequently associated with that other great female penitent, Mary Magdalene (Cahier and Martin, 1874, 62-67, pl. III). Bourges (Cahier and Martin, 1841-1844, 248-250, pl. XIB) and Auxerre produced windows of both Mary of Egypt and Mary Magdalene. Possibly the popularity of the shrine of the Magdalene at Vézelay influenced the depiction of both saints in these two programs. See also scenes of penitence and burial under standing figure of Mary of Egypt in Chartres clerestory (Delaporte and Houvet, 1926, 412-413, pl. CLXXXIII). The narrative parallels the *Golden Legend* closely (228-230).

MARY MAGDALENE

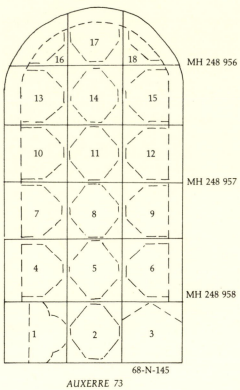

AUXERRE 73
MARY MAGDALENE

AUXERRE 73 MARY MAGDALENE

4. Mary and her brother Lazarus stand under arcade and preach to the crowd in Marseilles. MAGDALLENE.
5. Mary Magdalene appears to the ruler of Provence and his wife in a dream.
6. A woman takes Lazarus and Mary to speak to the provincial ruler.
7. A woman and two men, haloed, confronting a person dressed in a dalmatic and carrying a book. S. BAUSEMIN (restored?).

8. Ruler of Provence and wife on pilgrimage during storm at sea.
9. Ruler looks at his dead wife and dying new-born child that he is forced to abandon on the seashore.
10. Ruler and companion are instructed by Saint Peter in Rome.
11. Ruler and sailor in a ship on a calmer sea.
12. Ruler discovers his child sustained and his wife miraculously restored to life.
13. Ruler and wife return to Marseilles and present their son to Mary. A group observes the scene.
14. Saint Maximinus baptizes ruler and his family.
15. Mary, surrounded by angels, appears to Maximinus.
17. Maximinus says mass by the tomb of the saint.

For iconography, see remarks under Mary of Egypt and the *Golden Legend* (355-364).

At Auxerre, Guillaume de Toucy, 1167-1181, dedicated an altar in the Romanesque cathedral to Mary Magdalene (Lebeuf, *Mémoires*, I, 337; Bouchard, 1979, 89-90). Bishop Guy de Mello participated in the verification of the Magdalene's relics at Vézelay on April 24, 1267 (Petit, 1885-1894, V, 95-97; Lebeuf, *Mémoires*, I, 441-442). Erard de Lésignes, then canon, assisted him during the ceremony and when bishop, 1270-1278, gave the cathedral a relic of the saint's hair (Lebeuf, *Mémoires*, I, 454). The 1420 relic census lists three separate relics of Mary Magdalene (Lebeuf, *Mémoires*, IV, 421).

Mary Magdalene cycles in twelfth- and thirteenth-century French glass:

Chartres (Delaporte and Houvet, 1926, 164-168, fig. 10, pls. XIV-XVII); Lyon (Cahier and Martin, 1841-1844, planche d'étude VIII/1); Sées (Lafond, 1953, 72); Bourges (illustrated here, fig. 43, and Cahier and Martin, 1841-1844, 245-248, pl. XIA; Grodecki, 1948, 97, pl. 21a); Clermont-Ferrand (du Ranquet, 1932, 85-120); Semur-en-Auxois (de Tervarent, 1938); Le Mans (Grodecki, 1961, 84).

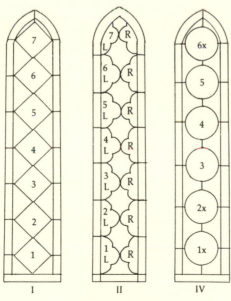

SEMUR-EN-AUXOIS
MARY MAGDALENE

II:7 L Mary in boat journeying to Marseilles (see below).
 R City of Marseilles (see below).
 L Christ confronted by Mary or Martha (Christ and the woman both hold books).
 R Christ telling Martha that Mary has the better part (Luke 10:42).
5 L Mary and Martha at sickbed of Lazarus.
 R Funeral of Lazarus.
4 L Mary falls at Christ's feet, "Lord, if thou hadst been there . . ." (John 11:32).
 R Christ instructs Martha, "I am the Resurrection and the Life . . ." (John 11:20-27).
3 L Resurrection of Lazarus.
 R Mary, Martha and Lazarus converse with Christ.
2 L Martha questions Christ about Mary's place (Luke 10:40).
 R Jews comfort Mary and Martha after Lazarus' death (John 11:31).
1 L Fourteenth-century angels.
 R Saint Peter with keys flanked by two figures (see below).

The iconography of the panels in this window follows very closely the unfolding of the biblical story in the Mary Magdalene window of the cathedral of Bourges (illustrated here, fig. 43, and Cahier and Martin, 1841-1844, 145-148, pl. XIA). Each one of the Semur panels has a parallel at Bourges. Both sites seem to favor instances of Christ interviewing one or another of the holy women, and frequently Christ and the women all hold books. Semur has lost the representation of Mary washing Christ's feet (John 12:3-8), however, and the panels are out of order.

I:7 Hand of God commanding Maximinus to say mass for the last communion of Mary Magdalene since it was not then the custom to preserve the Eucharist (or mass at Mary's tomb, as in the uppermost panel of Auxerre's Mary Magdalene window, 73:17).
6 Mary (or Martha) instructing the people of Provence, as in the Auxerre panel 73:13.
5 Death of Martha; demons appear in the dark and a nun relights the lamp.
4 Death of Mary Magdalene foretold; Mary is blessed by the hand of God and lifted up from the ground. Maximinus and spectators watch.
3 Abbot of Vézelay, at request of Duke of Burgundy, who had built the monastery, sends envoys to Provence to bring back the body of Mary Magdalene.
2 Abbot and monk discussing the translation of Mary's relics to Burgundy. The bones were mysteriously rooted to the spot until all the monks of Vézelay went to greet them.
1 Standing figure (from Saint Peter window, V).

This window and four panels from windows II and IV are based on traditions concerning Mary and Martha's stay in France and the history of their relics (*Golden Legend*, 355-364, 391-395). Many of the events also appear in the Auxerre window of Mary Magdalene. The Auxerre account of the legend of the ruler of Provence may serve to identify the single panel at Semur showing Saint Peter holding the keys (II:1 R). It was to Saint Peter in Rome that the ruler had journeyed to hear confirmation of Mary Magdalene's teachings. The identification of panels I:2 and 3 as relating to the translation of Mary's relics to Vézelay is conjectural. The extensive treatment of the entire legend in the Semur cycle, however, would argue that a reference to the peculiar position of Burgundy as a possessor of her relics might be intended. De Tervarent (1938) has argued that this window referred to the 1279 contention by Charles of Salerno that he had found the Magdalene's relics in Provence, an identification untenable because of the early date of the windows. For discussion of the relative claims of Burgundy and Provence, see *Acta sanctorum, supplementum*, vol. 1, Paris (1899), 22-24.

IV:(panels 1, 2, and 6 modern)
> 5 Christ siezes hand of Saint Thomas to guide it to the marks of his wounds (John 20:27).
> 4 Mary tells apostles that she has seen the risen Christ (John 20:18).
> 3 Mary Magdalene discovered by a priest in the wilderness of Provence. She is caught up to heaven seven times a day, similar to panel at Auxerre 73:15 (see p. 156).

Semur appears to have extended Bourges' biblical cycle to include the events of the Resurrection and later appearances of Christ. Grodecki (*Vitrail*, 139) identified this theme.

MOSES

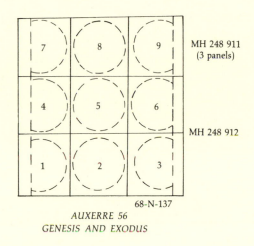

AUXERRE 56
GENESIS AND EXODUS

AUXERRE 51 and 56 GENESIS AND EXODUS (Moses)

> 51:2 Moses gestures toward the brazen serpent set on a pillar. Two Israelites hold their hands up to worship (see p. 139).
> 56:1 Three Israelites hold their hands up to worship; same pose and figure type as panel 51:2.
> 2 Moses descends from Mount Sinai holding the tablets.
> 3 A bust-length figure of God appears to Moses out of the burning bush.

The limited number of scenes in the third Genesis cycle (56) and in the Moses narrative, together with a similarity of style encourages one to think that they could have formed a single window. There is no precedent for this, however. There remain no extraneous New Testament panels with which one might reconstruct a typological window using the Genesis and Exodus scenes.

The 1420 list of relics begins with the notation: "the staff of Moses by which he produced water to drink for himself and for the people of Israel" (Lebeuf, *Mémoires* IV, 240). Glass in the Renaissance lancets below Auxerre's south rose (c. 1550) repeats the theme of Moses.

Moses cycles in twelfth- and thirteenth-century French glass:

Saint Denis (Grodecki, 1976, 93-102, figs. 104-121); Sainte-Chapelle (Grodecki, *Corpus, France* I, 107-141, pls. 19-24); four-panel medallion showing two scenes of Moses, Soissons (*L'Europe gothique, XIIe-XIVe siècles,* Musée du Louvre, *12e Exposition du Conseil de l'Europe,* Paris [1968], no. 196, fig. 66; *Corpus, France, Recensement* I, 170, pl. XXIIIb); Poitiers (Grodecki, 1951, 153-154).

NICHOLAS

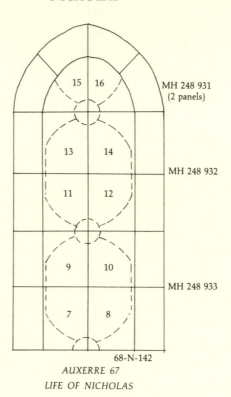

AUXERRE 67
LIFE OF NICHOLAS

AUXERRE 67 LIFE OF NICHOLAS

7. Bishop of Myra on his deathbed, a bishop and clerics in attendance.

8. Nicholas kneeling at the doorway of a church.

9. Ecclesiastics of province implore heaven for guidance in the selection of a new bishop; an angel appears in the upper left.

10. A bishop seizes Nicholas by the hand and brings him into the church; acolyte with holy water bucket.

11. Woman returns from witnessing Nicholas' consecration to find her child miraculously preserved from the demons who were fanning the fire under the infant's bath water with bellows.

12. Nicholas kneels to receive consecration from bishop; three clerics attend.

13. Impoverished father lies in bed; his three daughters stand to the right.

14. Nicholas under heavy architecture, distributes the gold pieces through an opening in the wall.

16. Child falls into the sea with a golden cup that had been promised to Saint Nicholas.

15. Miraculously saved, the child presents the cup at the altar of Saint Nicholas in the presence of his parents.

A popular saint throughout France, Saint Nicholas was particularly venerated at Auxerre, with two complete windows of the saint. The Romanesque cathedral possessed an altar dedicated to Nicholas during the episcopate of Humbaud, 1087-1114 (*Gesta*, LIII, 404). Bishop Guillaume de Toucy, 1167-1181, gave a substantial fund to the altar of Nicholas and Martin (Lebeuf, *Mémoires*, I, 337). The double dedication undoubtedly sprang from the relationship between Martin and Nicholas, the former the wonder-worker of the West and the latter the thaumaturge of the East (Mâle, 1923, 330-333; Timmers, 1947, 972-973; *Golden Legend*, 16-24 and 663-674). See especially the tympanum of the Confessor Portal, Chartres South (Sauerländer, 1972, 433, pls. 118-119). The 1420 list of relics mentions a tooth of Saint Nicholas (Lebeuf, *Mémoires*, IV, 241).

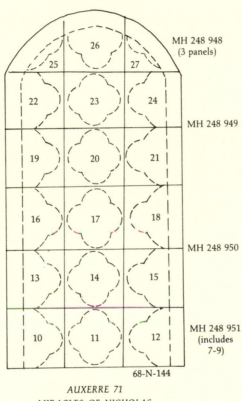

AUXERRE 71
MIRACLES OF NICHOLAS

AUXERRE 71 MIRACLES OF NICHOLAS

10. Dishonest borrower gives staff filled with gold to his Jewish creditor. Borrower would then swear that he had returned the money.
11. Cart runs over borrower, breaking his staff and revealing the ruse.
12. Man guiding the oxen drawing the cart.
13. Jew at prayer.
14. Saint Nicholas resurrects the dishonest borrower in the presence of the Jewish moneylender.
15. Nicholas baptizes the moneylender.
16. Another Jew confides his treasure to the protection of Saint Nicholas.
17. Two robbers break into the storehouse and seize the treasure.
18. They carry off the bags on their shoulders.
19. The robbers show their loot to a third companion.

20. The Jew strikes the image of Saint Nicholas with a bundle of sticks.
21. Nicholas appears to the three robbers. NCOLAS.
22. Two robbers carry sacks of gold on their shoulders.
23. They replace the money before the statue of Saint Nicholas.
24. The Jew finds his treasure intact and falls on knees before the statue.
26. Three-quarter length figure of Christ holding orb and blessing.

These two miracles are clearly described in the *Golden Legend* (22-23). Auxerre's window presents the most extensive depiction of the stories, but the legends also appear in the cathedrals of Chartres, Le Mans, Troyes, Rouen and Tours, and the church of Saint-Julien-du-Sault.

Nicholas cycles in twelfth- and thirteenth-century French glass:

Troyes, twelfth-century panels in the Victoria and Albert Museum, London, and the Cluny Museum, Paris (Grodecki, 1977, 140-144, figs. 123 and 124; idem, 1973, figs. 3 and 3a; idem, "Problèmes de la peinture en Champagne pendant la seconde moitié du douzième siècle," *Romanesque and Gothic Art; Studies in Western Art* [Acts of the 20th International Congress of the History of Art, I] Princeton [1963], 135, pl. XLVII/7); Troyes, choir triforium (Lafond, 1955, 46); Chartres, two windows that mingle scenes from Nicholas' life and miracles, even repeating similar episodes (Delaporte and Houvet, 1926, 260-266, fig. 26, pls. LXXI-LXXIV and 391-394, fig. 49, pls. CLVIII-CLXI, color plate XII); Bourges (Cahier and Martin, 1841-1844, 259-264, pl. XIIB; Grodecki, 1948, 93-95, pl. 21b); Rouen (Ritter, 1926, 8, 37-39, pls. I-VII); Le Mans (Hucher, 1864, unpaginated; Grodecki, 1961, 77, 86); Tours (Boissonnot, 1920, 100-103, pl. III, 1932, 23-25, pl. III; Papanicolaou, 1979, 103-106, pls. 63-68); Saint-Pierre at Saint-Julien-du-Sault (Rheims, 1926, 155-156; Lafond, 1958b, 366) Sées (Lafond, 1953, 69-70); Amiens, now reserves of château of Champs-sur-Marne (*Corpus, France, Recensement* I, 221).

NOAH, ABRAHAM AND LOT

Auxerre 52 Noah, Abraham and Lot

Reads from bottom to top.
1. Arc of Noah floating on the waters; dove with olive branch.
2. Devastation of the flood; dead horse, architecture.
3. Noah and family leave arc.
4. Man in short tunic cultivates tall plants (vineyard?).
5. Drunkeness of Noah; Ham pointing while Shem and Japeth shield their faces.
6. Tower of Babel constructed of brick and mortar by two masons.
7. Sacrifice of Abraham; Isaac bound on altar, angel seizing Abraham's sword.
8. Abraham receives three visitors at his table; Sarah turns away.
9. Angels announce destruction of Sodom to Abraham.
10. Abraham intercedes for condemned cities.
11. Lot greets two angels at the entrance of the city.
12. Lot's wife places food before two angels seated at table.
13. Crowd of Sodomites gather at Lot's door to demand the visitors.
14. Lot's departure from Sodom. Also interpreted as the expulsion of Hagar (Guilhermy, Auxerre, fol. 689), the parting of Abraham and Lot (Bonneau, 1885, 82; Porée, 1926, 87) and Abraham's separation of Isaac from the rest of his sons (Fourrey, 1929, 323).
15. Angel strikes a crouching figure; destruction of Sodom.
17. Lot between two daughters.

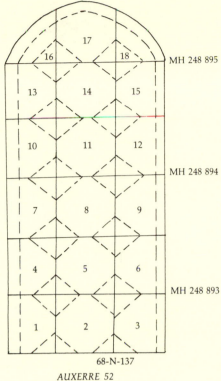

AUXERRE 52

NOAH, ABRAHAM AND LOT

Noah, Abraham and Lot cycles in twelfth- and thirteenth-century French glass:

Chartres, Noah (Delaporte and Houvet, 1926, 409-411, fig. 53, pls. CLXXIX-CLXXII); Poitiers, 3 windows, one dedicated to each patriarch (Grodecki, 1951; ibid., 1948; Auber, 1849, 349-352); Sainte-Chapelle, one remaining Abraham panel from Genesis window (Grodecki, *Corpus, France* I, 103, pl. 18).

PETER AND PAUL

AUXERRE 58 PETER AND PAUL

1. Peter sailing alone in a boat. (Double line in diagram indicates form before 1925-1927 restorations.)
2. Simon Magus followed by disciple; three gold coins with pagan images.
3. Miraculous draft of fishes; Peter and an apostle put down their net.
4. Christ, attended by a censing angel, beckons to Peter.
5. Peter confronts the apostle, "Peter do you love me?" (heavily restored).
6. Ananias cures Paul of his blindness (heavily restored).
7. Deceit of Ananias and Sapphira. They offer money to the seated Peter.
8. Peter resurrects Tabitha; a person supports her shoulders.
9. Peter led from prison by an angel.
10. Peter and Paul kneel in prayer while Simon Magus falls from a tower.
11. Nero, seated under arcade, commands a servant.
12. Simon Magus is supported by two disciples after his fall.
13. Peter dreams of the unclean animals presented to him in a sheet.
14. Peter confronts Christ, "Quo vadis, Domine?" (heavily restored).

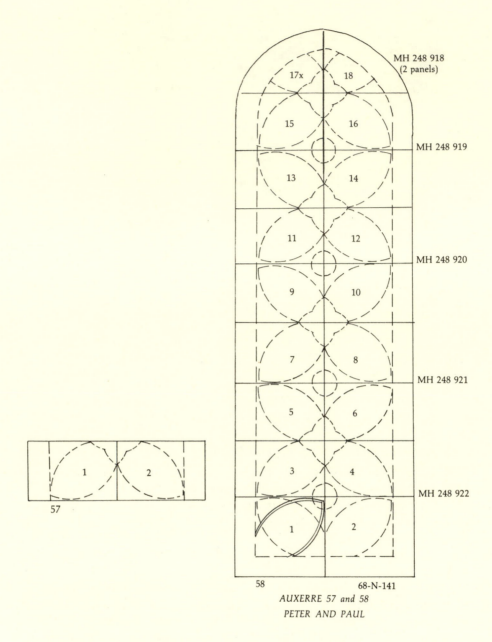

AUXERRE 57 and 58
PETER AND PAUL

15. The prefect Agrippa orders the deaths of Peter and Paul.
16. Peter nailed to an inverted cross; two guards at hands, one holds feet.
17. Angel with censer (modern copy).
18. Angel with censer.

AUXERRE 57 PETER AND PAUL ON MALTA

1. Saint Paul preaching to a group of converts on the island of Malta.
2. After shipwreck on Malta, Peter feeds a fire that causes a serpent to wake and bite a disciple.

Unusual episodes appear at Auxerre: Peter's dream of the unclean animals, 58:13, and the scenes on Malta, 57:1 and 2, are unique in thirteenth-century glass cycles. Ananias and Sapphira before Peter appears in France at Notre-Dame of Dijon. The Ananias scene once figured in the eighth typological window at Canterbury, now destroyed, forming a pendant to a scene of Christ casting the money-changers from the temple (Caviness, 1977, fig. 15). For further iconography, see Réau, 1955-1959, III/3, 1034-1050.

From early Christian times, a church in Auxerre was dedicated to Peter and Paul (*Gesta*, XIX-XX, 329 and 338; Louis, 1952, 16-17). Guillaume de Toucy, 1167-1181, dedicated an altar in the Romanesque cathedral to Saint Paul (Lebeuf, *Mémoires* I, 337; Bouchard, 1979, 89-90). Guillaume de Seignelay, 1207-1220, established a fund to provide greater pomp in the celebration of the feast of the Holy Apostles (Lebeuf, *Mémoires* I, 379; Bouchard, 1979, 136). The 1420 list of relics mentions relics of Saint Peter and Saint Paul in the altar of the Blessed Virgin (Lebeuf, *Mémoires* IV, 240). Scenes from the lives of Peter and of Paul appear in the early fourteenth-century voussoirs of the cathedral's central portal.

Cycles of Peter and Paul appear with great frequency in twelfth- and thirteenth-century French glass:

Clermont-Ferrand (Grodecki, 1977, 190); Rouen (Ritter, 1926, 48-50, pls. XXIV-XXVI); Sens (Bégule, 1929, 55-56; Chartraire, 1926, 88-89); Chartres (Delaporte and Houvet, 1926, 284-290, fig. 29, pls. LXXXVI-LXXXVIII, also window of the apostles, 296-301, fig. 31, pls. XCII-XCV); Lyon (Bégule, 1911, 31-32, fig. 14); Poitiers (Grodecki, 1951, 146-147; idem, 1977, 74, fig. 59); Tours (Boissonnot, 1920, 107-108, pl. VI, 1932, 29-30, pl. VI; Papanicolaou, 1979, 46-47, 151, pls. 32-37); Troyes (Lafond, 1955, 30); Angers (Farcy, 1910, 164-165; Hayward-Grodecki, 1966, 33-34); Le Mans (Grodecki, 1961, 74-75, 84-86); Bourges (Cahier and Martin, 1841-1844, 257-259, pl. XIIIA); Saint-Père-de-Chartres (Lillich, 1978, 156-167, pls. 59-68); Saint-Pierre of Saint-Julien-du-Sault (Rheims, 1926, 152; Lafond, 1958b, 366); Notre-Dame of Semur-en-Auxois (de Tervarent, 1939, 18); Notre-Dame of Dijon (Oursel, 1953, 115; idem, 1938, 81-85; Vallery-Radot, 1928, 68-70).

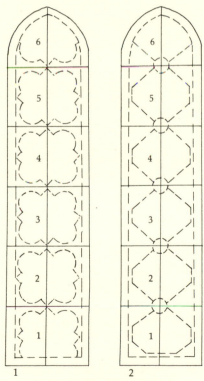

NOTRE-DAME OF DIJON
PETER

NOTRE-DAME OF DIJON PETER

First and second lancets under north rose.

1:1 Peter speaks to the faithful.
1:2 Death of Ananias and Sapphira.
1:3 Lame person at the temple asks for cure from Peter and John.
1:4 The lame person is healed.
1:5 Jesus walks on the water; Peter gestures to him from a boat.
1:6 Peter and Jesus both walking on the water.

2:1 Christ preaches to the apostles.
2:2 Christ gives the keys to Peter.
2:3 Peter addresses two men; Cornelius the centurion?
2:4 Inhabitants of Joppa show Peter the tunics and cloaks that Tabitha had made for them.
2:5 Tabitha shown lying on her death bed surrounded by friends.
2:6 Peter kneels down and obtains Tabitha's resurrection.

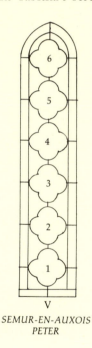

SEMUR-EN-AUXOIS
PETER

SEMUR-EN-AUXOIS PETER

V:6 Saint Peter before Judge.
   5 A guard thrusts Peter into prison.
   4 Peter converts guards in prison.
   3 Peter escapes from prison. An angel makes a speaking gesture while Peter steps over the wall.
   2 Peter lead by an angel. PETRUS.
   1 Peter in the house of Mary, the mother of John Mark (Acts 12:12). Peter strides toward a woman who looks at him.

Fragments from this cycle have been placed in panels in windows I and IV that relate the story of Mary Magdalene. I:1 shows an isolated striding male figure seen from the side.

The man is beardless and has a halo. In panel IV:5, showing Christ seizing the hand of Saint Thomas, a figure has been added to the right of the group of apostles. Due to the fragmentary nature of these scenes iconographic identification would seem unwarranted.

PRODIGAL SON

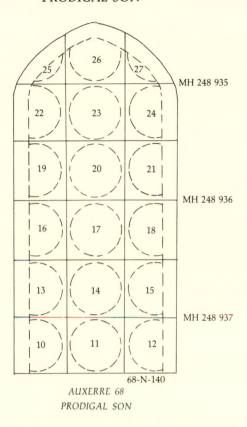

AUXERRE 68
PRODIGAL SON

AUXERRE 68 PRODIGAL SON

10. Prodigal, half naked, pushed away by a woman.
11. Another woman, without wimple, joins the first to see the departure.
12. Prodigal presents himself to a seated man to ask for work.
13. Prodigal leans on staff and watches his herd.
14. Prodigal turns away from his herd; he decides to return.
15. Father receives the prodigal with open arms.
16. A servant brings the prodigal a new robe.
17. A servant holds a calf while another prepares to strike it with an axe.
18. Two musicians playing viols.
19. Prodigal and a woman at table while a man serves them. This could be a panel left over from the days of debauchery.
20. The elder son, returning from the fields, speaks to a servant.
21. Elder son embraced by his father.
22. Servant with food in a bowl; servant with drum.
23. Father, woman and prodigal son at table.
24. Servant brings bowl with food; another brings jug of wine.
26. Prodigal son with mantle and long robe, holding scepter.

The story of the Prodigal Son occupies the right dado of the central portal of the cathedral. Stylistically, the sculpture recalls art of around 1260 (Sauerländer, 1972, 500-501, pl. 287). The Prodigal Son iconography, however, has been related to the marriage of Jean de Chalon in 1268 (Denny, 1976, 31-34, fig. 5). See also Porée (1926, 60-63, fig. p. 63).

Prodigal Son cycles in twelfth- and thirteenth-century French glass:

Chartres (Delaporte and Houvet, 1926, 381-383, fig. 47, pls. CL-CLIII); Poitiers (Grodecki, 1951, 154; Auber, 1849, 371-372, drawing p. 371); Bourges (Cahier and Martin, 1841-1844, 179-188, pl. IV; Amedée Boinet, *La Cathédrale de Bourges*, Paris [1925], 121-122; Grodecki, 1948, 88, pl. 19c); Sens (Bégule, 1929, 50-51, figs. 58-61; Grodecki, *Vitrail*, 139, fig. 22); Coutances (Lafond in Daage, 1933, 86-87, fig. p. 87).

SAMSON

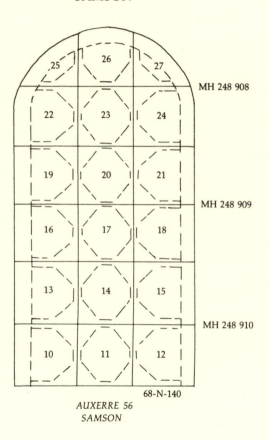

AUXERRE 56
SAMSON

AUXERRE 56 SAMSON

10. Samson gathering foxes; animals hung by their tails.
11. Foxes setting wheat fields on fire with the brands attached to their tails.
12. Samson carries off the Gates of Gaza into the mountains.
13. Samson prays to be delivered from thirst after slaying the thousand Philistines; water pours from jawbone of the ass (not rock).
14. Samson kneels to drink the water.
15. Samson enters a building with gates (Gaza?).

16. Delilah cuts Samson's hair as he sleeps in her lap.
17. Samson blinded by two men.
18. Samson labors at the grindstone.
21. Samson, his head shaved, is lead by a child.
20. Samson, with long hair, lead by child under architecture.
19. Samson stands under arcade, reaching out to shake the pillars of the Temple of Dagon.
22. Temple of Dagon destroyed; fragments of architecture and bodies.
23. Samson's body carried by mourners.
24. Annointing of Samson's body.
26. Angel.

Throughout the window, the inscription SENSUM FORTIN, or FOTIN, appears nine times. The inscriptions were noted in the nineteenth century (Guilhermy, Auxerre, fol. 691; de Lasteyrie, 1841, 44). Authentic for the most part, the formulas may be French-Latin corruptions meaning "the strength of Samson." For additional iconography see the mid-thirteenth-century Parisian Bible of the Morgan Library, New York (Morgan 638, fols. 14-15v. in John Plummer, *A Medieval Picture Book*, New York, 1969, 78-85).

Samson cycles in twelfth- and thirteenth-century French glass:

Sainte-Chapelle (Grodecki, *Corpus*, France I, 168-171, pl. 40).

STEPHEN

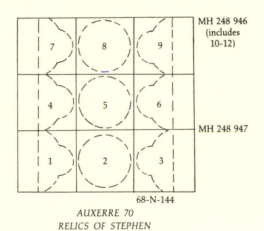

AUXERRE 70
RELICS OF STEPHEN

AUXERRE 70 STEPHEN (Relics of Stephen)

1. Lucien, preceded by a cleric, leads Bishop John of Jerusalem to the relics that had been revealed in a dream.
2. John presides over the opening of the sarcophagi of Nicodemus, Gamaliel and Stephen. IO/ES LUC/NU.
3. Bearded man with cap and sword under arcade; an angel.
4. A priest under an arcade preceded by a cleric.
5. Juliana rides in cart that brings Stephen's relics to Constantinople. A man rides the cart horse and a demon appears in the sky.
6. Three monks; one holds the hand of a smaller figure, possibly the healing of the

lame at the touch of Stephen's relics. ONAC (monachi); other inscriptions Renaissance or modern.

7. A man ties a standing bishop to a ladder.
8. Juliana anoints bodies on a table; the naked body of Stephen under that of a bishop, leading Juliana to mistakenly transport both bodies with her. ANA.
9. A cleric uses a ramp to enter a church.

Stephen, as patron saint of the cathedral, appears very early in the documents concerning Auxerre. In the late sixth century, shortly after the introduction of Stephen's relics to the west, the cathedral is referred to as "the basilica of Saint Stephen" (*Gesta*, XIX, 329; Louis, 1952, 16). Embellishments to the altar of Saint Stephen appear in the *Gesta* during the episcopates of Héribalde, 824-857, Gaudri, 918-933, and Humbaud, 1087-1114 (*Gesta*, XXVI, XLIV, LIII, 354, 375, 404). The monastery of Saint-Germain dedicated one of the oratories in the crypt to Stephen (Louis, 1952, 60-62), decorated the walls with frescoes of his life (Henri Focillon, *Peintures romanes des églises de France*, Paris [1967], 13-16), and produced the Carolingian scholars, Héric and Haymon, who composed widely read homilies for the feast of Saint Stephen (H. Barré, *Les Homélies carolingiennes de l'école d'Auxerre*, Vatican [1962], 148, 163).

Relics at the cathedral are mentioned in the 1420 inventory (Lebeuf, *Mémoires*, IV, 240) and during the episcopate of Hugues de Montaigue, 1115-1136 (Lebeuf, *Mémoires*, I, 294). Guillaume de Seignelay ordered an annual procession for the patron's feast (Lebeuf, *Mémoires*, I, 379; Bouchard, 1979, 136) and gave the cathedral a reliquary of the finger of Saint Stephen brought from Constantinople (Lebeuf, *Mémoires* I, 392-393). The thirteenth-century missal from Auxerre set off in red the celebration of the translation of Stephen's relics on November 18 (Leroquais, 1924, II, 87). The south transept portal, from the early fourteenth century, presents the life and martyrdom of the saint (Porée, 1926, 74-76).

For the history of Stephen's relics, see H. Leclercq and F. Cabrol, *Dictionnaire d'archéologie chrétienne et de liturgie*, X/1, Paris (1922), cols, 641-646; *Golden Legend*, 54-57, 408-412.

Relics of Stephen in twelfth- and thirteenth-century French glass:

Châlons-sur-Marne (Lucien Magne, *L'Oeuvre des peintres-verriers français*, Paris [1885], fig. 1; Grodecki, *Vitrail*, 107-108, fig. 78; idem, 1977, 125-126, fig. 105); Chartres (Delaporte and Houvet, 1926, 331-337, fig. 37, pls. CXIX-CXXII); Tours (Boissonnot, 1920, 96-98, pl. I, 1932, 21, pl. I; Papanicolaou, 1979, 124-126, pls. 88-92); Bourges (Cahier and Martin, 1841-1844, 232-234, pl. VIII; Grodecki, 1948, 88-89, pl. 9g; idem, *Vitrail*, 139, fig. 105; idem, *Year 1200* III, figs. 1, 5); Le Mans (Grodecki, 1961, 84); early fourteenth-century cycle at Saint-Ouen, Rouen, (Lafond, *Corpus, France* IV, 144-147, pls. 36-38; Aubert, *Vitrail*, 174, pl. XVIII).

THEOPHILUS

AUXERRE 63 THEOPHILUS

1, 2, 3. Theophilus takes leave of his bishop; he complains of his unjust treatment; he embraces a demon (modern).
4. A man presents Theophilus with a fish, a reference to his responsibilities over the bishop's material affairs.
5. Theophilus and Jew stand under arcades (modern).
6. Theophilus and the Jew are seated; a demon whispers in the Jew's ear.
7. Jew gives money to Theophilus.

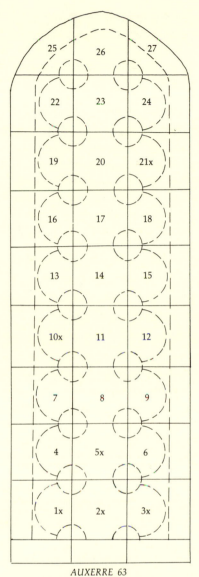

AUXERRE 63
MIRACLE OF THEOPHILUS

8. Guided by the presence of a demon, Theophilus distributes alms.
9. Theophilus hands a demon a long scroll containing the sale of his soul.
10. Two demons (modern).
11. Theophilus directs the construction of a church.
12. The repentant Theophilus prays before a statue of the Virgin and Child.
13. Theophilus raises hand to head in a gesture of despair.
14. The Virgin appears to Theophilus.
15. Three observers hold Theophilus' garments (should be in register above, 18, flanking Theophilus' penance).
18. Virgin strikes the demon with a cross and seizes the scroll.
17. Theophilus, stripped to the waist, is beaten by his bishop (much restored).
16. The Virgin gives the contract scroll back to Theophilus.

19. Theophilus presents his seated bishop with the scroll.
20. Demons try to destroy the church by striking it with hands and feet.
21. Two demons (modern).
23. Theophilus dies in the presence of his bishop and two clerics (much restored).
22. An angel holds Theophilus' soul in a cloth.
24. Censing angel (much restored).
26. Three-quarter-length figure of Christ holding orb and blessing.

All extant panels were identified in the nineteenth century (Guilhermy, Auxerre, fol. 691v.-692) but they had been haphazardly gathered together in window 58. Presumably the panels had been moved out of the axial chapel to make room for the Renaissance windows of 1587. The Renaissance glass was badly damaged by artillery during the Franco-Prussian War and Leprévost and Steinheil were commissioned to work repairs in 1879. Since the Miracle of Theophilus was traditionally associated with narrative cycles in honor of the Blessed Virgin, it would have been quite logical to move the glass back to the Virgin's chapel. For iconographic development, see A. C. Freyer, "Theophilus the Penitent in Art," *Archeological Journal* 92 (1935), 287ff.; Meyer Schapiro, "The Sculptures of Souillac," *Medieval Studies in Memory of A. Kingsley Porter*, II, Cambridge (1939), 359-387, nn. 15-17; for a discussion of the north transept portal sculpture at Notre-Dame in Paris, see Sauerländer, 1972, 472-473, pl. 186.

Theophilus cycles in twelfth- and thirteenth-century French glass:

Chartres, almost totally destroyed (Delaporte and Houvet, 1926, 189-195, pls. XXIX-XXXI see esp. n. 1, p. 195 for iconography); Le Mans (Hucher, 1864, unpaginated; Grodecki, 1961, 80, n. 3, 85); Beauvais (Leblond, 1926, 65-67; *Corpus, France, Recensement* I, 178, fig. 98); Laon (Grodecki, *Vitrail*, 123; *Corpus, France, Recensement* I, 163; Florens Deuchler, *Der Ingeborgpsalter*, Berlin [1967] 150-160, pl. LXII, psalter illustrations and iconography 67-70); Troyes (Lafond, 1955, 48); Saint-Pierre of Saint-Julien-du-Sault (Lafond, 1958b, 366; Rheims, 1926, 155-156); Gercy (Grodecki, 1953, 51-52, no. 13); Tours (Papanicolaou, 1979, 135-136, pl. 104).

VINCENT

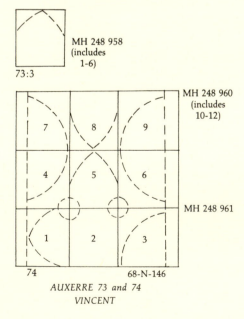

AUXERRE 73 and 74
VINCENT

Vincent's body carried by two women and a man.

AUXERRE 74 VINCENT

1. An angel visits Vincent in prison while two guards observe from the outside (heavily restored).
2. Vincent is led before Dacien (much effaced).
3. Vincent sleeps in prison while two guards observe the scene (heavily restored).
4. Dacien orders three servants to throw Vincent's body in the sea (Vincent's head modern). DATIANO.
5. Dacien observes two guards who tear at Vincent's body with rakes. Vincent is tied to a central column. S:VINCENTUS.
6. Dacien orders a guard to begin the torture (Vincent heavily restored).
7. Vincent tied to X-shaped cross by two guards. S.VINCENCIU (effaced).
8. Dacien confronts two guards holding the half naked saint between them (moderately restored).
9. Two angels support Vincent in a swath of cloth (heavily restored).

Auxerre's 1420 list of relics mentions those of Saint Vincent (Lebeuf, *Mémoires*, IV, 241).

Vincent cycles in twelfth- and thirteenth-century French glass:

Saint Denis (Grodecki, 1976, 106-107, Fig. XIII); Angers (Farcy, 1910, 150-153; Hayward-Grodecki, 1966, 21-22 fig. on p. 22); Chartres, in same window with saint Theodore (Delaporte and Houvet, 1926, 323-326, fig. 35, pls. CXI-CXIV); Bourges (Cahier and Martin, 1841-1844, 268-270, pl. XIV B); Rouen, with Lawrence and Stephen in window of three deacon martyrs (Ritter, 9, 50, pl. XXVII); Tours (Boissonnot, 1920, 98-100, pl. II, 1932, 21-22, pl. II; Papanicolaou, 1979, 113-115, pls. 75-80); Le Mans (A. Marquet, *La Cathédrale du Mans*, Le Mans, n.d., 30; Grodecki, 1961, 84); church of Saint-Germain-des-Prés, panels in Walters Art Gallery, Baltimore, Metropolitan Museum of Art, New York, and the Victoria and Albert Museum, London (Philippe Verdier, ''La verrière de Saint-Vincent à Saint-Germain-des-Prés,'' *Mémoires de la Fédération des sociétés historiques et archéologiques de Paris et de l'Ile-de-France* 9 [1957-1958], 69-87, predominantly iconography; idem. 1962-1963, mentions two additional panels of the saint's martyrdom that date from around 1250); Beauvais (*Corpus, France, Recensement* I, 178, fig. 99); Mantes-Gassicourt, in window with saints Stephen and Lawrence (ibid., 132).

Abbreviations

Acta sanctorum	*Acta sanctorum, quotquot toto orbe coluntur vel a catholicis scriptoribus celebrantur . . .* ed. Johan von Bolland, assisted by Godfried Henshen et al., Antwerp, 1643 and following, volumes indicated by month.
Corpus, France I	*Corpus Vitrearum Medii Aevi, France* I. Marcel Aubert, Louis Grodecki, Jean Lafond, and Jean Verrier, *Les Vitraux de Notre-Dame et de la Sainte-Chapelle de Paris*, Paris, 1959.
Corpus, France IV	*Corpus Vitrearum Medii Aevi, France* IV-2/1. Jean Lafond, *Les Vitraux de l'église Saint-Ouen de Rouen*, Paris, 1970.
Corpus, France, Recensement I	*Corpus Vitrearum Medii Aevi.* Louis Grodecki et al., *Les Vitraux de Paris, de la région parisienne, de la Picardie, et du Nord-Pas-de-Calais, Recensement des vitraux anciens de la France* I, Paris, 1978.
Corpus, Switzerland I	*Corpus Vitrearum Medii Aevi, Schweiz* I. Ellen J. Beer, *Die Glasmalereien der Schweiz vom 12. bis zum Beginn des 14. Jahrhunderts*, Basel, 1956.
Gesta	*Gesta pontificum Autissiodorensium, Auxerre, Bibliothèque municipale*, Ms. 142, ed. Louis Duru, *Bibliothèque historique de l'Yonne* I, Auxerre, 1850, 309-509.
Golden Legend	Granger Ryan and Helmut Ripperger, *The Golden Legend of Jacobus de Voragine Translated and Adapted from the Latin*, London, 2nd prtg., 1948.
Guilhermy, Auxerre	François de Guilhermy, Manuscript notes on the cathedral of Auxerre, visits of 1854, 1858, and 1864, Paris, Bibliothèque nationale, Ms. nouv. acq. fr. 6095.
Guilhermy, Saint-Julien-du-Sault	François de Guilhermy, Manuscript notes on the church of Saint-Pierre of Saint-Julien-du-Sault, visit of 1864, Paris, Bibliothèque nationale, Ms. nouv. acq. fr. 6108.
Lebeuf, *Mémoires*	Jean Lebeuf, *Mémoires concernant l'histoire civile et écclesiastique d'Auxerre et de son ancien diocèse*, ed. Ambroise Challe and Maximilien Quantin, Auxerre, 1848-1855, 4 vols.
New England Collections	*Medieval and Renaissance Stained Glass from New England Collections. Catalogue of an Exhibition Held at the Busch-Reisinger Museum, Harvard University*, Cambridge, 1978. Catalogue edited by Madeline H. Caviness.
Vitrail	Musée des Arts Décoratifs de Paris, *Le Vitrail français*. Paris, 1958. Text by Marcel Aubert, André Chastel, Louis Grodecki, Jean-Jacques Gruber, Jean Lafond, François Mathéy, Jean Taralon, and Jean Verrier.
Year 1200 I	The Metropolitan Museum of Art, *The Year 1200: A Centennial Exhibition at the Metropolitan Museum of Art I, Catalogue*

(The Cloisters Studies in Medieval Art). New York, 1970. Catalogue by Konrad Hoffmann.

Year 1200 III   The Metropolitan Museum of Art, *The Year 1200: A Symposium*, New York, 1975.

Selected Bibliography

Auber, Charles Auguste. *Histoire de la cathédrale de Poitiers*. Poitiers: 1849.

Bégule, Lucien. *Monographie de la cathédrale de Lyon*. Lyon: 1880.

————. *Les Vitraux du moyen-âge et de la renaissance dans la région Lyonnaise*. Lyon: A. Rey, 1911.

————. *La Cathédrale de Sens*. Lyon: A. Rey, 1929.

Boissonnot, Henri. *Histoire et description de la cathédrale de Tours*. Paris: Imp. Frazier-Soye, 1920.

————. *Les Verrières de la cathédrale de Tours*. Reprint. Paris: Imp. Frazier-Soye, 1932.

Bonneau, l'abbé. "Description des verrières de la cathédrale d'Auxerre." *Bulletin de la Société des sciences historiques et naturelles de l'Yonne* 34 (1885): 296-348.

Bony, Jean. "The Resistance to Chartres in Early Thirteenth-Century Architecture." *Journal of the British Archaeological Association* 20-21, 3rd ser. (1957-1958): 35-52.

Bouchard, Constance B. *Spirituality and Administration: The Role of the Bishop in Twelfth-Century Auxerre*. Cambridge, Mass.: The Medieval Academy, 1979.

Bouvier, Henri. *Histoire de l'église et de l'ancien archidiocèse de Sens*. Paris: A. Picard et fils, 1911.

Branner, Robert. *Burgundian Gothic Architecture*. London: A. Zwemmer Ltd., 1960.

————. "Westminster Abbey and the French Court Style." *Journal of the Society of Architectural Historians* 23 (1964): 3-18.

————. *St. Louis and the Court Style in Gothic Architecture*. London: A. Zwemmer Ltd., 1965.

————. "Le premier évangéliaire de la Sainte-Chapelle." *Revue de l'art* 3 (1969): 37-48.

————. *Manuscript Painting in Paris During the Reign of Saint Louis*. Berkeley: University of California Press, 1977.

Cahier, Charles, and Arthur Martin. *Monographie de la cathédrale de Bourges*. 2 vols. Paris: 1841-1844.

————. *Nouveaux mélanges d'archéologie* III. Paris: 1875.

Caviness, Madeline Harrison. *The Early Stained Glass of Canterbury Cathedral*. Princeton: Princeton University Press, 1977.

———— and Louis Grodecki. "Les vitraux de la Sainte-Chapelle." *Revue de l'art* 1, no. 2 (1968): 9-16.

Chartraire, Eugène. *La Cathédrale de Sens*. Paris: H. Laurens, Petite monographie, 1926.

Courtépée, Claude. *Description générale et particulière du duché de Bourgogne*. 2nd ed. 4 vols. Dijon: 1847-1848.

Daage, Colmet. *La Cathédrale de Coutances*. Paris: H. Laurens, Petite monographie, 1933.

Delaporte, Yves, and Emile Houvet. *Les Vitraux de la cathédrale de Chartres*. 4 vols. Chartres: E. Houvet, 1926.

Denny, Don. "Some Narrative Subjects in the Portal Sculpture of Auxerre Cathedral." *Speculum* 51 (1976): 23-24.

Duru, Louis M. *Bibliothèque historique de l'Yonne: Collection des légendes, chroniques, et documents divers pour servir à l'histoire des differentes contrées qui forment aujourd'hui ce département*. 2 vols. Auxerre: 1850-1863.

Dyer-Spencer, Jeannette. "Les vitraux de la Sainte-Chapelle de Paris." *Bulletin monumental* 91 (1932): 333-407.

de Farcy, Louis. *Monographie de la cathédrale d'Angers*. Angers: 1910.

Forestier, Henri. *Archives du département de l'Yonne: l'Yonne au XIXe siècle.* 2 vols. Auxerre: Imprimerie l'Universelle, 1959.

Fourrey, R. "Les verrières historiées de la cathédrale d'Auxerre." *Bulletin de la Société des sciences historiques et naturelles de l'Yonne* 83 (1929): 5-101.

Fyot, Eugène. *L'Eglise Notre-Dame de Dijon, Monographie descriptive.* Dijon: L. Damidot, 1910.

Gallia Christiana, ed. Congregation of Saint Maur, O.S.B., Paris, 1770.

Geoffroy de Courlon. *Chronique de l'abbaye de Saint-Pierre-le-Vif de Sens redigée vers la fin du XIIIe siècle par Geoffroy de Courlon.* Trans. and ed. Gustave Julliot: Sens, 1976.

Grodecki, Louis. "A Stained Glass Atelier of the Thirteenth Century." *Journal of the Warburg and Courtauld Institutes* 11 (1948): 87-110.

———. "Les vitraux de la cathédrale de Poitiers." *Congrès archéologique de France* 109 (1951): 138-163.

———. *Les Vitraux de France du XIe au XVIe siècle* (Exposition du Musée des Arts Décoratifs). Paris: 1953.

———. "Stained Glass Windows of Saint-Germain-des-Prés." *The Connoisseur* 140 (1957): 33-37.

———. "Les vitraux soissonnais du Louvre, du Musée Marmottan, et des collections américaines." *La Revue des Arts* 10 (1960): 163-178.

———. "Les vitraux de la cathédrale du Mans." *Congrès archéologique de France* 119 (1961): 59-99.

———. *Cathédrales: Sculptures, vitraux, objets d'art, manuscrits* (Exposition du Louvre). Paris: 1962.

———. "Le maître de Saint Eustache de la cathédrale de Chartres." In *Gedenkschrift Ernst Gall*, ed. Margarete Kühn and Louis Grodecki, pp. 171-194. Munich: Deutscher Kunstverlag, 1965.

———. "Nouvelles découvertes sur les vitraux de la cathédrale de Troyes," In *Intuition und Kunstwissenschaft: Festschrift für Hanns Swarzenski*, ed. Peter Block et al., pp. 191-203. Berlin: Gebr. Mann, 1973.

———. *Les Vitraux de Saint-Denis.* Paris: Arts et Métiers graphiques, 1976.

———. *Le Vitrail roman.* Fribourg: Office du Livre, 1977.

———. "Les problèmes de l'origine de la peinture gothique et le 'maître de Saint Chéron' de la cathédrale de Chartres." *Revue de l'art* 40-41 (1978): 43-64.

Hautecoeur, Louis. *L'Architecture. La Bourgogne (Les richesses d'art de la France).* Paris and Brussels: G. Van Oest, 1927.

Hayward, Jane, and Louis Grodecki. "Les vitraux de la cathédrale d'Angers." *Bulletin monumental* 124 (1966): 7-67.

Hucher, Eugène. *Calques des vitraux peints de la cathédrale du Mans.* Paris: Didron, 1864.

Lafond, Jean. "Les vitraux français du Musée Ariana de l'ancienne vitrerie de Saint-Fargeau (Yonne)." *Genava* 26 (1948): 115-132.

———. "Les vitraux de la cathédrale de Sées." *Congrès archéologique de France* 111 (1953): 59-83.

———. "Les vitraux de la cathédrale Saint-Pierre de Troyes." *Congrès archéologique de France* 113 (1955): 28-62.

———. "Les vitraux de la cathédrale Saint-Etienne d'Auxerre." *Congrès archéologique de France* 116 (1958a): 60-75.

———. "Les vitraux de l'église de Saint-Julien-du-Sault." *Congrès archéologique de France* 116 (1958b): 365-369.

de Lasteyrie, François. "Description des verrières peintes de la cathédrale d'Auxerre." *Annuaire statistique et monumental du département de l'Yonne* 5 (1841): 38-46.

————. *Histoire de la peinture sur verre en France d'après ses monuments* Vol. II. pp. 184-190. Paris: 1857.

Lebeuf, Jean. *Histoire de la prise d'Auxerre par les Huguenots*. Auxerre: 1723.

Leblond, Victor. *La Cathédrale de Beauvais*. Paris: H. Laurens, Petite monographie, 1926.

Leroquais, Victor. *Les Sacramentaires et les missels manuscrits des bibliothèques publiques de France*. 3 vols. Paris: Protat Frères, 1924.

————. *Les Psautiers manuscrits latins des bibliothèques publiques de France*. Macon: Protat Frères, 1940-1941.

Lillich, Meredith Parsons. "The Band Window: A Theory of Origin and Development." *Gesta* 9, no. 1 (1970): 26-33.

————. *The Stained Glass of Saint-Père de Chartres*. Middletown, Conn.: Wesleyan University Press, 1978.

Louis, René. *Autessiodurum christianum; Les Eglises d'Auxerre des origines au onzième siècle*. Paris: Clavreuil, 1952.

Mâle, Emile. *L'Art religieux du XIIIe siècle en France*. 5th ed. Paris: Armand Colin, 1923.

Molinier, Auguste, with Alexandre Vidier and Léon Mirot. *Recueil des historiens de la France: Obituaires de la province de Sens; Diocèses d'Orléans, d'Auxerre, et de Nevers*. Vol. III. Paris: Imprimerie nationale, 1919.

Mortet, Victor. *Recueil de textes relatifs à l'histoire de l'architecture*. 2 vols. Paris: Alphonse Picard, 1911-1929.

Oursel, Charles. *L'Eglise de Notre-Dame de Dijon*. Paris: H. Laurens, Petite monographie, 1938.

————. *L'Art de Bourgogne*. Paris: B. Arthaud, 1953.

Panofsky, Erwin. *Abbot Suger on the Abbey Church of St.-Denis and its Art Treasures*. Ed., trans. and ann. Erwin Panofsky. 2nd ed. rev. Gerda Panofsky-Soergel ed. Princeton: Princeton University Press, 1979.

Papanicolaou, Linda Morey. "Stained Glass Windows of the Choir of the Cathedral of Tours." Ph.D. dissertation, New York University, Institute of Fine Arts, 1979.

Perrot, Françoise. "Note sur les arbres de Jessé de Gercy et de St.-Germain-lès-Corbeil." *Year 1200* III, pp. 417-424. 1975.

Petit, Ernest. *Histoire des ducs de Bourgogne de la race capétienne*. Vols. 4 and 5. Paris: 1885-1894.

Petit-Dutaillis, Charles. *The Feudal Monarchy in France and England from the Tenth to the Thirteenth Century*. Repr. 1936 rev. ed. New York: Harper and Row, Harper Torchbooks, 1964.

Porée, Charles. "Le choeur de la cathédrale d'Auxerre," *Bulletin de la Société des sciences historiques et naturelles de l'Yonne* 60 (1906): 231-239.

————. *La Cathédrale d'Auxerre*. Paris: H. Laurens, Petite monographie, 1926.

Prache, Anne. *Saint-Remi de Reims, l'oeuvre de Pierre de Celle et sa place dans l'architecture gothique*. Paris: Arts et Métiers Graphiques, 1978.

Quantin, Maximilien. *Cartulaire général de l'Yonne* (Société des sciences historiques et naturelles de l'Yonne). 2 vols. Auxerre: 1854-1860.

————. *Dictionnaire topographique du département de l'Yonne comprennant les noms de lieux anciens et modernes*. Paris: 1862.

————. *Répertoire archéologique de l'Yonne* (Société des sciences historiques et naturelles de l'Yonne). Paris: 1868.

————. *Inventaire sommaire des archives départementales antérieures à 1790, Yonne*. 4 vols. Auxerre: 1868-1873.

————. *Recueil de pièces pour faire suite au cartulaire général de l'Yonne, XIIIe siècle*. Paris: 1873.

Raguin, Virginia. "The Genesis Workshop of the Cathedral of Auxerre and its Parisian Inspiration." *Gesta* 13, no. 1 (1974): 27-38.

———. "Windows of Saint-Germain-lès-Corbeil: A Travelling Glazing Atelier." *Gesta* 15, nos. 1 and 2 (1976): 265-272.

———. "The Isaiah Master of the Sainte-Chapelle in Burgundy." *The Art Bulletin* 59 (1977): 483-493.

du Ranquet, Henri. *Les Vitraux de la cathédrale de Clermont-Ferrand*. Clermont-Ferrand: Paul Vallier, 1932.

Réau, Louis. *Iconographie de l'art chrétien*. 3 vols. Paris: Presses universitaires de France, 1955-1959.

Rheims, Gabrielle. "L'église de Saint-Julien-du-Sault et ses verrières." *Gazette des beaux-arts* 14 (1926): 139-162.

Richard, Jean. *Les Ducs de Bourgogne et la formation du duché du XIe au XIVe siècle*. Paris: Société des Belles Lettres, 1954.

Ritter, Georges. *Les Vitraux de la cathédrale de Rouen*. Cognac: Impressions d'art des Etablissements FAC, 1926.

Robert of Saint-Marien. *Chronicon*. ed. O. Holder-Egger. Vol. 26, *Monumenta Germania Historica, Scriptores*, pp. 219-287. Hanover: 1882.

Runciman, Stephen. *A History of the Crusades*. 3 vols. New York: Harper and Row, Harper Torchbooks, 1967.

Salet, François. "La cathédrale de Sens et sa place dans l'histoire de l'architecture médiévale." *Académie des inscriptions et belles-lettres. Comptes-rendus de séances* (1955): 182-187.

Sauerländer, Willibald, and Max Hirmer. *Gothic Sculpture in France 1140-1270*. New York: Harry N. Abrams, 1972.

Stoddard, Whitney S. *Art and Architecture in Medieval France*. New York: Harper and Row, 1972.

de Tervarent, Guy. "Les vitraux de Semur-en-Auxois," In *Les Enigmes de l'art du moyen-âge* 1, pp. 17-24. Paris: Les Editions d'art et d'histoire, 1938.

Theophilus. *On Divers Arts: The Treatise of Theophilus*. Ed. John G. Hawthorne and Cyril S. Smith. Chicago: University of Chicago Press, 1963.

Timmers, Jan Josef. *Symboliek en Iconographi der Chrislijke Kunst*. Roermond-Masseik: J. J. Romen and Zonen, 1947.

Tonnelier, J. "Saint-Julien-du-Sault." *Annuaire statistique et monumental du département de l'Yonne* (1842): 99-118.

Vallery-Radot, Jean. "L'église de Notre-Dame de Dijon." *Congrès archéologique de France* 91 (1928): 39-70.

———. "La cathédrale Saint-Etienne d'Auxerre: Les principaux textes de l'histoire de la construction." *Congrès archéologique de France* 116 (1958a): 40-50.

———. "L'église de Saint-Julien-du-Sault." *Congrès archéologique de France* 116 (1958b): 353-365.

Verdier, Philippe. "The Window of Saint Vincent from the Refectory of the Abbey of Saint-Germain-des-Prés." *Journal of the Walters Art Gallery* 25-26 (1962-1963): 38-99.

Viollet-le-Duc, Eugène. *Dictionnaire raisonné de l'architecture française*. Vol. 9. Paris: 1875.

Index

Illustrations

1. Auxerre Cathedral, the interior of the choir

3. Auxerre Cathedral, detail of choir clerestory and triforium

2. Auxerre Cathedral, axial chapel from south ambulatory

5. Dijon, Notre-Dame, detail of north transept and lancets of Gothic glass

4. Dijon, Notre-Dame, interior

7. Saint-Julien-du-Sault, Saint-Pierre, north ambulatory

6. Semur-en-Auxois, Notre-Dame, interior

8. Auxerre 51:7-12, Creation window, creation of man and woman, Adam naming animals, God warning Adam and Eve

9. Auxerre 51:17, Creation window, God creates the stars

10. Paris, Cluny Museum, Saint Martin window from Gercy, detail of Christ in majesty

humilite

11. Sketchbook of Villard de Honnecourt, Paris, Bibl. nat. Ms. fr. 19093, fol. 3v., Humility

12. Auxerre 52:7-12, Noah, Abraham and Lot window, story of Abraham and Lot

13. Auxerre 52:9, Noah, Abraham and Lot window, angels announce the destruction of Sodom

14. Auxerre 56:16-18, Samson window, blinding and servitude

15. Auxerre 54:7-12, Saint Margaret window, confrontation with Olybrius and tortures

16. Auxerre 54:14, Saint Margaret window, mass martyrdom

17. Paris, Cluny Museum, Saint Martin window from Gercy,
miracle of the tree

18. Paris, Cluny Museum, Saint Martin
window from Gercy, detail of Saint Martin
from the miracle of the tree medallion

19. Paris, Cluny Museum, Saint Martin window, detail of fallen
pagans from the miracle of the tree medallion

20. Auxerre 56:23, Samson window, funeral procession

21. Paris, Cluny Museum, Saint Martin window
from Gercy, detail of angel

22. Auxerre 55:5, Saint Andrew window, demons exorcised in the form of dogs

23. New York, Metropolitan Museum, Saint Vincent window from Saint-Germain-des-Prés, Dacien and guards

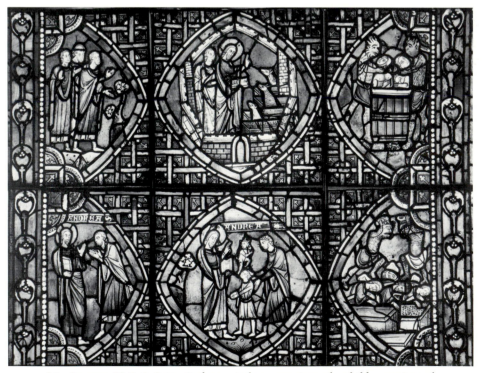

24. Auxerre 55:1-6, Saint Andrew window, exorcism of a child, exorcism of
the demons of Nicea

25. Auxerre 68:16-21, Prodigal Son window, return, banquet preparations

26. Auxerre 68:15, Prodigal Son window, reunion with father

27. Auxerre 74:13-15, Saint Bris window, discovery of relics in a cistern

28. Auxerre 56:5, Genesis and Exodus window, God confronts Adam and Eve

29. Auxerre 56:1-6, Genesis and Exodus window

30. Auxerre 53:13-18, Joseph window, dream of Pharaoh, release from prison

31. Auxerre 53:17, Joseph window, Joseph explains Pharaoh's dreams

32. Auxerre 70:23, Saint James window, baptism

33. Auxerre 61:11, Tree of Jesse window, seated king

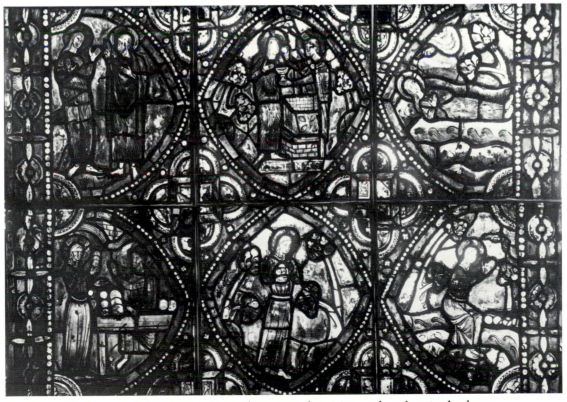

34. Auxerre 73:7-12, Saint Mary Magdalene window, legend of provincial leader on a pilgrimage

35. Auxerre 72:7-12, Saint Mary of Egypt window, Mary seeks refuge in the desert,
receives communion, dies

36. Auxerre 49:13-18, David window

37. Auxerre 50:16-21, Saint Mammès window

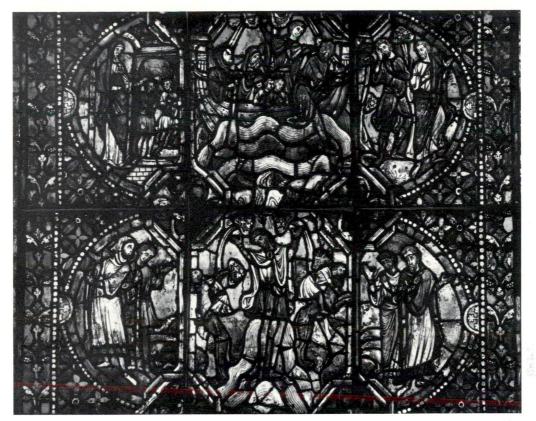

38. Auxerre 66:13-18, Saint Eustache window, Eustache witnesses sons carried away by a wolf and a lion, Eustache expelled from ship

39. Chartres LXII, Saint Eustache window, Eustache is expelled from ship

40. Auxerre 66:13, Saint Eustache window, two shepherds

41. Auxerre 63:8, Theophilus window, Theophilus distributes money

42. Auxerre 63:11 and 12, Theophilus window, building a church, Theophilus asking the Virgin
to redeem his soul

43. Bourges, Saint Mary
Magdalene window

44. Auxerre 57:15-20, Saint Lawrence window, scenes of torture, Lawrence
baptizes his jailers

45. Chartres VI, Good Samaritan window, lower portions, traveler is set upon by robbers, neglected by priest and Levite, rescued by Samaritan

45a. Chartres VI, Good Samaritan window, detail of innkeeper

45b. Chartres VI, Good Samaritan window, detail of robbers

46. Auxerre 57:13, Saint Lawrence window, scene of torture

47. Auxerre 71:19-24, Miracles of Saint Nicholas window, legend of the Jew who confided his treasure to a statue of the saint

48. Auxerre 72:22, Miracles of Saint Nicholas window, two robbers returning stolen gold to the statue of Saint Nicholas

49. Chartres LX, Saint Nicholas window,
detail of border

50. Auxerre 75:7, Saint Catherine window, flagellation

51. Auxerre 75:7-12, Saint Catherine window, tortures of the saint, tortures and death of the empress

52. Ardagger, Saint Margaret church, Saint
Margaret window, upper part

53. Auxerre 67:1-6, Saint Germain window, miracles

54. Saint-Germain-lès-Corbeil, Tree of Jesse window, Virgin flanked by two prophets

55. Moralized Bible, Vienna, Österreichische Nationalbibliothek, 1179, fol. 174, Susanna taken by the elders, Susanna before Daniel

56. Saint-Germain-lès-Corbeil, Passion window, Flagellation, Crucifixion with Sol and Luna, Ecclesia and Synagoga

57. Moralized Bible, Vienna, Österreichische Nationalbibliothek, 2554,
fol. 1, creation of the world and establishment of the church

58. Semur-en-Auxois, Saint Peter window, Peter
at Mary's house

59. Semur-en-Auxois, Saint Peter window, Peter led by an angel

62. Auxerre 67:7-10, Saint Nicholas window, selection of Nicholas as bishop

60. Troyes, Saint Andrew window, Andrew greeted by inhabitants of a city

61. Troyes, Saint Andrew window, exorcism of a child

64. Auxerre 67:8, Saint Nicholas window, Nicholas in prayer at the door of the church

65. Auxerre 70:3, Relics of Saint Stephen window, tracing of head of angel

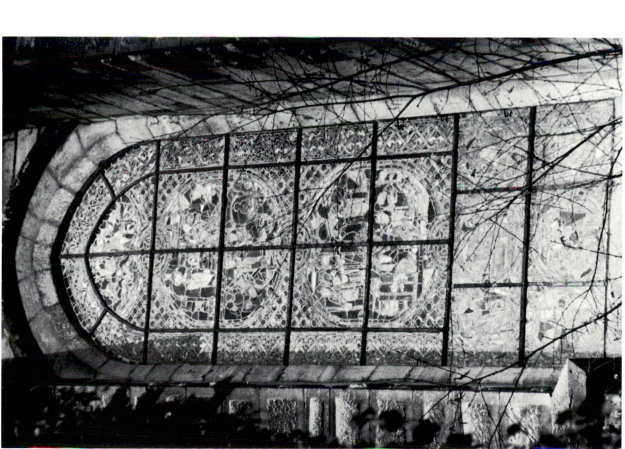

63. Auxerre 67, Saint Nicholas and Saint Germain window, exterior

66. Auxerre 70:1-6, Relics of Saint Stephen window

67. Auxerre 68:1-6. Apocalypse window

68. Paris Apocalypse, Paris, Bibl. nat. Ms. fr. 403, fol. 7v., the first horseman

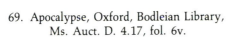

69. Apocalypse, Oxford, Bodleian Library, Ms. Auct. D. 4.17, fol. 6v.

70. Auxerre 68:7-9, Apocalypse window, John withstands the test of the poisoned cup

71. Paris Apocalypse, Paris, Bibl. nat. Ms. fr. 403, fol. 44v., John withstands the test of the poisoned cup

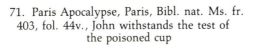

72. Chartres, XXXV, Saints Simon and Jude window, detail

73. Auxerre 71:1-6, Saint Eloi window, early miracles as goldsmith, consecration

75. Evangeliary of the Sainte-Chapelle, Paris, Bibl. nat. Ms. lat. 8892, fol. 6, Circumcision and Magi before Herod

74. Auxerre 71:7-9, Saint Eloi window, Eloi and Saint Ouen, procession

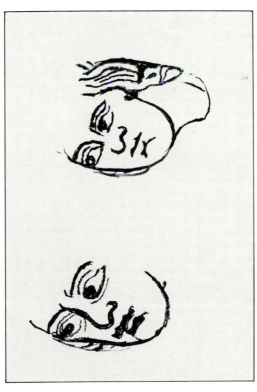

76. Auxerre 71:2, Saint Eloi window, tracing of the head of Saint Eloi. Auxerre 68:2, Apocalypse window, tracing of the head of an angel

77. Auxerre 68:4, Apocalypse window, Christ surrounded by seven trumpeting angels

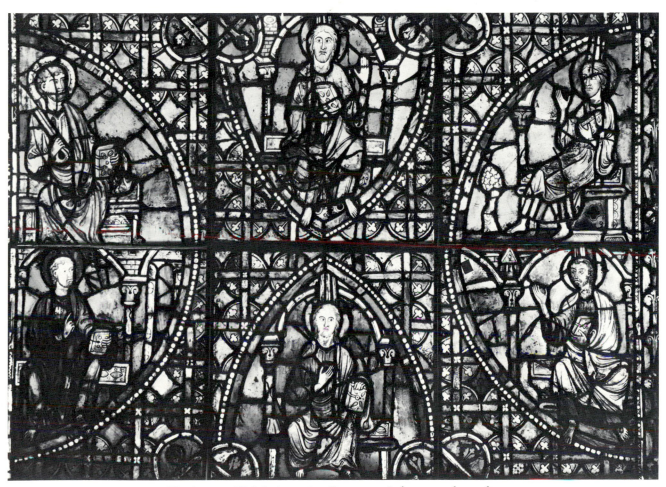

78. Auxerre 57:3-8, Ascension-Pentecost window, seated apostles

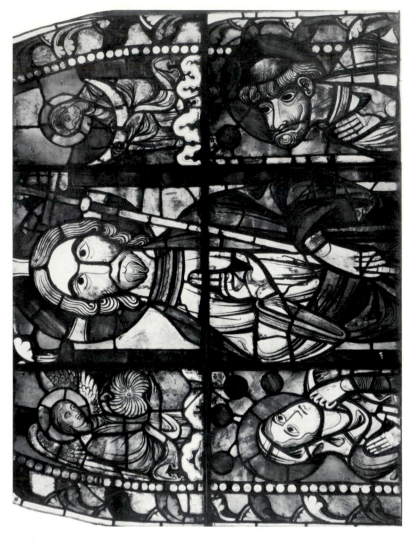

81. Auxerre 12a, north choir clerestory, Christ between the Virgin and Saint John

79. Auxerre 15, rose of north choir clerestory, Jeremias

80. Auxerre 19:26, axial rose of choir, clerestory, censing angel

83. Vivian Bible, Paris, Bibl. nat. Ms. lat. 1, fol. 329v., Christ in a majesty surrounded by prophets and evangelists

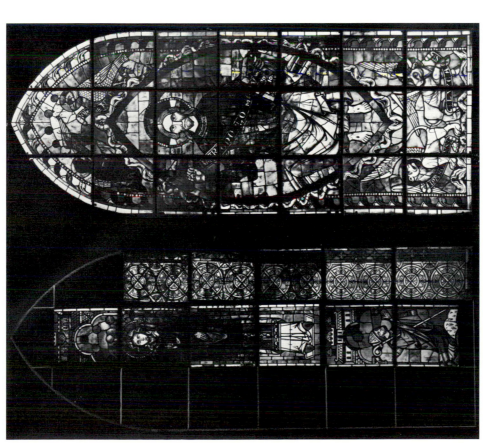

82. Auxerre 26a and b, south choir clerestory, female saint, Christ in mandorla surrounded by the tetramorph

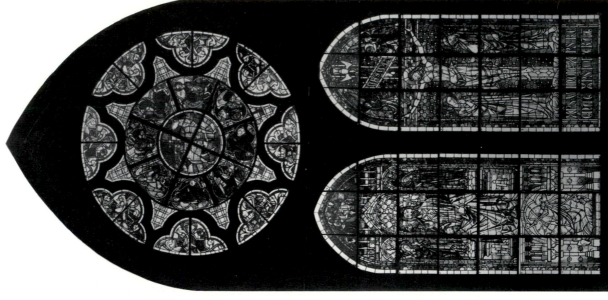

85. Auxerre 19a and b, axial bay of choir clerestory, Christ enthroned and Crucifixion, rose of Lamb of God

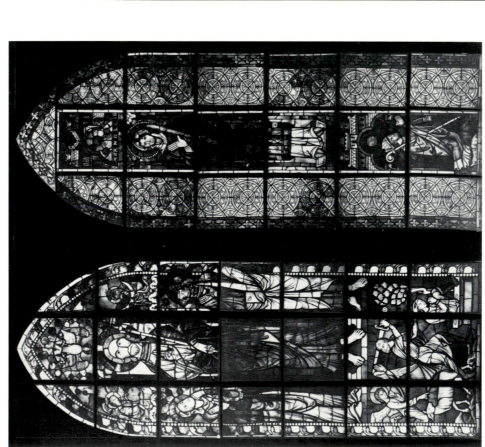

84. Auxerre 12a and b, north choir clerestory, Christ between the Virgin and Saint John, Saint Camille

87. Auxerre 65, Saint Stephen and donor

86. Auxerre 20, south choir clerestory, Saints Lawrence and Amâtre

88. Auxerre 25, south choir clerestory, Ezekiel

90. Reims Bay 2P, choir clerestory, Philip

89. Auxerre 18, north choir clerestory, Saints Germain and Stephen

91. Auxerre 74:5, Saint Vincent window, Vincent tortured with iron rakes

92. Saint-Julien-du-Sault 9:23, Saint Nicholas window, Jew strikes statue of Saint Nicholas

93. Saint-Julien-du-Sault 6:18, Saint John the Evangelist window, John blesses the poisoned cup

94. Saint-Julien-du-Sault 3:13, Saint Margaret window, Margaret led from prison

95. Geneva, Musée d'Art et d'Histoire, Passion window from Saint-Fargeau, Flagellation

96. Geneva, Musée d'Art et d'Histoire, Passion window from Saint-Fargeau, Kiss of Judas

97. Evangeliary of the Sainte-Chapelle, Paris, Bibl. nat. Ms. lat. 8892, fol. 14, Christ exorcises a demon

98. Geneva, Musée d'Art et d'Histoire, window from Saint-Fargeau, apostles

99. Wellesley College Museum, apostles
from Saint-Fargeau

100. Bryn Athyn, Pitcairn collection,
window from Saint-Fargeau, Christ and
apostles

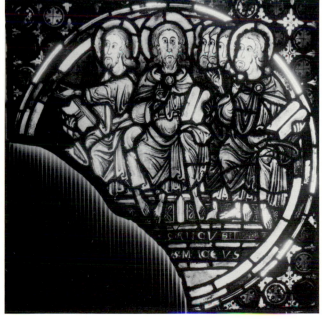

101. Bourges, Apocalypse window,
detail from central quadrilobe

102. Saint-Julien-du-Sault 10,
Legend of Theophilus window

103. Saint-Julien-du-Sault 11,
Infancy of Christ-Glorification of the
Virgin window

104. Saint-Julien-du-Sault 11:6, Infancy-Glorification
window, Magi before Herod

105. Detroit Institute of Arts, reconstructed panel after Saint-Julien-du-Sault,
Theophilus window 10·17

106. Saint-Germain-des-Prés, Saint Anne and Life of the Virgin window, Joseph protests his selection as Mary's betrothed

107. Montreal Museum of Fine Arts, glass from Saint-Germain-des-Prés, Joachim and a priest of the Temple

108. Paris, Sainte-Chapelle, interior

109. Sainte-Chapelle L:115, Joshua-Deuteronomy window, ruse of the Gabonites

110. Sainte-Chapelle L:156, Joshua-Deuteronomy window, Moses receiving the Law

111. Sainte-Chapelle L:130, Joshua-Deuteronomy window, king of Jericho interrogating Rahab (Isaiah Master)

112. Sainte-Chapelle J:44, Isaiah
window, Isaiah foretells the coming of
Christ

113. Sainte-Chapelle J:37, Isaiah
window, Annunciation

114. Sainte-Chapelle J:8, Isaiah
window, martyrdom

115. Saint-Julien-du-Sault 8:18, Passion
window, Crucifixion

116. Saint-Julien-du-Sault 4:21, Infancy
window, Massacre of the Innocents

117. Saint-Julien-du-Sault 8:12, Passion
window, Flagellation

118. Saint-Julien-du-Sault 4:16, Infancy window, Presentation
in the Temple

119. Twycross, Passion window of the Sainte-
Chapelle, Deposition

120. Saint-Julien-du-Sault 7, Saint Blaise and Saints Peter and Paul window

120a. Saint-Julien-du-Sault 7:14, Saint Blaise and Saints Peter and Paul window, Peter and Paul

121. Twycross, Saint John the Evangelist window of the Sainte-Chapelle, John followed by a woman

122. Saint-Julien-du-Sault 5, John the Baptist
window, beheading

123. Auxerre 57:1, Saints Peter and
Paul window, tracing of the head of
seated auditor

124. Auxerre 57:2, Saints Peter and
Paul window, tracing of the head of
disciple

125. Auxerre 66:1-6, Saint Martin window, miracles and death

126. Chartres XVI, Life of the Virgin window, central medallion

127. Auxerre 66:6, Saint Martin window, miracle of the tree

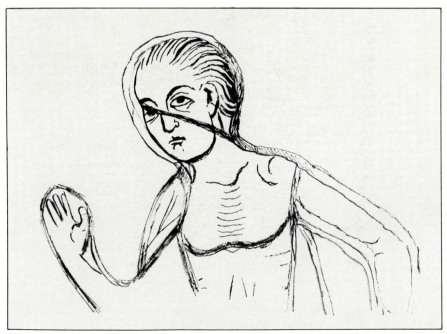

128. Auxerre 66:1, Saint Martin window, tracing of the head of
revived catechumen

129. Auxerre 58:9-12, Saints Peter and Paul window, Peter led from prison, fall of
Simon Magus, Nero gives orders to a servant

130. Auxerre 58:11, Saints Peter and Paul window, Nero gives
orders to a servant

131. Auxerre 19b, axial bay of choir clerestory, detail of Crucifixion

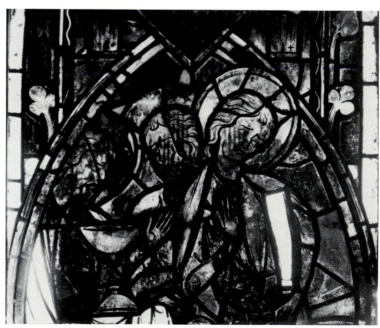

132. Tours 8, axial bay of choir clerestory, Passion window,
detail of Last Supper

133. Tours 13, north choir clerestory, Saint Nicholas
window, impoverished father

134. Le Mans, bay C, triforium, Life of Saint Julien of
Le Mans window, Julien resurrects a dead child

135. Clermont-Ferrand Ec:20, Saint Bonitus
window, Bonitus presented to the Virgin by
an angel

136. Semur-en-Auxois IV:4, Mary Magdalene tells the apostles she has seen
the risen Christ

137. Semur-en-Auxois I:3, Abbot of Vézelay sends envoys to Provence to bring back the
body of Mary Magdalene

138. Semur-en-Auxois II:3r, Jews
comfort Mary and Martha
after Lazarus' death

139. Semur-en-Auxois I:4, death of Mary Magdalene foretold

140. Semur-en-Auxois IV:3, Mary Magdalene discovered by a priest in the
wilderness of Provence

141. Bourges, Passion window, Crucifixion

142. Lausanne, Musée Historique de l'Ancien Evêché, John the Baptist window from the cathedral of Lausanne, detail of servant from martyrdom panel

143. Lausanne, Musée Historique de l'Ancien Evêché, John the Baptist window from the cathedral of Lausanne, John before Herod

145. Clermont-Ferrand Fc:35, Nativity

144. Poitiers, Lot window, Lot and daughter

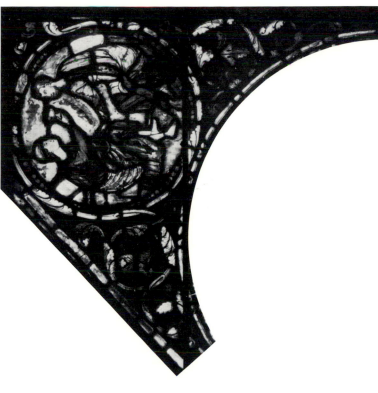

147. Chartres LXII, Saint Eustache window, detail of side medallion

146. Notre-Dame of Dijon 4:2, second Saint Andrew window, Andrew expels demons from Nicea in the form of dogs

148. Notre-Dame of Dijon 3:3, first Saint Andrew window, demons strangle people of Nicea in their bath

149. Notre-Dame of Dijon 2:2, second Saint Peter window, detail of Christ giving the keys to Peter

150. Bourges, New Alliance window, Moses
before the Brazen Serpent

151. London, Victoria and Albert Museum, Tree of
Jesse window associated with Troyes, Ezekiel

152. Notre-Dame of Dijon 2:1, second Saint Peter
window, detail of Christ preaching to the apostles

153. Notre-Dame of Dijon 2:2, second Saint Peter window, detail of Christ giving the keys to Peter, apostles

154. Troyes, axial chapel, window of Infancy with Typological Subjects, Purification

155. Notre-Dame of Dijon 1:2, first Saint Peter window, detail of Sapphira

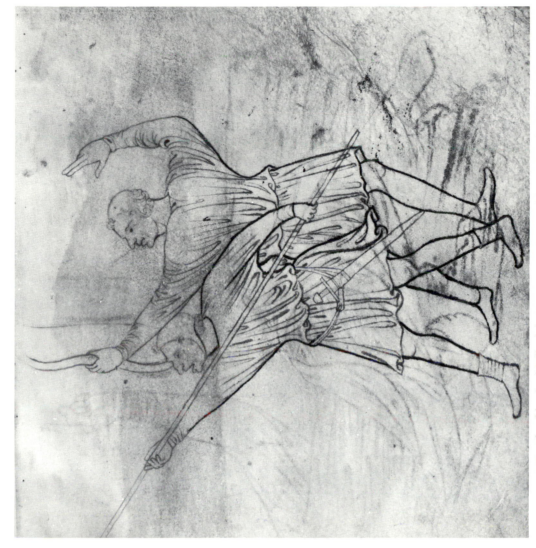

157. Sketchbook of Villard de Honnecourt, Paris, Bibl. nat. Ms. fr. 19093, fol. 25v., soldiers

156. Notre-Dame of Dijon 3:1, first Saint Andrew window, detail of donor panel, blacksmith

158. Notre-Dame of Dijon 5:1, third Saint Andrew window,
tracing of executioner stripping off his cloak

159. Notre-Dame of Dijon 5:1, third Saint Andrew
window, detail of executioner

160. Notre-Dame of Dijon 5:3, third Saint Andrew window, Andrew crucified

161. Notre-Dame of Dijon 5:4, third Saint Andrew window, exorcism of a child